THE BEST BASS FLIES

HOW TO TIE AND FISH THEM

Jay Zimmerman

STACKPOLE
BOOKS

Guilford, Connecticut

Published by Stackpole Books
An imprint of Globe Pequot
Trade division of The Rowman & Littlefield Publishing Group, Inc.
4501 Forbes Boulevard, Suite 200, Lanham, Maryland 20706
www.rowman.com

Distributed by NATIONAL BOOK NETWORK
800-462-6420

British Library Cataloguing in Publication Information available

Library of Congress Cataloging-in-Publication Data available

ISBN 978-0-8117-1998-8 (paperback)
ISBN 978-0-8117-6598-5 (e-book)

♾™ The paper used in this publication meets the minimum requirements of American National Standard for Information Sciences—Permanence of Paper for Printed Library Materials, ANSI/NISO Z39.48-1992.

Printed in the United States of America

DEDICATION

For Dad.
You showed me how to fish, tell a story, and be a man.
I am gladly spending my life trying to keep up.

CONTENTS

FACING PAGE: Top left: Erik Johnson. *Cliff Watts* photo. **Top right:** Erin Block. **Middle:** Jay Zimmerman. *Erin Block* photo. **Bottom:** Ted Calcaterra. *Thomas Ziegler* photo.

ACKNOWLEDGMENTS

Thank you, Joy Hart, Mildred Zimmerman, Vanda Parker, Katy McElroy, Kendall Zimmerman, Eva Zimmerman, and Erin Block. I dedicated this book to the guy who taught me how to fish, but it is the strong women I have had in my life who I have to thank for making me a person both capable and willing to write this book. If it were not for these women, I most likely would be living in a van under a bridge down by the river with the ghost of Chris Farley.

FOREWORD

Bass fishing and tying can be enjoyed by almost anyone and anywhere.

The danger in thinking of fly tying as an art is that you ignore that at its heart, tying is practical, like a grandmother's rag quilt. Sure, it might be beautiful and made with love and any number of other feel-good things, but it's also useful. It keeps you warm and uses up scraps like a compost bin. That's to say, a fish doesn't care how beautiful or meaningful a fly is to you personally, it cares that it looks like something it's eaten before. Something that moves and acts like food. And above a great many other things I've learned from Jay Zimmerman, that truth rises to the top.

Jay taught me to tie shortly after I started fly fishing because, he said, it would make me a better angler. And I think what he was saying is that if I was going to be fishing with him, he didn't want me raiding his boxes. Point taken.

So I listened as he told me how to start the thread and how to wind the marabou so it wouldn't bunch and lump and generally look awful. He laughed at the first fly I tied—it deserved it—and I thought he'd given up on me when he left to go pet his cat in the corner. But as it turns out, that's just classic Jay.

Each week he presented me with a new pattern. New materials. What the fly called for and extra options too. This intimidated me because I don't like to make decisions—I'll stand for 15 minutes staring at my opened fly box wondering what I should tie on, already anticipating it won't work. But he told me to have fun. So I tried lime-green Woolly Buggers and Foxy Clousers made from a mink stole my dad had found at Goodwill. Jay taught me classic patterns, how to modify them, and then how to create some of my own.

And I discovered that my designs I liked best didn't catch many fish because I was tying what looked good to me, a land-dwelling human being. I learned the importance of mechanics and swim tanks, movement and action, how to flip a hook and make sure it stays flipped when it swims through the water. I learned that Jay's obsession with these things is not just OCD, as I once suspected—it's good engineering and smart design. And that's what makes the best bass flies.

—Erin Block, *Trout Magazine* deputy editor,
author of *The View from Coal Creek* and *By a Thread*

Erin Block casts a bass fly along an edge of dead cattails with her constant companion Banjo at her side.

FLY FISHING FOR BASS

"Indeed, there is probably as much genetic disparity—and, hence, real-life difference—between a bass and a trout as between a cat and a cow."
—Keith A. Jones, PhD

Bass can be found in abundance in each of our Lower 48 states. *Erin Block* photo.

Black bass in aggregate are the most sought-after gamefish in the United States of America. Fourteen species of fish fall under the genus *Micropterus* (known as the black basses), though largemouth, smallmouth, and spotted bass are the three commonly found and fished for, be it in their original native range or in the rivers, lakes, and reservoirs where they have since migrated or been introduced. Black bass have been one of the most widely stocked fish in the United States for 150 years—this has to do with their ability to survive and thrive in a variety of conditions and their popularity among anglers. Bass in one form or another can now be found in abundance in each of our lower 48 states, as well as several other countries.

The popularity and accessibility of bass have not been lost on fly anglers; in fact, a 10-inch largemouth bass caught on a cork popper is responsible for converting many longtime conventional-gear anglers and tricking the rest of us into falling in love with fishing in the first place. Bass are almost everywhere; they are an accessible learning aid when a friend or family member wants to learn to fly fish, and bass and small sunfish are often willing to take even a sloppily laid cast.

As convenient as these quintessential unpressured bass ponds are to furthering the sport, they can also give new anglers misconceptions about the ease of fooling a bass at a formative moment in their development. Fishing may never again be as easy as it was that one afternoon in the pond behind grandpa's barn. As anglers grow and expand their roam, so to speak, they will inevitably find themselves on a river with no old guiding hand pointing out the spots to cast to, or staring blankly out over an expansive public reservoir in a new hometown a thousand miles from the comfort of that old Mail Pouch Tobacco barn of their youth and the naive largemouth and bluegill living behind it.

Bass *are* everywhere, but sometimes hard to find . . . and even harder to catch. The learning curve is gentler if you respect the intelligence of your quarry and are forever observant of the environment in which they live. All animals (fish and humans included) are in some way products of the environment they live in, so if you recognize most of the variables that affect how a bass lives and eats, you will be a more successful angler.

THE ENVIRONMENT

The environs in which a bass can live are greatly varied and always changing. River smallmouths in late summer are going to act differently than they did in early spring; although they

A young Sam Barnett hoists up a largemouth bass at the bow of his father's boat. Bass are a crucial fish early in the lives of many hard-core anglers because they are plentiful and accessible. Many of my earliest fishing memories are with this boy's father, Steve, on a farm pond back in Ohio.

may be living in the same stretch of water, their environment has changed. Likewise a largemouth in a lake is not making a living in the same situation in August as it is in November. Anglers may "dial in" a particular piece of water one day, but that does not mean they will have the answers the next time they fish it. The obvious physical characteristics of the body of water where a bass lives are always important, but often not the main environmental factors that define a fishery—seasons and water temperature, forage, structure and cover, and pressure and competition all factor into the riddle.

The Body of Water

Bass can live in a perfectly still lake, a swiftly moving river, and about everything in between. However, it is more likely to find smallmouth bass in moving water and largemouth bass in still water. This is a generalization, of course, and each fishery is at least somewhat unique.

Smallmouth bass can be found in large, clear lakes and reservoirs but usually thrive only if there is at least some current or water movement. The Great Lakes have ideal habitat for smallmouth, but in the 18 years I lived on the southern shore of Lake Erie, I can only remember seeing a handful of largemouth bass caught in the lake itself. Largemouth are better suited for warmer, more turbid and sluggish to still water. Most of the man-made impoundments, ponds, and other such bodies of water scattered across the country are the perfect places to find largemouth. Spotted bass, as a riverine species, prefer water conditions more akin to that of a smallmouth, but when found in a river will be occupying the slower stretches less desirable to smallmouth, which may also be in the same body of water.

Moving water or stillwater, the size, depth, and shoreline configuration often dictates the best angling approach. The larger the body of water, the more practical some form of watercraft becomes for ease of mobility and access, and a boat with a V hull and outboard motor will always be best for the largest lakes and reservoirs. Steep banks or heavily vegetated shoreline on a smaller body of water can force an angler into an inflatable belly boat or canoe. However, much of bass fishing is done while wading midsize and smaller rivers and casting from the shore of ponds ("tanks" in Texas) and reservoirs.

Seasons and Water Temperature

Bass populations are widely spread over the lower half of the North American continent, and this covers several distinctly different regions. The seasons are vastly different for a smallmouth bass in Ontario, Canada, and a largemouth bass in south Texas. Despite this wide range and great disparity in the timing and length of seasons within their range, some generalizations can be made regarding water temperature preference for most bass. Bass from different geographical locations will adapt to temperature variations, so use these numbers purely as a starting point for a more detailed and regionalized fishing journal. Yes, *your fishing journal.*

Largemouth and smallmouth bass both function well in water between 50 and 85 degrees Fahrenheit, though they are most active and begin feeding more aggressively once the water has reached 65 degrees, and this accelerated feeding behavior steadily increases as the water temperature rises. Activity will begin to decline if the water heats up

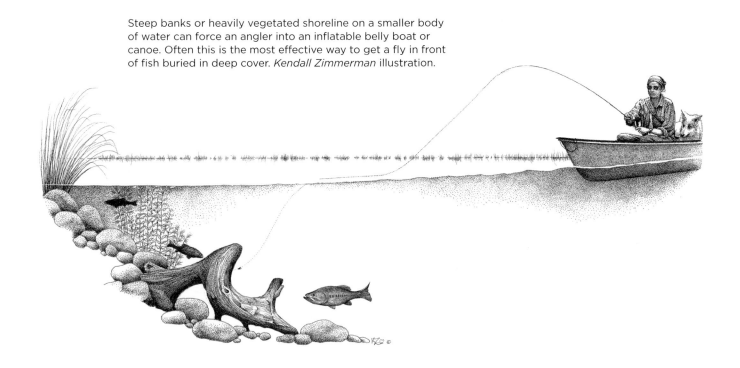

Steep banks or heavily vegetated shoreline on a smaller body of water can force an angler into an inflatable belly boat or canoe. Often this is the most effective way to get a fly in front of fish buried in deep cover. *Kendall Zimmerman* illustration.

much past 85 degrees. Bass spawn in the spring when the water temperature is still in the low 60s. Several different species are included in this generalization and each has its idiosyncrasies, but I have found the environment has far more bearing on a particular fisheries' seasonal life cycle. Learn your water.

Because season and water temperature have such an impact on bass behavior, anglers will benefit greatly from maintaining a journal. You don't need to write about how amazing the sunrise was and how much your neighbor's dog underappreciates you . . . just the nitty-gritty numbers will do. I keep separate notes on each bass water that I regularly visit because *I may have mild OCD* and it removes much guesswork, especially in the early part of the year when it gets sunny and warm for a few days and I am jonesing hard to get on some bass water. The journal reminds me it is still only the second week in March in Colorado and the secret pond behind the

baseball diamond is probably only 42 degrees, and I would do better heading to a trout stream.

In your journal you should note what the weather and nighttime lows have been in the past week or so, as well as what the actual water temperature is and what bug, frog, and fish activity you observe. When you are taking water temps, keep in mind the fish are not being affected by how warm it is in the shallow water right at your feet—they live out deeper where it may be many degrees colder. Have your thermometer on a long tether and get a reading that means something.

It is always wise to know when the bass in the areas you fish tend to spawn, and this you can bracket pretty accurately after only a few years fishing a new area. In Florida the spawn can take place as early as February; in Ohio it can take until sometime in May. I am not suggesting taking advantage of a vulnerable female while she is guarding her bed (you have to

Greg Pearson with a big smallmouth bass taken on a big baitfish streamer at Lake St. Clair between Ontario, Canada, and Michigan. *Brooks Montgomery* photo.

make your own ethical judgment call on that), but knowing when and how long the spawn happens in your favorite spots can allow you to hit the *pre-spawn* window when some of the largest fish are moving into shallow water and eating heavily. There is a two- to three-week period immediately after the spawn known as *post-spawn* when most of the sexually mature bass are quite lethargic and don't eat much. This is not the best time to invite your boss out to your best spot if you're looking to finagle a raise.

Forage

Bass (especially largemouth) have a reputation for being gluttons willing to eat anything they can catch and fit in their mouth. There is a certain amount of truth here: Bass are known to eat small birds, bats, baby turtles, salamanders, mice, rats, crayfish, frogs, dragonflies, damselflies, and other fish. Like most stereotypes, this is based on only half the information. Or, approached via another perspective, this reputation *is entirely true*, but can cause misconceptions about the intelligence of bass and how easy it is to fool them with a fly or other artificial lure.

We fly anglers have a tendency to hold trout species up as the standard for how a fish should recognize and eat food and mistakenly use a trout's selectiveness as an indicator of intelligence and the yardstick to measure the "smarts" of other fish species. We assume that if a fish eats something it has never seen before, it must mean the fish is dumb—again, we have an image of a rainbow trout rising to an adult mayfly and refusing to eat it because it is not quite the right shade of olive as the rest of the "hatch." Bass have evolved in environments where they must recognize something as potential food by its general shape and the way it moves—anatomical details in prey such as coloration, surface markings, and the exact placement of body parts are far less important.

The wide diversity of things bass are willing to eat certainly adds to the complexity and wow factor of an avid bass angler's fly collection. There can be all sorts of creative variations on crustaceans, amphibians, and evil-looking baby ducks crammed together waiting to escape like creatures in Maurice Sendak's plastic Pandora's fly box. This is one of the many fun parts about bass fishing—and also why tying bass flies may be one of the more complex forms of the craft. *There is just so much you can do!* Keep one thing paramount in your mind as you venture down the creative fly highway: Bass may eat birds and bats, but they are primarily piscivores. Large bass mainly eat other fish. *Period.* Even smallmouth bass, which are known to love crayfish, *actually* eat other fish 10-to-1 over anything else.

Structure and Cover

Structure and cover are two things bass anglers never get bored talking about, partly because together they define so much of bass fishing, but they are also really fun to talk about. When shown an aerial photo of a lake they have never been on, an experienced bass angler's eye will immediately be drawn to the back cove littered with stumps and lily pads. They know this is where the best bass are, and they may get goose bumps imagining making their first cast . . . *right up along that fallen tree.*

Little of bass fishing is sight fishing (casting to individual fish the angler has seen)—it is more often spent looking for specific places within the body of water where bass are likely to be. In some instances bass inhabit a mere 10 percent of the lake or reservoir, so having knowledge of what sort of places within an aquatic environment bass are drawn to is the key. Bass anglers eventually develop a Pavlovian conditioning to the sight of promising structure and cover. Most of us don't actually drool, but a neuroscientist observing brain activity may not be able to distinguish between a young college volunteer being shown a nudie slide show and a bass bum viewing photos of a well-endowed weed line near deep water.

Sometimes the terms *structure* and *cover* are used interchangeably; they are similar and often relate to each other, but they are very different. Structure is a change in the lake bottom, whether it be a change in depth or a point, bump, or channel. Cover is the stuff a bass can hide and hunt in—the weed beds, rock piles, stumps, fallen trees, and old docks. In topographical terms we land dwellers can better understand, structure is the mountain (or valley) and cover is the trees and abandoned stills.

Structure on large bodies of water can be located easily with the aid of sonar or maps showing underwater contour. Look for points (miniature peninsulas, often completely underwater), sudden drop-offs, submerged humps, islands, troughs, and channels (sometimes the original bed of the creek or river that was dammed to create the reservoir) as well as subtle things such as changes in the bottom composition. On smaller bodies of water locating bass-holding structure becomes less relevant, as all the structure in the entire pond is so close together. Good cover, however, is important no matter how large or small the water. I will add, before leaving the subject of structure, that these changes

Largemouth bass can live for a long time, getting bigger and smarter than most freshwater fly anglers are used to chasing. *Erin Block* photo.

in the underwater topography do not normally attract bass on their own, but when coupled with or adjacent to proper cover can be a serious fish magnet. Find the cover first, and then look for the structure that concentrates the active bass.

Cover is simply the stuff fish hide in, for concealment from whatever is trying to eat them or from what they are about to pounce on and eat themselves. Underwater weeds are almost always the number one cover in any body of water; these come in the form of water lilies (pads), water hyacinth, cattails, coontail, bulrushes, milfoil, hydrilla . . . all briars in the underwater briar patch. Uneven, haphazard weed lines with sudden breaks and pockets of open water make the best ambush areas for bass to lurk in: Think like a middle-school bully—it is easier to catch a little fourth-grader in a corn maze than a long, wide hallway where they can see you coming.

Although living aquatic weeds provide the best and most abundant cover for bass, there is an array of other natural submerged cover—rock piles, brush piles, stumps, and trees.

Then there is the man-made cover—the sunken cars and concrete foundations, the bed springs and shopping carts. Not all man-made cover is accidental or even refuse. Some farmers I have known wire a cluster of discarded Christmas trees together and attach a few cinder blocks, then drag the lot out onto the ice of their bass ponds after the holidays. When spring comes and the ice melts, the pond life will prosper. This is a small-scale version of what happens when old warships are towed out to sea and sunk to form a man-made reef.

Structures such as docks, floating gazebos, and boathouses are not considered "structure" in the world of bass fishing, they are "cover." *Good cover, too!* The perfect dock for the best bass cover has wooden pilings (not floats), sits low to the water, has tight decking (to reduce vulnerability from above), and is as large as possible . . . maybe even have a T or L shape at the very end. A long, wide wooden dock buried in a dense but broken bed of weeds is the fanciful scenario of bass-fishing dreams.

Pressure and Competition

Of all the variables that affect a bass fishery, often it is the amount of pressure and type of competition that is the hardest to predict and adjust to. Other pieces of the puzzle an angler is attempting to piece together to understand a particular body of water are visual, albeit often underwater. Anglers can record weather reports, drop a thermometer in the lake, observe large schools of shad, and map the entire bottom with sonar if they are so inclined. Gauging the amount of fishing pressure from other anglers and competition from other predatory fish species are two intangibles that can take a lot of time on the water before you get a good feel for the situation.

Popular public water can present a real challenge. Bass are a fish that learns quickly and has memory associated with bad experiences that will last for months. Pair these smart fish with a long history and culture of catch-and-release, and a quite difficult and technical fishery develops. I have seen the transition from an easy *they'll-eat-anything* bass fishery to *lucky-to-catch-a-couple-even-on-a-good-day* happen within a few seasons. Sometimes this occurs when a group of avid anglers stumble onto a semisecret and neglected spot, or a landowner discovers he can turn his lake into a bass lease and charge for access. The bass need only be caught one or two times before they realize there is potential danger in what they choose to eat.

In small bodies of water, bass are often the sole large predator fish, and they rule the roost hunting wherever they like, so can be found right where you think they should be. Some larger fisheries are more diverse, and the bass may have to share their home with bigger bullies and find a way to get by somewhere more toward the middle of the food chain. Get to know what baitfish are present in your favorite waters, but also figure out what the competition is like. If there is a significant northern pike or musky population, the bass will tend to avoid them. Largemouth bass will hole up in shallow coves and stay clear of the outside edges of weed lines. Smallmouth bass will hang out in rocky, weedless areas that are poor ambush spots for toothy critters, but where they can still find enough grub to get by. In some large reservoirs with threadfin and gizzard shad populations, bass

Always be careful handling bass before releasing them.

will spend much of their time suspended out in open water where the getting is good, but add stripers or wipers (large temperate bass) to the mix and the black bass will stick close to shore and their diet will consist mainly of bluegill and other sunfish. White bass (a smaller temperate bass) present no threat to black bass, so their presence may only encourage a joint-force shad-busting out in open water.

TACTICS AND FLIES

Understanding the environments bass live in and how their behavior is altered by changes in that environment is the first part of learning your quarry—it's the amateur fisheries biologist stuff. The next part is taking what you already know (or have just learned or observed on the water) and figuring out how to take advantage of that knowledge—this is the transition from backyard scientist to angler. When you sit down at the tying bench in the evening or open your fly box on the water with your rod under your arm, there are several things to consider as you choose a tactic and corresponding fly.

Type of Water

Locating bass in a river is different from finding them in stillwater, as there is the added variable of current. In a slow-moving river bass will be drawn to certain areas because of desirable structure and cover, but if the flow is more substantial, the current itself will be the defining variable and being able to read the water and recognize current seams and eddies becomes important.

The practical approach to a river with obvious current is to work downstream, as your fly and line will be swept that way and the retrieve will make the fly swim against the current. The weight of the fly you choose becomes the most important deciding factor (assuming you are using a subsurface fly, as you probably should in these situations). Getting a bass fly sunk to the bottom of stillwater is doable even if the fly is slightly underweight, so long as your leader is long enough and you are patient. This is not the case in current: The fly will be swept downriver too fast to sink to where the fish are and then ride just below the surface on the retrieve. You may have found the fish, but they never see the fly or are not willing to leave their spot near the bottom of the river or behind a rock to battle the current to get the meal. Choose a fly with enough weight to counter the current. Using a sink-tip fly line can help in this situation, but is limiting if you are carrying just the one rod and reel and may encounter

slack water where you might want to try a topwater fly. A loop knot will allow a fly to sink significantly faster than one cinched tight to the leader without adding weight, so learning a new knot (any of the many nonslip loop knots) can help get the fly where it needs to go—besides, the loop knot will increase the erratic action of almost all bass flies.

Ponds and large reservoirs are the same type of water at opposite ends of the size spectrum, but each particular body of water will present different obstacles and opportunities based on its size and depth. A lake that got its start as a stone quarry may have bass holding at depths out of the normal comfort range of most fly anglers, where extra-heavy flies on jig hooks fished with long leaders or sink-tip fly lines are necessary. Where you are on the body of water is also important. The lake may be large and deep, but if you are shorebound and can't wade out enough to access anything but the shallow flats, then lighter-weight flies and floating line will rule the day. Usually the larger and deeper water is best fished from the vantage of a boat or float tube.

Water Temperature

As the water temperature increases, the metabolism of bass living in that body of water increases, thus so does their need for food and willingness to chase prey more aggressively. Bass are most active in water temperatures between 65 and 85 degrees, and the warmer the water is within this range, the more energetic they tend to be. Hungry, aggressive bass are more easily taken advantage of, so choose larger flies that make noise, cause commotion in the water, and move quickly and erratically.

The best chance an angler has at getting an explosive topwater take is when the water temperature is at its peak for fish activity. Bass continue to feed even when the water is as low as 40 degrees, so can still be taken on a fly. However, the colder the water gets below what is optimal, the more your fly selection and strategy should change. At any time anglers should match their presentations and retrieves to bass aggressiveness, so a slow, deliberate retrieve through heavy, weedy cover with a well-weighted (and weedless) fly often works the best in cold water.

Type of Forage

Knowing what particular bass are used to hunting and most likely to chase and eat is an important part in determining the right flies and tactics. Stomach pumps are used by some trout anglers to better understand the current diet of the

All fishing is fun, but bass fishing is the most fun. *Erin Block* photo.

fish they are after, but I always felt this was peeking at other players' cards at a poker table; besides, most things bass eat are too large to be sucked out easily anyway. As a boy I fished (and hunted) solely to put meat in the family freezer. I am a fairly strict catch-and-release bass angler as an adult, but I have not forgotten all the things I found in the belly of fish I gutted—*bass sometimes eat interesting things.* However, once bass get larger than about 3 pounds they eat mostly other fish—it's what's most constantly available as forage year-round and of a serving size worth pursuing. Baitfish fly patterns rarely don't work, so are a great choice to start with, especially on unfamiliar water.

Frogs and crayfish can also play crucial roles in some bass fisheries. The more time you spend on any body of water, the more you will learn about what makes its fishery tick. Spend time exploring the shoreline, and wade in and pick up rocks and lift weed beds to see what flees or clings. Not every bit of bass water is easily stereotyped, and they can change. I grew up fishing a river in northern Ohio that had

an incredible smallmouth bass population in the spring when the flows were strong and weighted baitfish patterns were the only flies needed, but come late summer when the water was slow and low and most of the bass and shad and other fish had retreated back to Lake Erie, everything was different. The main food source for the remaining smallmouth was crayfish, and the water was low and clear so a lightweight fly that could enter the water quietly and scoot around on the bottom was called for.

Another time, many years later, a friend showed me a bass pond in Colorado that I came to know well (mainly because it was just five minutes from the fly shop we were both working for). It was small and weedy in the summer but full of largemouth bass. The odd thing with this pond was that it had no fish other than the bass. No bluegill, no pumpkinseed . . . nothing. There were plenty of frogs around to keep the bass full as well as swarms of damselflies so thick they outnumbered the mosquitoes. I spent countless evenings after work stripping size 12 damsel nymph patterns

It takes skill and a heavy leader to wrestle a bass out of heavy cover.

over the slop and catching as many 1- to 2-pound bass as I liked before dark. It pays to know what the fish know, but even in that little Colorado bass pond, the biggest bass I ever caught was on a baitfish streamer.

The action and movement of a fly is almost always more important than what the angler believes the fly imitates in nature. When choosing a fly for bass, an angler should be aware of the available forage and use that knowledge simply as a starting point.

Cover and Water Clarity

The physical characteristics of a body of water will sometimes need to be considered when choosing the right fly and rigging. The type and density of cover and the clarity level of the water are often two pertinent factors. The presence of good, thick cover is crucial for thriving bass habitat, but can create obvious problems for an angler.

If there are a lot of sticks, logs, and other obstacles that can easily snag a fly, select flies tied on jig-style hooks that make them more snag-resistant. If the water is clogged with aquatic weeds, using flies with some form of weed guard or anti-snagging mechanism built into the pattern will drastically decrease frustration levels and increase odds of catching fish. When bass fishing in heavy cover, it is best to use a heavy fly rod with fast (stiff) action, as any of the flies with weed guards will need a bit more *oomph* to get the hook properly set. Strong leaders are a good idea as well, to avoid snapping off on a powerful hook set or while pulling the fly free from the almost inevitable snag in deep water or in brush well over your head.

Water clarity plays a large part in not just the flies an angler should choose, but also how the angler approaches the water. If the water is clear enough for you to spot bass, the bass can spot you. Wear drab clothing and always be aware of your shadow and silhouette when fishing in clear water. Bass

Urban areas are often close to home and can offer great bass-fishing opportunities. *Erin Block* photo.

are less skittish in deeply stained or muddy water because they are safer from other (usually feathered) predators that have being trying to snatch or spear them since they were wee young fry. Often a finesse rig works better in clear water—a slimmer leader with a lighter-weight, more subtle fly.

In extremely off-color water, bass can no longer locate prey by sight, so must rely on other senses to find food. Bass are equipped with great hearing and lateral-line sensory organs nearly as reliable as their eyes at pinpointing something to eat. A larger, more bulky fly that displaces more water when it moves will be easier for a bass to find using these nonvisual senses. Exaggerated flash and fly rattles are also used in off-color water for the same purpose. When fishing in clear water a hyper-erratic retrieve can be what is needed to trigger an aggressive strike from otherwise unwilling bass, but in murky water it is usually best to slow down your retrieve to a more steady, predictable pace to make the fly easier to locate and intercept. Any of the advice given for murky-water bass fishing also applies to night fishing in clear water.

Amount of Pressure

The tactics and flies you choose for a public bass lake that receives many anglers throughout the season should be different from those you go with when the opportunity to fish an untouched private pond or stretch of river arises. Bass may be curious and adventurous feeders, but they learn fast and remember longer than most other fish, and this creates an interesting and often confusing situation for anglers. Unpressured bass are more predictable and have aggressive feeding instincts that can be taken advantage of—obnoxious flies with lots of flash and fast retrieves can be incredibly productive given that all *natural* variables that can alter the day have lined up positively. A body of water with similar natural conditions will not fish as well if the bass have bachelor's degrees in buzz baits and PhDs in whatever spun deer hair concoction you were just about to tie onto your leader.

The first step in overcoming the stinginess of pressured bass is to know what you are up against. Look for signs the place has excessive angler traffic, such as well-worn fishermen's trails through tall grass along the back side of a pond, tangles of monofilament line caught in trees, loose bobbers along the shoreline, and empty chicken liver containers. Bait fishers tend to leave more trash behind than conventional-gear and fly anglers combined, and finding signs of their presence adds another negative element to an already difficult situation. Bait-caught bass are usually kept for dinner and those released often have swallowed the hook and will die slowly later—either way, there will be fewer mature bass in that body of water and those remaining will be less likely to do anything foolish. A pressured fishery that is predominantly catch-and-release may educate bass, but a fishery that has large numbers of bass repeatedly removed in this way will have inadvertently eliminated not only many of the biggest bass, but much of the aggressive genetics within the population.

It is sometimes frustrating as an angler with no private water connections to hear about a friend's day on a bass lease, or see 8-pounder after 8-pounder being hoisted out of the net on Saturday morning television. If this strikes a tender nerve, don't beat yourself up too much—there should be far more satisfaction in finding one solid bass on public water, or having a great day on some neglected property on the sketchy side of town that you sniffed out for yourself. These are the results of hard homework and persistence. Sometimes catching smart bass means you must scale down in size of line and fly, fish slow, and be as subtly enticing as possible. Steer away from common bass flies, and leave the flashy and rattled ones at home. Maybe try some of your favorite carp and trout flies? *Something smaller, something different.* Find parts of the lake that are hard to get to, or focus your energy on unlikely spots that get bypassed regularly because they look like less-than-ideal holding areas for bass. If you are in a real jam, try fishing public water during foul weather or at different times of the day (or night) than the bass are used to being pressured—fish can pattern us just as we can pattern them.

TYING BASS FLIES

"Elk don't know how many feet a horse has!"—Bear Claw, *Jeremiah Johnson*

The wide diversity of things bass are willing to eat certainly adds to the complexity and wow factor of an avid bass angler's fly collection. Flies out of box, top to bottom: Bellyache Minnow (Olive), Stuntman Eddy (Creek Chub). Flies on lid of box, left to right: Bass Bug, Bellyache Minnow (Brown/Tan), Bellyache Minnow (White). Flies in box, starting from row 1, top to bottom: Geezus Lizard (Crayfish), Geezus Lizard (Black & Olive), Stuntman Eddy (Threadfin Shad), Stuntman Eddy (Rainbow Trout); row 2: Finesse Worm (Pearl), Finesse Worm (Purple), Finesse Worm (Olive), Meat Whistle (Black 'N Blue), Meat Whistle (Crawfish Orange), Meat Whistle (Olive Variant).

More fly anglers are adding bass as a targeted species every year. As famous trout streams become crowded and rely more and more on stocking-truck conservation, the romance is weakening in those areas once thought to be hallmarks of traditional fly fishing and growing stronger in the areas of the sport that have been historically less respected. The experience is what we are all after, so it stands to reason that we as anglers seek out aggressive fish away from crowds. The lack of pretty spots along the flanks of the quarry is an easy price to pay for the fun and solitude an angling life has always promised. *Isn't it?*

I live in Colorado and work in a fly shop at the foot of the Rocky Mountains. This is deep in trout country, and the majority of anglers I introduce to bass fishing are those who have been fly fishing for a long time (often longer than I have been alive) yet have never strayed from the pursuit of trout. When I show most trout anglers a typical bass fly, the usual response is, "What is *that* supposed to be?" Sure, many bass-specific fly patterns are easily identified as frogs, crayfish, and baitfish imitations (even to the frog-water virgins who have never left tailwater midge factories), but many of the best bass flies can confuse someone whose extent of scientific angling goes no further than "match the hatch."

Trout have evolved to remain single-minded during much of their feeding, so as not to waste precious energy moving through heavy current to eat something they have never seen before. The majority of what a trout eats is tiny, and if any measurable amount of what it routinely puts in its face hole turns out to have the protein content of a piece of dead leaf (because it *is* a piece of dead leaf), the trout will starve to death. Dead trout don't spawn. This particular evolutionary paradigm does not encourage free thought. In a sense, most trout are stuck in the aquatic culinary Dark Ages.

Bass, on the other hand, have grown up as a species in a much different environment. The places bass live have generally warmer water, longer growing seasons, and fewer environmental hurdles, which result in a higher diversification of potential prey, coupled with less risk in making a mistake about dinner. Up until us humans began pestering them with flies and lures, bass could feel pretty safe having a go at anything that looked alive and could fit in their mouth.

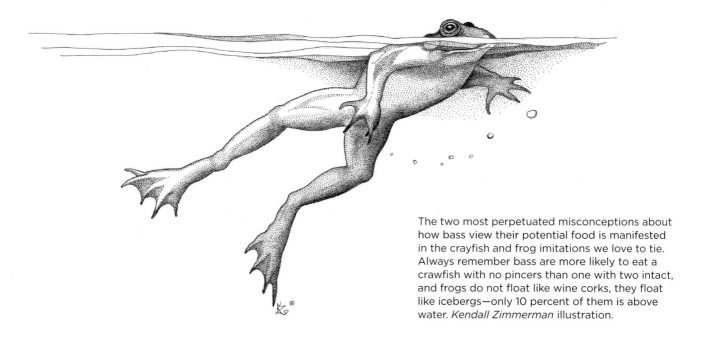

The two most perpetuated misconceptions about how bass view their potential food is manifested in the crayfish and frog imitations we love to tie. Always remember bass are more likely to eat a crawfish with no pincers than one with two intact, and frogs do not float like wine corks, they float like icebergs—only 10 percent of them is above water. *Kendall Zimmerman* illustration.

I have heard some anglers claim this makes bass dumb, because *they will eat anything*. But this logic is flawed. Bass have developed a keen ability to know if something is alive and worth eating, even if they have never seen or swallowed that particular creature before. This constant brain exercise partially explains why a bass can learn and remember better than most species we fly anglers pursue.

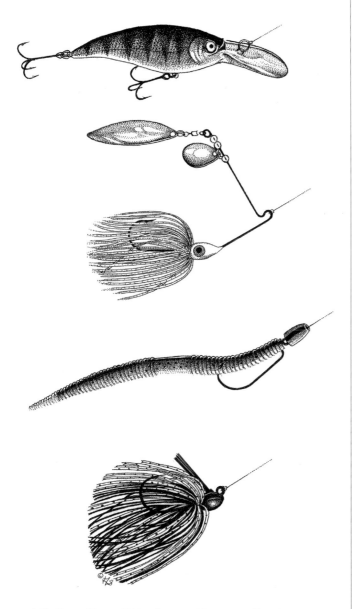

A fly tier with a solid background in conventional-gear fishing will have a distinct advantage on bass water. Far more than "matching the hatch," bass fishing is about presenting a fly or lure that moves like it is alive and is of the shape or has an action that triggers aggressive feeding behavior. Common conventional bass lures are (from top to bottom) diving plug, spinner bait, Texas-rigged rubber worm, and bass jig. *Kendall Zimmerman* illustration.

Dr. Keith Jones, a fish biologist, documented the years of laboratory work he oversaw while employed by Berkley & Company in a book called *Knowing Bass* (Lyons Press, 2002), where he illustrates how quickly bass can learn from bad experiences (being caught on a particular lure) and how long (years) they can remember the experience and let it dictate their actions and willingness to repeat that behavior. This partially explains the vastly different approaches an angler must take when fishing private, unpressured bass waters versus heavily fished waters. The purpose behind the work Dr. Jones was doing was to better understand how bass think and what triggers them to eat, then focus on these things to make lures with better action and shape, and bait with a more attractive scent.

If there is one sound bite from the extensive tome of information that best encompasses what I have learned from Dr. Jones, it's: "Anglers would be better to focus on the *features* of shape that activate strike behavior, and then exploit those features for greater effect." This knowledge has helped me catch more fish and enjoy time on the water. It also begins to demystify some of the odd flies and lures used by bass anglers. After all, elk don't know how many feet a horse has . . . and bass don't know how many toes a frog has or antennae a crawdad has, or how long worms are. What matters is whether it moves like it is alive and whether the shape or action of the fly takes one of these living traits (be it the length/width ratio of a baitfish, or the top-dark/bottom-light color scheme) and amplifies it to make the fly even more appealing to the feeding instinct of a bass.

THE TOOLS

Bass live in many different environments and eat whatever is there for them. With this in mind, you need to be prepared to tie flies in a wide array of sizes and styles if you are serious about tying for bass. You need all the basic tools an average trout tier owns, plus some weird stuff to help with, well . . . the weird stuff.

Tying Vise

If you already own a fly-tying vise, don't use bass flies as an excuse to buy a new vise unless, of course, you are planning on buying it from me, then by all means treat yourself, don't cheat yourself! I believe in making do with what you have for as long as possible. I am frugal. I buy my clothing at Goodwill and my wine glasses at the dollar store. But

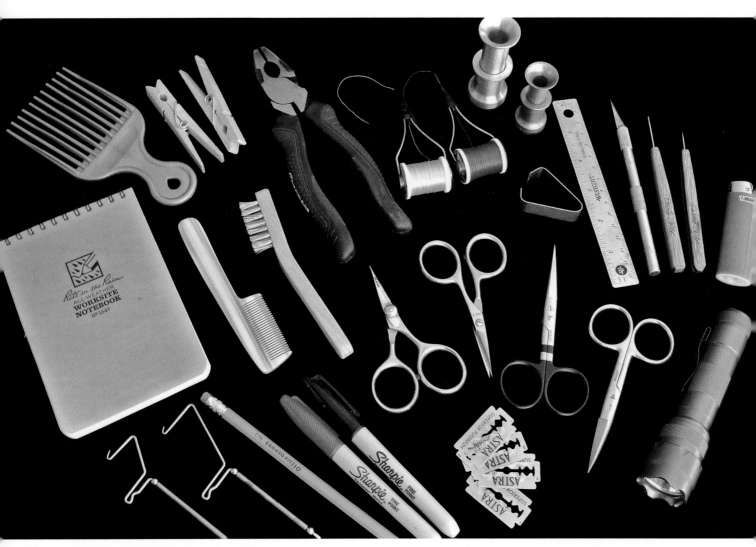

From top to bottom, left to right, the basic fly-tying tools I use for bass flies: large hair pick, waterproof note pad, standard and extended-reach whip-finish tools, wooden clothespins, small hair comb, coarse wire dubbing brush, graphite pencil, red and black Sharpie markers, heavy side cutters, multiple ceramic bobbins, various straight and curved-blade scissors, flexible double-sided razor blades, large and medium hair stackers, hair-packing tool, straight-edge ruler, X-ACTO knife, long- and short-spear bodkins, lighter, and a powerful UV lamp.

tools are more important and worth spending some money on—and your vise will always be the most important tool.

Most decent fly-tying vises are great for bass flies, but steer away from ones with weak jaws or those that do not have the ability to rotate the fly around easily. You will see during the course of the tutorials in this book that turning a bass fly into different positions during the tying process is done on a regular basis. If you are using a vise that you must disengage the jaws and reposition the fly each time, you will quickly become frustrated. I have tied on the same Renzetti Presentation 4000 Cam model with a sturdy pedestal base for over 15 years without having to replace the standard jaws the vise came with. I can comfortably tie anything from a size 28 midge pupa to a 5/0 musky fly.

Bobbins

What I like in a bobbin is exactly what I like in a bow—the less moving parts, the better. One end of a bobbin is meant to hold the thread, and the other is meant to make precise thread wraps easier without fraying the thread. *Simple.* Anything more, the manufacturer is trying to pitch you a gimmick. If you have any bobbins with all-metal tubes, pitch them. Don't keep them around to use in a pinch, or to give to your niece when she is old enough, unless you are still holding a childhood grudge and want to make your sibling's kid miserable—gift her stilts or a trombone, or both, so she at least has fun while terrorizing your intended target. Throw the cheap metal-tubed bobbin away. It is worthless and should never be on a fly-tying

Many of the best bass flies are tied on heavy hooks and in a way that allows the fly to swim hook point up to avoid snagging. A fly-tying vise with strong jaws and the rotary ability needed to turn a fly over is important.

bench, let alone in every $50 fly-tying kit ever sold in America (which it is).

I have found no better bobbins than the Tiemco ceramic bobbins. Tiemco makes curved and straight bobbins as well as standard and heavyweight ceramic shafts. As much as I love and promote these tools, I have never found a practical difference between any of the four varieties they make. However, I do own them in all configurations. I like using the standard/curved Tiemco bobbin for any thinner, weaker threads and the heavy/straight bobbin for the thicker, stronger threads. The ceramic bobbin shafts are white on the former and black on the latter, and this color difference immediately reminds me how much tension I can apply to the thread as I am tying.

Scissors

I recommend owning good scissors regardless of what you are tying. Bass flies tend to be bigger, so there is rarely need for small, fine-tipped scissors. However, large quantities of hair and other materials often need to be cut when tying bass flies, so good sharp scissors are a must. The nicest pair on my own bench at the moment are $60 Tiemco razor scissors, but the ones I use day in and day out are $30 Dr. Slick razor scissors, usually in the 4-inch, but occasionally I need the 5-inch scissors when trimming up larger deer hair flies.

Once you have a few good scissors, be protective of them. Never use them to cut wire (even lead), and don't let cats or kids (or your elbows) knock them off your tying bench, as they will always land tip down and never close right again. And never let non-tying family members "borrow" them for random household cutting cores—scrapbooks, new toy packaging, and clogged sink drains have all killed their share of expensive fly-tying scissors.

Dubbing Brushes

The majority of dubbing blends used with bass flies are of the longer, coarser-fibered variety, so wire dubbing brushes tend to be the most useful. There are seldom any delicate features on a bass fly, so anytime you are using dubbing it is to add bulk or bushiness to a fly, and the best way to achieve this is to use the burly stuff. Leave the fine stuff for the trout flies.

The best way to take full advantage of this sort of dubbing is to use a dubbing loop to get the dubbing onto the hook shank, but this means twisting the thread loop and then wrapping it onto the fly. Both of these actions will mat down and diminish the desired effect unless you vigorously brush out the dubbing after twisting it in the loop and after wrapping it onto the hook shank.

Whip-Finish Tool

Having a standard whip-finish tool at your tying bench is often all that is needed, but because bass flies tend to be larger and often more complex than what the average fly tier tackles, there are occasionally times when an extended-reach whip-finish tool can make the job easier and faster. The purpose of an extended-reach whip-finish tool is to allow the fly tier to "reach" over the bulky front end of a fly and tie a knot farther back on the hook shank instead of directly behind the hook eye. There is seldom need to do this, but seldom is not never.

Matarelli used to make a whip-finish tool far superior to any other, but sadly they have been discontinued. Dr. Slick tools will suffice, but if you have the time and want the best, get online and track down someone selling a used Matarelli. I have several still in their original paper packaging hoarded away like collector *Star Wars* toys, and *no*, I will not sell them.

Specialty Items

This is the part where we talk about the weird stuff. To be fair, these are not necessarily weird tools, just stuff you sometimes won't find at a fly shop but need to tie the bass flies in this book. Have a set of heavy pliers with side cutters handy for clipping heavy-gauge hooks. Have two sets if you intend to tie with articulated shanks, as they rarely come perfectly aligned and two pliers are needed to straighten them. A comb and plenty of flexible, double-sided razor blades are needed if you will be spinning and/or packing deer hair for a textbook deer hair "bass bug." Next time you

are at a hardware store or backpacking specialty shop, pick up a waterproof notepad with a heavy plastic cover and graph paper, as this is the best way to create patterns and templates to aid in cutting tail or body shapes out of foam or leathery material. Also, have a few wooden clothespins to hold flies as they dry.

THE MATERIALS

When a serious fly tier walks into a fly tiers' fly shop, it is like a chef walking through a farmers' market or high-end grocery store. There are aisles and piles of magic and inspiration. Beams of light come down from the sky, and sometimes harp music can be heard. I grew up fawning over fly-tying catalogs and still look through every page twice when they come in the mail at the shop, even though I work in one of the best-stocked tiers' shops in the country. I can't help myself. I love ingredients. Fresh produce.

Hooks

Hooks are the meat of a fly-tying recipe—what everything else is built around. An undercooked turkey can send Thanksgiving guests home early, and sloppy processing can turn your prize venison "gamey." Poor hook choice can ruin a fly, a fish-of-a-lifetime, a trip . . . even a season. Never use cheap hooks. I tie most of my bass flies using only two brands and 10 styles of hook: Tiemco 811S (sizes 4, 2, and 1/0), 8089 (sizes 6 and 2), 600SP (size 2), 5262 (size 8), 9395 (size 4), and 3769 (size 6); and Gamakatsu B10S (sizes 6, 4, 2, and 2/0), Jig 90 (sizes 1/0 and 2/0), Jig 60 (size 3/0), and SC15 (size 1/0). These are not the only two quality manufacturers of fly-tying hooks, just the two I have the most confidence in and the easiest access to.

Every well-designed fly pattern is tied on a specific hook for a reason; it may be the gauge/weight of the hook, direction of the hook eye, gape style, or length of the shank. If you are playing around with a variation of a fly you have used before, or making something entirely new, think hard about your hook choice and how different styles of hook will make the fly act in the water and function as the tool it is.

Threads

Just like every fly should be tied on a particular hook chosen with deliberation, every well-designed bass fly uses a certain thread for a reason. Color of thread is almost always not as important as we tiers think—it is usually purely aesthetic.

Most bass flies are not small and often large amounts of material are needed to be secured to the hook, so stronger threads are called for. The threads I most often use when tying bass flies are UTC Ultra Thread 140, 210, and 280 denier; UNI-Thread 6/0; Danville's Waxed Monocord 3/0; and UTC G.S.P. 100 and 200 denier.

That being said, I always choose thread color very carefully. I have more confidence in a good-looking fly with obvious attention to detail involved in its creation, so will naturally fish it a little bit harder and with more concentration—confidence in fishing is never overrated. At times thread color choice in a pattern may seem odd at first, but look ahead (or *think* ahead if you are working up a recipe for a new fly) and take note where on the finished fly the thread is visible—most times it is just at the head, behind the hook eye.

Aesthetics aside, there are real considerations as to what thread is best for a given fly pattern. The three main variables that dictate thread choice are strength, bulk, and cost. Obviously a thread that is thicker is usually stronger, and there is no reason to not use a heavy thread unless excessive thread buildup is a concern. However, although bass flies tend to be large and not "delicate flowers," bulkiness is often a reasonable concern in certain areas of the fly, which forces a compromise.

Even if excess thread bulk is not a concern, there is another reason to dial back from the strongest threads. Gel-spun polyethylene (G.S.P.) is the strongest thread, but can slice through other tying materials as well as add unnecessary cost to a pattern. I reserve the use of G.S.P. thread for lashing down large clumps of deer hair that often need above-average thread tension to remain sturdy, or for securing clumps of synthetic material such as EP Fibers that cannot be severed by thread tension. G.S.P can be slick if used as a thread base, which is something to keep in mind and be either utilized or avoided.

Some threads, such as UTC Ultra Thread as well as UTC G.S.P., are more "fibrous" and, if wrapped without added twist, will lie flat on the hook shank. The thicker, non-G.S.P.

flat threads (UTC 210 and 280 denier) are ideal when tying down foam, as they are the least likely to cut this material. Other threads, such as UNI-Thread and Danville's, are round, which provides the best traction when used as a thread base on a hook shank—when material slippage is a concern, these are good thread choices. The threads I most often use when tying bass flies are UTC Ultra Thread 140, 210, and 280 denier; UNI-Thread 6/0; Danville's Waxed Monocord 3/0; and UTC G.S.P. 100 and 200 denier.

Weights

Traditionally, weight is added to a fly by wrapping lead (or lead-free substitute) wire around the hook shank during the beginning stages of tying the fly. Nowadays, most subsurface bass flies are weighted with brass or lead barbell eyes, or brass or tungsten cones. Lead wire can still be added to a pattern in addition to whatever original hardware is called for in the recipe to increase the sink rate, but I would hesitate to use it to *replace* some hardware. Cones and large beads can be easily replaced with wire with only minor cosmetic changes to the fly, but barbell weights are often crucial to the way a fly rides in the water. Barbell eyes are an ideal way to add weight to a fly while also counterbalancing the fly and causing it to ride hook point up—which is important with any subsurface warmwater fly.

Be aware of the weight of the hardware you are incorporating into a bass fly pattern. It is important to have a general sense of what each finished fly weighs, as this will likely dictate the areas the fly can be fished with either better success (because it can quickly sink to the desired depth) or less likelihood of getting hung up on the bottom (because it is not *too* heavy). Typical small lead barbells weigh .68 gram, medium are 1.02 grams, and large are 1.34 grams—this is significant, especially once you consider the overall weight of most weighted bass flies is only a gram and a half. It would take nearly 6 inches of the heaviest lead wire (.035) to equal the weight of medium lead barbell eyes.

Dubbing

Dubbing is an underrated tying material in larger flies, overshadowed by hide, hackle, and other materials that are easier and faster to make into a fly. However, dubbing is one of the most versatile materials once a tier becomes comfortable with application techniques beyond simply rolling it onto waxed tying thread and wrapping it onto a hook shank. Also, the options in dubbing blends and

consistencies have improved greatly in recent years, which makes finding just the right material for a particular part of a recipe much easier.

There are natural and synthetic dubbings (as well as blends of both), and as much as I like tying with natural materials, the purely synthetic dubbings tend to have longer fibers, lending themselves better to most of the bass flies I tie. Apart from color, length of fiber is the primary characteristic I am looking for in a dubbing for bass flies. For "buggy" flies, such as crayfish (and actual aquatic insects), I usually use either Dave Whitlock SLF dubbing or Crawdub. For flashy baitfish-type flies, I prefer either Hareline Ice Dub or Wapsi Prism dubbing.

If you find Ice Dub in a color you like, be sure to look closely or even open the package to see exactly how long the dubbing fibers are—there is a drastic inconsistency in fibers between colors. For example, the rusty brown Ice Dub and copper Ice Dub are similar colors, but very different dubbings. Both have fibers that are roughly 2 inches (5 cm) long, but the rusty brown fibers are slimmer and softer and so have more "curl," making them seem shorter than the copper Ice Dub, which has thicker, straighter fibers that look a bit like small strands of Micro Flashabou. The softer-fibered Ice Dubs are easier to insert into thread dubbing loops and make fuller, more natural dubbed bodies on flies.

The Wapsi Prism blends are consistent throughout the style, and I prefer them when tying flies that use multiple colors of flashy dubbing, as I am guaranteed consistency in appearance, even if I decide to switch up a color scheme. However, the pearl Ice Dub is my go-to dubbing for shad and other baitfish bellies.

Feathers

Hackle and marabou are the two primary types of feathers used in the bass flies I tie. The most useful hackle is wide, long, and generally softer than what is used on trout dry flies. There is rarely a need for expensive genetic dry-fly hackle when tying bass flies. Schlappen feathers (think chicken tail feathers), hen saddles and necks, and inexpensive strung hackle make up the bulk of what you need for these flies. However, Whiting Bugger Hackle and select feathers out of Hebert Miner saddles are some of my most coveted bass fly feathers.

Hackle feather selection always hinges on what the intended purpose of the feather is and how it is going to be incorporated into the fly. If the feather is going to be wrapped onto the hook shank, it needs to be long enough to cover the intended section of hook shank, and if just the tips are being used, they need to be wide enough to achieve the desired effect.

"Marabou" is a fluffy feather that originally came from an African stork that is now endangered and protected. The feathers of that name used in modern fly tying usually come from turkeys and are legally sold for fly-tying purposes. These feathers have amazing undulating action when wet and are used as tails in Woolly Buggers, Super Buggers, and many other well-known fly patterns. Marabou can also be used as a "topping" ingredient for a streamer, or wrapped on a hook shank to form an ultra-webby hackle if the feather is of a proper length.

Hair

A deer hair bass bug is what most anglers immediately think of when they think about flies for bass. This quintessential bass fly is tied using multiple clumps of deer hair (usually whitetail) placed or allowed to spin around the hook shank.

Large or small square/rectangular patches of deer hair suitable for this application can be purchased, usually bleached and dyed to an assortment of common fly-tying colors.

Natural deer body hair has a gray/brown/black mottled look on the animal (as you are only viewing the tips of all the hair), but viewed as a clump of hair about to be lashed to a hook, it graduates from light gray at the very butt end to medium gray mid-fiber to dark gray before reaching the mottled tip. This coloration varies slightly from animal to animal, as well as where on the hide the patch is from or how late in the season it was harvested. When deer hair is bleached, it turns a light cream to tan color (not pure white), so when the hair is later dyed, it takes on the dye but retains some of the mottling and has a somewhat dirty appearance. This look is great for bass flies, but if you are after a bright color or a band of drastic contrast color in your fly, steer away from the dyed body hair and find a patch of dyed belly hair. The belly hairs on whitetail are naturally white, so when bleached and dyed will be vivid and true to color.

White-tailed deer provide fly tiers with one of the most important natural materials used in bass flies. Their body and belly hair are hollow and are ideal for packing and trimming into topwater bass bugs, and the long white hair on their tails can be dyed any color and used in almost any type of bass streamer.

Bucktail is the hair from the tail of the same white-tailed deer most of the body and belly patches come from, but has very different characteristics that concern fly tiers. The tail hair is much longer than any other hair on a deer (averaging 4 to 5 inches, or 10 to 13 cm) and not as hollow, so will not flare as much when thread tension is applied. These traits make this hair an ideal material for use in large streamers.

Rabbit is a frequently used natural hair in tying bass flies that is usually mounted onto the fly while still attached to the tanned strip of hide. Rabbit strips can be purchased in "standard" ⅛-inch (3 mm) wide strips and "magnum" ¼-inch (6 mm) wide strips. The rabbit hides are tanned and then usually cut down the length of the animal (nose to tail), so the cut is following the direction the individual hairs are lying. A rabbit strip designated as "crosscut" is one with the hide cut across the grain, so to speak, leaving the hairs extending out over one of the sides of the strip of hide. The theory of crosscutting rabbit strips is to allow fly tiers the ability to wrap the material around a hook shank as they would hackle. In reality the straight-cut strips work better for this application, as the hair is not allowed to fall back naturally on the body of the fly as it is moving through the water, so the hair remains fluffed out better and has more movement.

Straight-cut rabbit can be used for all applications, but crosscut rabbit can *only* be used for wrapping, which leads tiers to the inevitable conundrum of finding just the right color and width of rabbit strip in their collection, but if it is crosscut they may not be able to use it. For this reason alone, I never recommend buying crosscut rabbit strips.

Deer and rabbit are the two mammals most commonly victimized for bass flies, but there are a slew of other great furbearers that you should not overlook. Arctic fox and Icelandic sheep both have soft, long fur that can give a subsurface bass fly great action. More importantly, these hides are dyed and readily available in hobbyist-size portions at most fly shops.

Synthetic Fibers

Every year more fibrous synthetic fly-tying materials are available, but few ever look as good as natural materials do on a fly. There are some huge advantages to using synthetics, as they are sold in lengths much longer than any natural hair ever grows and are almost always more durable and won't absorb water like natural materials, which make them easier to pick up off the water and cast. But fake fiber will never look or act as alive as natural fur or feather. The trick to making the best flies is using a mix of natural and synthetic

materials in the same fly—this gives you all the advantages of both while diminishing either's drawbacks.

The majority of synthetic fiber I use in bass flies can be better classified as *flash* that I use to add accent and glitter to an otherwise drab fly—this is usually more important when imitating baitfish, but if used sparingly can add a bit of an attractor to any fly. The two main flash fibers I use on bass flies are Flashabou and Krystal Flash. Flashabou is the wider and limper of the two materials, and even a little bit can be a flashbulb underwater. Krystal Flash adds subtle flash and is stiff enough to hold the shape with stiff natural fiber such as bucktail.

Enrico Puglisi (EP) Fibers are the one non-flash, body-building material I often use. These fibers are the perfect combination of supple and stiff—easy to tie down and manipulate, but make almost indestructible flies if G.S.P. or Kevlar threads are used. However, a fly tier can get into too much trouble with any long, soft synthetic fiber, including EP Fiber. It is tempting to use this material as a bucktail replacement to create long, sweeping bodies of Deceiver- or Clouser-style streamers. The finished fly usually looks great right off the vise, but more often than not will have serious problems once wet and being flung around at the end of a fly line. If the fibers are left long, they have a tendency to foul in the hook bend or tangle into a giant dreadlock. If used in the same manner but trimmed short, the fly looks and swims as naturally as a sock being dragged behind a boat. I prefer to tie EP Fiber onto the hook shank in multiple short clumps that stand up straight off the shank and then trim the fly to shape afterward. This method is tedious, but results in very lifelike and durable streamer bodies that never foul or tangle.

Rubber Legs

There is a drift-boat-load of different rubber strands meant to be used as legs on flies. All these products may have forty different names, but can easily be broken down into three distinct categories: rubber floss, round rubber, and flat legs.

Of the three, rubber floss is the thinnest but the strongest and is sold by several wholesalers under different names (Spanflex, UNI-Flexx, Super Floss, Life Flex, Flex Floss, and Sexi Floss). There are slight variations between brands, but most are thin and fibrous. Rubber flosses can be found in a decent number of colors but not nearly as diverse as other rubber leg material, and only a handful are available with very basic variegation. These are best suited for smaller bass flies.

Round rubber is the standard rubber leg material and is commonly found in two sizes, small and medium. The medium round rubber is the size most often used for bass flies. This material is perfectly round, so it has the same look viewed from all angles (unlike other rubber leg material), and is almost as strong as any of the rubber floss. Round rubber can be found in a lot of barred or variegated colors by a few different names—barred round rubber, Tarantu-Leggs, and Centipede Legs.

Flat legs are either Wapsi Sili Legs or Hareline Crazy Legs. The Wapsi product comes in two sizes, standard and a smaller size called "nymph." The standard Sili Legs come in a ton of different colors and color schemes—barred, speckled, chrome, and accent tipped. The vast amount of color options is certainly this material's major plus factor; however, these rubber legs are the weakest of all those listed here and rather flimsy, so are best used as tailing rubber instead of protruding from the side of a bass fly.

Foam

Foam can be used in many ways in fly tying, almost always incorporated into a pattern to make it float higher and longer. I am not a huge fan of foam on flies because I don't like the look of synthetic material on a fly. I realize the importance of synthetics, however, and use them in my own tying, but will always try to hide them among natural stuff. It is almost impossible to conceal foam. My material prejudices are strictly based on cosmetics, not function, and in the end, function always trumps.

Hard, closed-cell foam is stiffer, more durable, and all-around better suited for use in the rough-and-tumble life of a bass fly. Fly shop foam is usually sold either in flat sheets (2 mm and 3 mm thick) or cylinders in a range of diameters. There are many other foam popper heads and the like available for those who dig on prefab fly assembly, and some of them are pretty cool. I especially like the Boobie Round Eyes from Rainy's—they are fat barbell eyes that float.

Chenille

Chenille is a type of yarn originated in France and thought (as the name in French insinuates) to look like a caterpillar. In fly-tying circles chenille is used to make a fast nymph or streamer body, commonly used in Girdle Bugs and Woolly Buggers. This material genre long ago evolved into a never-ending wave of new types of fly body wrap for those too afraid to twist a dubbing loop. The corner of the fly shop that once had a simple color selection of rayon chenille now has variegated chenille and variegated tinsel chenille.

It does not stop there. There is the flashier Estaz chenille, Polar chenille, and Cactus chenille. But wait . . . there's more. There is Palmer chenille and dozens of other body wraps that can add inches of flashy, pulsating girth to a streamer body in an instant. Order now and they will be shipped in a discreet package to your home.

Eyes

Eyes on a fly (be it a shad, frog, or dragonfly) are far more important to *us* the angler than *them* the bass. Just as flames painted on the hood of a '58 Thunderbird do not make it any faster, eyes on a fly do not catch more fish. I have experimented for decades but it does not matter—I can't help myself. Eyes are fun and eyes are good. I don't care. I am putting eyes on every streamer I tie.

You will see white or yellow eyes with black pupils painted onto the thread heads of Lefty's Deceivers, and you can certainly keep it old school if you like, but there are some options available these days. I tend to use the simple, round-pupil 3-D and dome eyes for most of the bass streamers I tie. However, there are some crazy realistic, oval-pupil stick-on eyes being made by a couple companies that really look good on the face of a fake minnow. If you decide to use some of these lifelike eyes, *please* for the love of all things proper put them on your fly facing the right way! It will not make a damn bit of practical difference in how the fly works, but will drive anyone with even mild OCD absolutely mad. If you are going to make your fly more realistic (with eyes that are often six times more expensive than simpler ones), why make it look like it's been whacked on the head with a rock?

Varnish, Adhesives, and Resin

Beginning fly tiers often confuse varnishes and adhesives. Most "head cements," including Hard as Hull (my preferred head cement), are not meant to glue two things together but to add a protective layer. This protective coating of varnish will make a fly more durable if applied to the thread head after the fly is completed, as even the tightest, well-tied whip-finish knot is susceptible to loosening and coming undone if the fly is used long enough. A glossy head cement can add a very larva-like glisten to a thread body as well.

Adhesive is what you use to bond things. Zap-A-Gap is a fly tier's superglue, which I use liberally throughout the construction of most of my larger flies to ensure durability. The standard green-labeled Zap-A-Gap with the brush applicator is the best and easiest to use. There are occasionally times when this adhesive in its liquid form is too much of a liability (it can easily wick into hackle fibers or other natural materials and make them as rigid as the hook shank) and Zap Goo must be used instead. Bish's Original Tear Mender is an instant fabric and leather adhesive I like to use when gluing eyes onto the heads of streamers or sticking two pieces of rabbit strip together—it binds well yet (unlike Zap-A-Gap) remains flexible.

Ultraviolet (UV) curing resins are relatively new on the fly-tying scene, but they have become a huge part of it rather quickly, especially in big fly/bass fly circles. UV resins are incredibly useful and have made Softex, Hard Head, and epoxy almost obsolete for most fly tiers. (However, commercial tiers concerned about the cost of fly manufacture should continue using the much less expensive alternatives when practical.) Many companies make UV resins in several viscosities, as well as expensive lamps to cure their products. The products I most frequently use are UV Knot Sense, Clear Cure Goo, and Solarez UV Resin. I have found that

in most instances these resins work equally well and it comes down to application preference (what kind of container it is in) when deciding which one to use—the brushable stuff in a bottle or the others in tubes. I have also found the tackiness of the cured resin (or lack of) has more to do with the power of the UV lamp than the actual resin used. Invest in the best lamp you can afford.

TECHNIQUES

Tools and materials are fly tying's baseball and bat—the items we collect and love about the game. But before we can have a walk-off homer in the bottom of the ninth, there has to be skilled hands on the bat and a few hard-earned lessons up your pin-striped sleeve. Like veteran closers on the mound, instructions for bass flies can throw some complicated spin on fly tying. Consider me Susan Sarandon and the following tricks the little black girdle you have under your uniform the next time you take the field. And watch *Bull Durham* again. It's a great movie.

Ultraviolet curing resins are ideal for creating durable heads on large bass streamers.

Mounting Barbells

Subsurface bass flies need to do a few things well. They obviously need to sink, but also sometimes need to flip around to a hook-point-up position once in the water. Using a barbell (sometimes called a dumbbell) to add the necessary weight to the fly has some advantages over simply wrapping lead wire onto the hook shank. A barbell will add weight to only one side of a hook shank and, if large enough, will be a sufficient counterweight to force it to flip hook point up—almost all barbells used in bass flies are heavy enough to flip almost any hook. If the barbell is placed at the forward end of the hook shank, it will make the fly tilt head down and dive for the bottom, which helps it sink faster and accentuates the downward motion in a "jigging" retrieve. Also, many of the lead barbells are painted and with pupils, so they double as eyes at the head of the fly.

Mounting barbells onto a hook shank is fast and easy; mounting them properly takes a bit more time and thread.

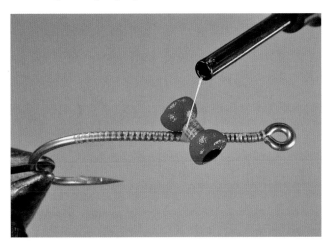

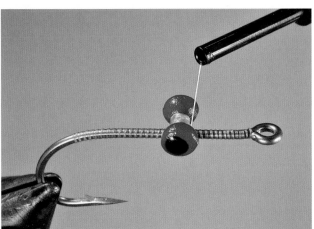

Mounting barbells onto a hook shank is fast and easy; mounting them properly takes a bit more time and thread. If the mounted barbell can be moved with gentle twisting, it certainly will be yanked out of place when bounced off a rock with an errant cast or when mauled by a hungry bass.

It is easy to see if the barbell is tied down less than perfectly perpendicular to the hook shank, but it takes further hands-on inspection. Grip the body of a finished streamer with one hand and the barbell with the other and twist gently—if the barbell moves, that is bad. If the barbell can be moved with gentle twisting, it certainly will be yanked out of place when bounced off a rock with an errant cast or when mauled by a hungry bass. And once the barbell is out of place, it no longer does all the things it was meant to do for balancing the fly.

Often the mounting of the barbell is one of the first steps taken in tying a pattern, so it will be lashed directly to the bare hook shank. This causes a problem, as the hook shank is narrow, slick, and easy for whatever is lashed to it to be twisted. Be sure to build a heavy thread base to create more girth on the hook shank before mounting the barbell. Build the thread base as long as possible as well. Lastly, coat the thread with Zap-A-Gap to ensure the tightest grip possible to the hook shank.

Once the hook shank has been properly prepared for the mounting of the barbell, be sure to tie it down as tight as possible. One sure way to get the tie-down tight is to begin by using multiple one-directional thread wraps to come around the hook shank and over the arbor of the barbell—this will temporarily mount the barbell crookedly. Then use your thumbnail to push the barbell into the desired position (perpendicular to the hook shank)—this will twist and tighten the thread wraps. Now, use more thread to create wraps crossing over the original wraps to lock the barbell in place. Lastly, make horizontal thread wraps that get thread in between the hook shank and the arbor of the barbell, but do not actually wrap over either—these thread wraps will gather all the previous thread wraps tightly together. Once the barbell is tied down, apply Zap-A-Gap to the entire thread tie-down area.

Articulation

Articulated, or jointed, streamers are fun to fish, as they have incredibly lifelike action that is hard to achieve in a larger fly tied on a single, fixed hook shank. An articulated fly can move through the water as though it were truly alive, but like any tool, toy, or piece of machinery, the more moving parts, the more chance of something going wrong. If not made properly, jointed flies can easily foul, ruining a retrieve (or multiple retrieves if not noticed right away). Moving parts on a fly raise durability concerns as well. If you are going to take the additional time and spend the extra money, be sure

Articulated, or jointed, streamers are fun to fish, as they have incredibly lifelike action that is hard to achieve in a larger fly tied on a single, fixed hook shank. An articulated fly can move through the water as though it were truly alive.

to tie your articulated bass flies properly—they are worth doing the right way.

Articulated trout streamers have become all the rage recently, and you can certainly mimic their design for a bass fly. Almost all jointed trout streamers follow the same general blueprint, which is two long-shank, down-eye hooks connected by a cord (often Dacron fly line backing or other braided line) with three or four plastic beads strung on the cord to provide just enough rigidity to keep the fly from folding over onto itself. The rear hook is usually tied like a large Woolly Bugger, and the front hook is the same plus painted lead eyes and deer hair or dubbing used to fill out the weighted head. Hundreds of variations of these streamers are being tied today, as a quick perusal of social fly-tying media will show, but take a closer look and you will notice there are really just two or three patterns being reinvented over and over with sexier/hipper-sounding names.

I don't like the use of plastic beads on a bass fly (or any fly, for that matter). If one of the beads cracks and breaks,

the fly will become too limp and foul readily. If you insist on going this route to achieve articulation, because you succumbed to peer pressure from your trout bum friends, at least have the decency to use a straight-eye hook for the rear part of the fly—when the beads get pushed back on a down-eye hook, the rear end of the fly gets cocked out of line, making the fly swim weird.

Articulated metal shanks are a fast and extremely durable way to build a joint into a large fly. Several companies now offer an array of different-length shanks from 10 mm to 80 mm. The shank I use most frequently is the 40 mm Blane Chocklett's Articulated Big Game Shank paired with either a #2/0 Gamakatsu B10S or #5/0 Umpqua Beast Hook. There is only one limitation to using shanks to achieve articulation in a streamer, and that is the thickness of the shank. Most shanks are not made of the same quality tempered steel that good hooks are, so they need to be thicker to maintain strength—and that is a problem when you are tying smaller articulated flies, as the shank won't thread the eye of a smaller hook.

When tying small to medium-size articulated bass flies, my primary method of building a joint is with twin wire loops. This is a labor-intensive way to achieve articulation in a fly, but it both moves naturally and is durable. The fly tier is in complete control of the size and spacing of the joint this way, and having more control in the outcome of a fly is always more desirable.

As with other articulated flies, tie the rear half first and then use strong thread to create a thread base along the entire front hook shank. Once there is a sufficient thread base, tie down two long strips of 20- to 30-pound wire bite tippet so they extend at least a hook-shank length out behind the hook. The tie-down for the wire should be tight and thorough. Sometimes I even fold the wire over or run it through the hook eye to ensure it will never pull free. The rear of the wire tie-down is important. Tie the wire well down onto the bend of the hook—this way the wire will form an in-line loop behind (and perfectly even with) the front hook shank once the wire is threaded through the straight eye of the rear

hook and laid down on the front hook shank. If the eye on the rear hook is too small, you will have to make due with one strand of 20-pound wire, but whenever possible, use two strands of 30-pound, as the twin heavy wire will allow up-and-down and side-to-side movement freely, but will never cock to the side or twist.

Use Zap-A-Gap liberally over the thread base between every stage if tying down both ends of the wire, as this will ensure the most secure grip on the wire possible. If you intend to clip the hook point off the forward hook of the articulated fly, be sure to get as close to the bottom of the twin wire loop as you are able, without accidentally clipping the wire with your side cutters.

Weed Guards

I hate weed guards. I also hate my bass fly getting snagged up in weeds. I don't know which I hate more . . . and herein lies the dilemma. Weed guards affect both a fly's appearance

The most common weed guard used in bass flies is the hard-mono loop over the hook point. The guard is tied to the hook shank at the start of the tying process and then looped under the fly and through the hook eye after the fly is completed.

and ability to hook a bass on the set—both pretty big deals. In the end it usually comes down to where the fly will be fished and at what time of year—the amount of aquatic vegetation being the deciding variable. Something to keep in mind at the vise: Weed guards can be easily cut off on the water, but not added if needed.

The most common weed guard used in bass flies is the hard-mono (or fluorocarbon) loop over the hook point. The guard is tied to the hook shank at the start of the tying process and then looped under the fly and through the hook eye (and tied off) after the fly is completed. I prefer to use fluorocarbon when making these weed guards because it is far stiffer than monofilament, so a thinner material can be used. RIO 25-pound (.017") Fluoroflex tippet is the best, I have found.

Spinning and Packing Hair

Crafting flies, or parts of flies, from packed and clipped deer hair is the quintessential bass fly-tying method. When most anglers think of a bass fly, they think of a deer hair topwater popping bug. The only two trout flies that call for this technique (that I can think of off the top of my head) are the body of an Irresistible and the head of a Muddler Minnow, two great flies that rarely get tied anymore. If it were not for bass flies, the practice may have gone the way of the dodo and the VCR.

Mounting deer hair onto a hook shank in this way takes advantage of the hollowness of the hair, which causes it to flare and stand up on the hook shank. The clump of deer hair is then packed back to compress the flared hair and make room for more hair. It is a time-consuming process—one fat clump of hair will take up 3/16 inch of hook shank when first tied in, but after being packed tightly will only take up 1/16 inch of space on the hook shank. The messy trimming part begins once the hair has all been tied in and packed tight. Flexible razor blades are the best way to get crisp and clean cuts that will define the shape of the finished fly.

Furled Dubbing Loop

The furled dubbing loop is an underutilized fly-tying technique, but one that is incredibly valuable to a bass fly angler. This trick is by and large the best way to duplicate the long wormlike style of lure so popular among conventional bass anglers. A furled dubbing loop uses thread and dubbing, two inexpensive and seemingly inconsequential materials, to make a tail, leg, or body of almost any size, color, or length

Crafting flies from packed and clipped deer hair is the quintessential bass fly-tying method. Mounting deer hair onto a hook shank in this way takes advantage of the hollowness of the hair, which causes it to flare and stand up on the hook shank. The hair can then be trimmed or shaved into shape.

needed—the fly-tying equivalent of Native American creation stories of Coyote making humans out of mud. Something out of nothing . . . this will always get my attention.

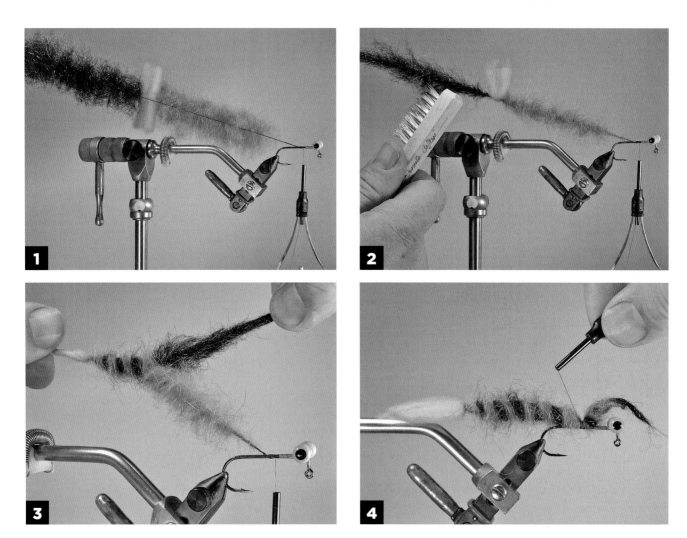

The furled dubbing loop is an underutilized fly-tying technique, but one that is incredibly valuable to a bass fly angler. This trick is by and large the best way to duplicate the long wormlike style of lure so popular among conventional bass anglers.

A traditional dubbing loop is created by first building a thread base to anchor the thread to the hook shank, then pulling 4 to 8 inches of thread from the bobbin, looping the thread around two fingers of your non-tying hand (or a tool), and bringing the thread back to the hook shank and tying it off. This thread loop is then waxed (to better hold the dubbing in place) and loaded with clumps of dubbing until the desired length is achieved. Lastly, the thread loop is spun or twisted, creating a sturdy, homemade chenille of sorts that can then be wound onto the hook to create a fly's body.

A furled dubbing loop takes this idea one important step further. Once the chenille-like dubbing rope has been properly twisted, it is pulled from its middle (like a bowstring) and then, when the tension is relaxed, the built-up twist furls the two ends of dubbing rope into one self-sustaining and durable length of twisted dubbing. Some tiers use a dubbing twirl tool to aid in the spinning process, but I don't

like them—I feel they are cumbersome, and I like to twist the rope by hand a little at a time and stop to brush out the long dubbing fibers before twisting some more. Often I will stop and brush out the dubbing several times before furling to keep the dubbing as bushy as possible and the entire rope as even as possible.

A heavy round thread such as 3/0 Danville's Waxed Monocord is ideal for furled dubbing loops—when twisted, round thread grips dubbing better than flat thread. Depending on the desired rigidity in the finished dubbing "appendage," I will use one to three strands of thread in the loop. Three strands of 3/0 thread twisted and furled (to make six) will be plenty stiff yet still flexible enough to be lively. As tempting as it may be to use some of the strongest Kevlar or G.S.P. threads, don't do it—they may be strong but are some of the slickest threads, so dubbing can be more easily pulled out.

FLY-TYING TIPS

Every Saturday morning during the winter months, I can be found lurking somewhere behind the back row of onlookers watching a guest fly tier show off his or her skill at the vise. I have worked at four different fly shops in Colorado over the past 15 years, and each one has hosted a two-hour free-admission fly-tying demonstration on otherwise slow Saturdays to bolster winter business. I have made bad shop coffee for the crowd, fed them supermarket pastries, and kept an eye on what the tier I invited was up to. I have seen some of the best fly tiers in the country show off their favorite patterns. I have also seen tiers whom I remember teaching how to tie (years before and in another town) put on a show that taught *me* new tricks. Sometimes it is the use of a new material I have never thought of using, or maybe something as simple as holding a tool slightly different that drastically improves my own game. You never know what can be learned with two open eyes and an ego checked at the door.

Movement vs. Action

When describing the prowess of a favorite bass fly, anglers and tiers often use the words *movement* and *action* somewhat interchangeably when, in fact, they are referring to two very different characteristics. A fly that has good movement is tied with materials such as marabou or rabbit that undulate seductively in the water whether or not it is resting or being retrieved—this is a desirable trait in a fly designed for *any* species of fish. Action is what a fly does when moved, jerked, or retrieved by the angler. A lively, or even erratic, action is often vital to the success of some bass flies. Almost none of the larger trout streamers I have fished had anything slightly resembling *action*—often they just swim like a wet sock or clump of moss being pulled back to shore.

To design better action into a bass fly, you have to add a flexible tail or articulation or trim the fly down to give it a sleek profile—sometimes all three. The fly must be able to go from standing still to warp speed with just one slight twitch of the rod tip, and change directions . . . or glide for a foot or two once the line goes slack. *That is good action.* A perfect bass fly has the best of both—sweet movement and wicked action—but it is almost impossible to have a solid dose of both in a single fly. The materials that provide the best movement are often the same things that will slow down and dampen the action.

The direction I go with a particular pattern is dictated by how I will be fishing the fly and what food-source genre the fly is intended to mimic. Crayfish and other bottom-dwelling patterns that I am often "slow playing" get the *movement* preference, while baitfish and the like get the *action* treatment to tap into the aggressive triggers predatory piscivores are prone to. Sometimes I still attempt to have my cake and catch bass, too . . . which takes a bit of a balancing act. To get both movement and action in the same pattern, you need to first ensure it has action (by tightly clipping and streamlining the hair or synthetic material at the head and body) and then leave some bushy marabou or rabbit off the back end.

Tying Durable Flies

There is hardly much point in tying a good fly if it unravels or falls apart after the first fish or two, or even before it is cast. I was on a two-week canoe float down a remote river in Alaska not long ago and had a commercially tied pike fly completely self-destruct in my hand as I was tying it onto my leader. I held the fly in one hand and pulled the leader knot tight with the other and the entire fly slid off the hook. No kidding. When a fly I tied "chucks a wobbly," as some members of my family would say, it gets shit-canned. No excuses.

Before a bad fly is discarded, you should take a hard look at it to identify exactly where the problem is, as this will enable you to fix the problem. Even if a particular fly has held up for more tours of duty than Colonel Hackworth but finally has an eye pop off, take a close look, take note, and make the next fly you tie even more indestructible.

If your flies are tied with a solid, tightly wrapped thread base on the hook shank at the start of the tying process, you will likely never have the problem I had on that river in Alaska. However, there will be times when a particular fly pattern calls for the majority of the hook shank to be left bare and the thread base kept to a minimum directly behind the hook eye. In this case, using what I call an "eye-locked thread base" can prevent the embarrassment of having that part of the finished fly slide down or completely off the hook shank. Simply "thread" the end of the thread through the hook eye before you begin the thread base, then hold the thread end down onto the hook shank and wrap the thread base over it—this single strand of thread through the eye can be just enough to prevent slippage.

The first place most flies begin to fall apart is at the thread head, right at the finish knot. As most bass flies tend to be on the larger side of average and the threads used are often thicker, the thread heads can quickly become bulky. Keep in mind, the more wraps of thread you have right behind the hook eye has no bearing on the durability of the knot tied over the top of it all—in fact, thread tends to

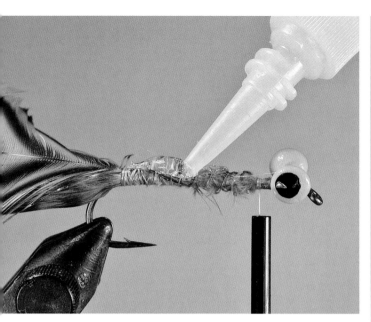

Applying a coat of Zap-A-Gap or Zap Goo adhesive to base thread layers and material tie-downs between tying steps greatly increases the life expectancy of a bass fly.

slip and become loose the bulkier the thread head. If I have spent more than five minutes or a dollar on a fly, I will finish it with two whip-finish knots and a touch of head cement (or even better, Zap-A-Gap). This only adds a second or two to the tying time, but can drastically increase the life span of a fly.

The quill of palmer-wrapped hackle is often another potential weak point in a fly, and if it snaps will completely unwind and ruin the fly. Cross-wrap a thin piece of wire over the hackle feather to give it reinforcement. In lieu of wire you can coat the body of the fly with Zap Goo and wrap the hackle through it, but this is a method I use only if wire is out of the question. I will only resort to it for the Super Bugger pattern, as the body is bare and the hackle is wrapped densely up the hook shank, making a wire support too likely to mat down the hackle fiber.

The aspects of durability that have an immediate effect on a fly's function are the things I obsess about first, and then come the issues of cosmetics. Usually anything involving eyes at the head of a fly I consider purely cosmetic, as they are there for our viewing pleasure and have little to do with the lethalness of the fly. However, the confidence we anglers feel in a particular fly will often translate into real-world effectiveness because we fish harder and better with something we trust, so I still take it seriously.

Dome-shaped stick-on eyes are best attached to the head of the fly with either Tear Mender or Zap-A-Gap, although both adhesives will eventually be compromised once the fly has been bashed against enough rocks and bridge pilings. Make the eyes more durable by dripping a UV-curing resin onto the eye (once it is mounted with adhesive). Allow the resin to evenly disperse over the face of the eye until it oozes off the entire round edge, then let it soak into the surrounding material slightly before curing it with a UV lamp. Also, a light coating of UV resin over painted lead eyes will reduce the chances of paint chipping.

Tying Flies Faster

I would make the world's poorest commercial fly tier. It is not the speed in which I tie flies, it is the hours I spend in between each fly that would get me laughed out of Sri Lanka. I can get away with it here because I call myself a fly *designer*. Sometimes I walk around for hours holding up the one fly I tied, looking at it from every angle and in every light . . . even bringing it to work the next day in my shirt pocket. I will peek in periodically to see how it is doing. This is part of how patterns get developed and tweaked, after all—but not how work or chore fly tying gets done.

Over the years I have figured out some tricks to fill fly boxes faster when trips are looming or winter is waning— they were painfully learned tricks born from necessity, as are most practical things. A hundred and one little tricks can be utilized at the vise to save tiny increments of time, such as always keeping your scissors in hand, keeping your work surface uncluttered, and thinking ahead well past the next step. All these small things add up over the course of an evening and boil down to being better organized and having the ever-desirable *economy of motion*.

The two best time-saving tricks (we really should call them *disciplines*) are batch tying and stage tying, and these can be used in conjunction. Batch tying is everything that tinkering is not . . . and most fly tiers are forever guilty of tinkering—tying a couple hair-wing dries, five midge pupa patterns, and an attempt at the cool streamer they saw on *InTheRiffle*. Batch fly tying is planning ahead and preparing for and knocking out four dozen of one size and color of a proven pattern you know you need . . . even if 48 of them will last you three years. Stage tying is batch tying in increments. If the pattern has a point in the tying process that calls for something to be set aside to dry, or a change of thread or hooks, this is the perfect place to stage-tie up to, and then resume once all four dozen are tied up to that point. Repetition builds speed.

1 Meat Whistle
2 Dahlberg
   Diving Frog
3 Krystowski
   Minnow
4 Grim Reaper
5 Geezus Lizard
6 Stealth
   Bomber
7 Stuntman
   Eddy
8 Clouser
   Minnow

9 Tri-Minnow
10 Finesse
   Worm
11 Texas
   Ringworm
12 Ball Peen
   Craw
13 Booby Frog
14 Booby Mouse
15 Super Bugger
16 Bass Bug
17 Bellyache
   Minnow
18 Snapback
19 Gartside
   Gurgler

Tying Less Expensively

The first thing too many tiers will consider when cost becomes a problem is to use cheaper hooks—*never* resort to cheaper hooks. There are many ways to cut the cost of your flies without compromising the quality or effectiveness of the pattern. Buy your hooks in bulk whenever possible and you will save roughly 15 percent (depending on the company). This is more practical than you may think, as many bass flies are tied on the same size and style of hook.

Stick-on eyes add a lot more to the per-fly cost than most tiers realize. A standard set of hologram dome or 3-D adhesive holographic eyes adds 30 to 35 cents to a fly, which is a lot considering the actual hook itself may only be 40 cents. Painting your own fly eyes can save a packet if you have the time and a steady hand, and building a batch of epoxy dome eyes on wax paper using a paper punch to make pupils can be as rewarding as baking a tray of homemade cookies. If you are willing to tie blander, slightly pedestrian bass flies (that usually work just as well as their fancy cousins), you can shave even more off the cost. Using single-color round rubber legs instead of barred rubber can save you 20 cents or more per fly. Standard lead barbells instead of painted lead eyes will save you 10 cents per fly. The more flies you tie, the more these little things add up.

Fly Name	Time to Tie (in Minutes)	Cost to Tie (in US Dollars)	Weight (in Grams)
Clouser Minnow	5	$1.80	1.83
Dahlberg Diving Frog	29	$2.90	1.28
Gartside Gurgler	9	$1.60	.67
Grim Reaper	9	$2.90	3.94
Krystowski Minnow	6	$1.10	.98
Meat Whistle	8	$2.00	1.54
Super Bugger	5	$1.20	1.48
Booby Frog	9	$2.90	.80
Finesse Worm	14	$1.00	.75
Stealth Bomber	6	$1.40	.55
Geezus Lizard	16	$3.00	2.56
Ball Peen Craw	9	$1.00	.65
Tri-Minnow	27	$3.40	1.87
Texas Ringworm	19	$3.50	1.27
Stuntman Eddy	42	$7.20	1.86
Bellyache Minnow	9	$2.50	1.73
Snapback	25	$4.90	3.25

CLOUSER MINNOW

Over the past six decades, Bob Clouser has been tying flies for bass, and it can be argued that he and his longtime fishing buddy, Lefty Kreh, have in some small form or another influenced nearly all modern streamer flies. Bob has created many innovative flies over these years but is best known for his groundbreaking pattern the Clouser Deep Minnow, or as it is more commonly referred to in fly shops and fishing circles around the world, simply the Clouser Minnow.

The Clouser Minnow was designed for river smallmouth but works equally well in reservoirs.

Bob Clouser had been guiding fellow fly anglers for smallmouth bass on the Susquehanna, his home river in Pennsylvania, for almost 30 years and was tinkering with flies and fly design long before he hit the jackpot with his Clouser Minnow. He perfected the fly in 1987—the result of three years of tinkering and field-testing after he received some of the first-ever packets of lead dumbbell eyes from the fly material wholesaler Wapsi Fly Company. Before that, Bob (and every other serious fly angler) had been attaching split shot to the hook shanks of streamers to get them to sink deep and fast.

The Clouser Minnow is simply a weighted version of a bucktail streamer, tied on a good stainless steel, saltwater-worthy hook. Besides thread, it has only four ingredients: lead dumbbell eyes, Krystal Flash, and two shades of long hair from the tail of a white-tailed deer. The concept for this sturdy and incredibly effective baitfish imitation may be simple, but it is also one of the most important warmwater flies ever conceived. Adding the ability to put weight on the top of just about any fly hook, and not only giving suggestive eyes to a baitfish pattern but also flipping the hook so that it swims through the water in the hook-point-up position, seems now like common fly-tying sense.

After catching over 70 species of fish on this fly, Lefty Kreh—not only Bob's friend, but also one of the most famous and respected ambassadors of our sport—wrote, "I consider the Clouser Minnow to be the single-most effective underwater fly to be developed in several decades!" This fly has become so popular among streamer anglers and tiers that it is almost no longer thought of as a pattern but rather as a style of tying. Bob Clouser has had the same degree of influence on contemporary warmwater and streamer fly tying as Bob Dylan has had on modern music and songwriting.

The Clouser Minnow can be tied in several sizes and countless color combinations, depending on the body of water or species being targeted; however, the overall crowd favorite is chartreuse, silver, and white.

If you hook into a 20-inch smallie while in a float tube, you better hope you have a stiff rod, a long net, and the arm strength of an oilman. *Herman de Gala* photo.

CLOUSER MINNOW (CHARTREUSE)

Hook: #1/0 Tiemco 811S

Thread: White 3/0 Danville's Waxed Monocord

Eyes: Red painted lead eyes (medium)

Belly Hair: White bucktail

Center Flash: Silver Krystal Flash

Top Hair: Chartreuse bucktail

Adhesive: Zap-A-Gap

Head/Body Resin: Tack Free Clear Cure Goo

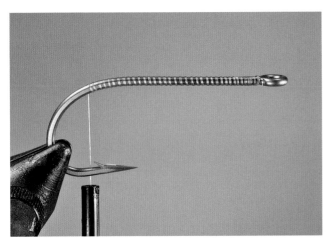

1. Secure the hook firmly into the jaws of the vise. Begin the thread wraps immediately behind the hook eye and spiral wrap the thread all the way to the rear of the straight hook shank and then slightly back onto the beginning of the hook bend. If the bobbin is allowed to hang free, the thread should come even with the very tip of the hook's barb. This thread base provides you with a rearward marker for where the first clump of deer hair should be tied and adds traction to the slippery hook shank so that material does not easily get pulled back or pushed forward on the shank.

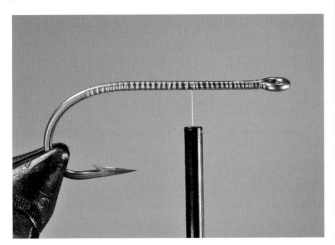

2. Spiral wrap the thread forward on the hook shank and stop the thread exactly between the point of the hook and the rear of the hook eye—this is where the lead eyes will

be mounted. Because these two points of measure are on different planes, it is sometimes difficult to park the thread at the exact in-between spot, so I will hook one thumbnail on the hook point and the other thumbnail behind the hook eye to enable a better sight picture. The location where the lead eyes are mounted is important—often they are mounted too close to the hook eye.

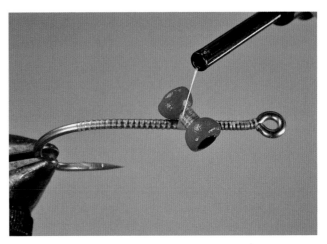

3. Begin mounting the painted lead eyes by cocking them on the top of the hook shank and tying them down with a liberal number of tight thread wraps that cover the entire interior arbor of the eyes.

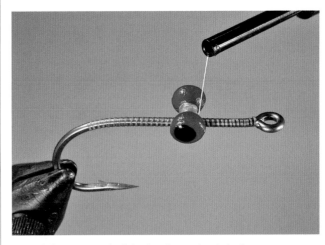

4. Pull the near end of the lead eyes back (using your thumbnail) so the eyes are neatly perpendicular to the hook shank. Tie the eyes down so they stay in this position.

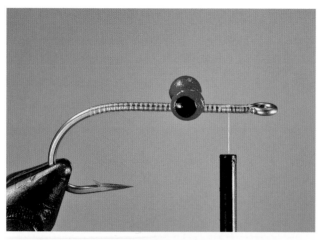

5. Wrap the thread forward and let the bobbin hang free so the thread is directly between the forward edge of the painted lead eyes and the rear edge of hook eye.

6. Select a long and clean clump of white bucktail (tail from a white-tailed deer). Trim the hair as close to the hide as possible to allow for maximum length.

7. Grip the clump of deer hair firmly near the tips end with one hand and use your other hand to pull out the finer underfur and any short hairs. Also pluck out any abnormally long hairs from the tips end.

8. Once the clump of hair is properly tidied up, trim the butt end so that all the ends are even.

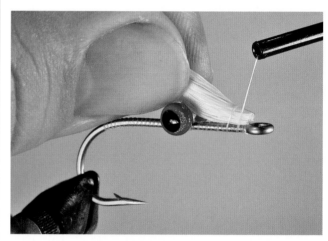

9. Lay the butt end of the clump of deer hair down on top of the hook shank and secure it in place with several tight thread wraps. No hair should stick out, obscuring the hook eye. Be sure to keep all the hair on the top side of the hook shank. Also be sure to keep the tie-down area just at the very front of the fly—only from the thread starting point forward.

10. The white bucktail should lie down in the middle of the barbell eyes. With the thread beginning at a point just behind the hook eye, pull the thread under the hook shank and to the rear of the painted lead eyes to begin tying the deer hair down to create the belly of the streamer.

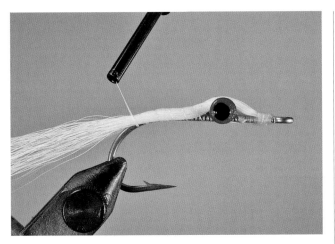

11. Once you have crossed the thread over to the back side of the painted lead eyes, pull the clump of deer hair down onto the top of the hook shank and secure it in place with spiral thread wraps all the way to the very rear of the original thread base. When you get to the very rear of the thread base (where it dips down slightly onto the bend of the hook), go easy on the tension of the thread wraps. Tight thread wraps at the end would squeeze the hollow hairs and make them flare up and out at every angle. These not-so-tight wraps will enable the clump of deer hair to remain together. You will also notice that because the hair is tied down slightly onto the bend of the hook, all the hair is being pushed downward at an angle—this will help the finished fly swim true and look better.

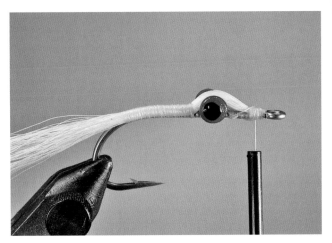

12. Wrap the thread forward, creating a solid thread base between the rear of the hook shank and the painted lead eyes. Cross the thread under the hook shank and back to the front of the fly. Let the bobbin hang free so that the thread rests at the middle of the hair tie-down point. Notice that the deer hair is tied down tight and snug to the rear of the painted lead eyes, but allowed to slope gently down to the hook eye at the front end.

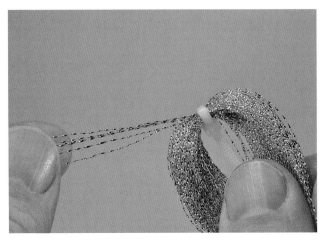

13. Select six strands of Krystal Flash. You will need the entire length of this flash material, so pull the complete strands free of the plastic zip tie that holds them all together.

14. Flip the hook over so that the painted lead eyes are on the bottom and the hook point is up (this is the position the fly will swim once finished). Tie the six strands of Krystal Flash in at their middle, just behind the hook eye. The fast and easy way to accomplish this is by looping the Krystal Flash around the exposed thread, grasping all 12 ends with one hand and then drawing the material down onto the proper tie-down spot with the thread.

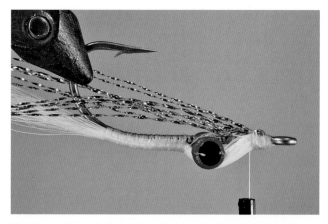

15. The end result should be 12 long strands of flash laid down over the fly and well past the tips of white deer hair. I like to put half the strands on one side of the upturned hook and the other half on the opposite side, then cross them over each other behind the hook so they all stay temporarily up and out of the way.

16. Select a long and clean clump of the secondary, or top, color bucktail (in this case chartreuse). Trim the hair as close to the hide as possible to allow for maximum length. This clump of hair should be larger than the first—not double the size, but nearly.

17. Prep this clump of deer hair the same as you did the first. Grip the hair firmly near the tips end with one hand and use

your other hand to pull out the finer underfur and any short hairs. Also pluck out any abnormally long hairs from the tips end. Once the clump of hair is properly tidied up, trim the butt end so that all the ends are even.

18. Secure the top clump of deer hair with two wraps of thread directly behind the hook eye. Be sure to pull the hair back slightly if the butt ends are protruding out over the hook eye.

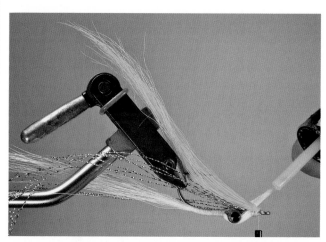

19. Brush a small amount of Zap-A-Gap onto the top of the tied-down deer hair. This clump of hair is only being held in place by two wraps of thread so that the hollow hairs are not completely compressed, thus allowing the Zap-A-Gap to penetrate through the entire clump of hair. Applying the Zap-A-Gap before completely tying down the clump of hair also allows the top and head of the streamer to remain full, not matted down by the tension of many tight wraps of thread. Notice how the jaw assembly of the vise is keeping this clump of hair up at an angle—this also helps keep the fly from becoming mashed and too narrow once finished.

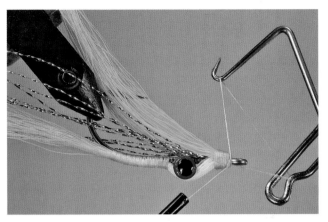

20. Complete the fully wrapped thread head of the fly and end with a whip-finish knot. Trim the thread.

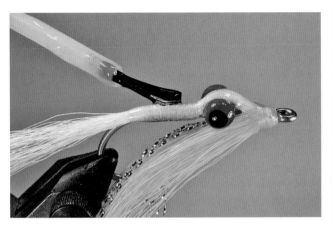

21. Rotate the fly over, exposing the belly and eyes. Be sure all the deer hair and Krystal Flash is swept down and out of the way in preparation for applying UV resin. For this fly I prefer any of the resins that are thick and come with an applicator brush, as you should coat the entire thread-base belly, the painted lead eyes, and the deer hair arched over the arbor of the lead eyes, as well as the entire thread head of the fly. This will create a super-durable bass streamer.

22. Cure the resin with a UV light. I have found that most UV resins will cure with a tack-free finish if the light used is powerful enough. If you find the finish is still a tad tacky, brush on a light coat of head cement and hook the fly to a piece of foam out of the way to dry.

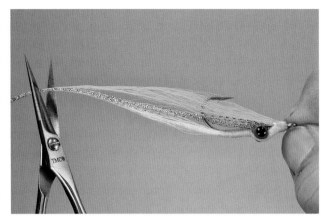

23. Remove the fly from the vise, slick all the hair and flash material back to see what you have (maybe lick your fingers first), and trim the Krystal Flash out just past the very tip ends of the longest deer hair. The overall length of a 1/0 Clouser Minnow should be roughly 4½ inches (114 mm).

PATTERN VARIATIONS

CLOUSER MINNOW (BLUE)

Hook: #1/0 Tiemco 811S

Thread: White 3/0 Danville's Waxed Monocord

Eyes: Red painted lead eyes (medium)

Belly Hair: White bucktail

Center Flash: Pearl Krystal Flash

Top Hair: Fluorescent blue bucktail

Adhesive: Zap-A-Gap

Head Resin: Clear UV resin

CLOUSER MINNOW (GRAY)

Hook: #1/0 Tiemco 811S

Thread: White 3/0 Danville's Waxed Monocord

Eyes: Red painted lead eyes (medium)

Belly Hair: White bucktail

Center Flash: Purple Krystal Flash

Top Hair: Gray bucktail

Adhesive: Zap-A-Gap

Head Resin: Clear UV resin

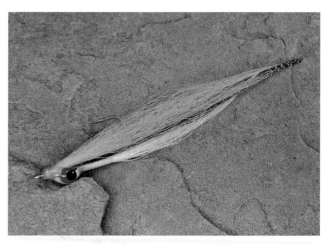

CLOUSER MINNOW (MICKEY FINN)

Hook: #1/0 Tiemco 811S

Thread: White 3/0 Danville's Waxed Monocord

Eyes: Red painted lead eyes (medium)

Belly Hair: White bucktail

Center Flash: Red Krystal Flash

Top Hair: Yellow bucktail

Adhesive: Zap-A-Gap

Head Resin: Clear UV resin

CLOUSER MINNOW (OLIVE)

Hook: #1/0 Tiemco 811S

Thread: White 3/0 Danville's Waxed Monocord

Eyes: Red painted lead eyes (medium)

Belly Hair: White bucktail

Center Flash: Olive Krystal Flash

Top Hair: Olive bucktail

Adhesive: Zap-A-Gap

Head Resin: Clear UV resin

CLOUSER MINNOW (LIGHT OLIVE)

Hook: #1/0 Tiemco 811S

Thread: White 3/0 Danville's Waxed Monocord

Eyes: Red painted lead eyes (medium)

Belly Hair: White bucktail

Center Flash: Olive Krystal Flash

Top Hair: Light olive bucktail

Adhesive: Zap-A-Gap

Head Resin: Clear UV resin

4

DAHLBERG DIVING FROG

Larry Dahlberg is on the short list as the most important and influential person in every sect of the American angling world. Larry's contributions and shared knowledge transcend all the petty bickering between those who dig and cut their bait, throw plugs, or cast a fly. He is loved and respected by every devoted angler, lure maker, and fly designer I have ever met. Read any article by or about Larry, or watch a video or television show with him in it, and you will forever embrace the inner obsessive compulsive geek gene you were born with—be it tying at the bench, tweaking hardware in the garage, or spending days on the water analyzing every slight variation in a retrieve.

I have always been partial to the frog version of Larry Dahlberg's fly. I believe the concept lends itself perfectly to the behavior and tendencies of these tailless amphibians.

Bass feed in bad weather. Put on a rain jacket and string a fly rod.

Larry was born in Minnesota and spent the 1960s and early '70s growing up in the northern end of the state. By age 11 he was guiding other anglers and while still a teenager had invented a bass fly that is to this day considered one of the best of all time—the Dahlberg Diver. The original was tied in the spring of 1977 to fool a very specific largemouth bass. The bass was big (nearly 7 pounds), and a standard deer hair bass bug was getting attention, but not enough to get eaten. Larry had always been fond of conventional jerk baits and their sudden diving action, so set out to modify a fly rod bass bug to achieve something similar. And he did. The first Dahlberg Divers were long and flashy, imitating a struggling baitfish more than anything, but his design concept became so popular among bass fly tiers that you can now find his fingerprint on countless hundreds of patterns. There are variations of his fly tied for maybe every fish, both fresh and salt water, including trout, pike and musky, bass, and brim.

I have always been partial to the frog version of Larry's fly. I believe the concept (both in fly design and presentation) lends itself perfectly to the behavior and tendencies of these tailless amphibians. The natural progression of fly design, both mine and a million others, has taken the same path, with one of the current results being what is sold commercially as the Umpqua Swimming Frog. This fly retains the hallmark shaved deer hair head and collar of the original Diver, but sexes it up with a froggy color pattern, eyes, and even rubber legs out the sides. The tail of the fly has lost its long, flashy baitfish look and adopted the twin set of feather legs common on both cork- and deer-hair-bodied bass bugs. There is still some marabou tied between the feather "legs" and shaved deer hair head. This variation is very good, and the fly featured in this tutorial is similar enough to be called either a Dahlberg Diving Frog or an Umpqua Swimming Frog—at this point in the design lineage, it is purely semantic.

If fished on a floating fly line, the Dahlberg Diver can take the place of most topwater bass "poppers," with the added bonus of occasionally diving a few inches under the surface of the water. The raised collar at the rear of the head will still make pops and gurgles when jerked hard enough.

However, this fly really comes into its own when fished on a long leader and sinking or sink-tip fly line. When the end of the fly line is below the surface, a strong pull will plunge the fly all the way to the bottom if the line is deep enough and the pull is long enough, leaving a trail of bubbles behind it. Then, when the line is left motionless, the fly will point its nose to the surface and "swim" back to the top. Bass will eat at any point in this retrieve, so be ready.

DAHLBERG DIVING FROG

Hook: #6 Tiemco 8089

Thread 1: White 140-denier UTC Ultra Thread

Weed Guard: RIO Fluoroflex tippet (.017"/25 lb.)

Adhesive: Zap-A-Gap

Flash 1: Olive Krystal Flash

Flash 2: Rusty brown Krystal Flash

Flash 3: Black Krystal Flash

Tail Feather 1: Olive grizzly saddle hackle

Tail Feather 2: Chartreuse saddle hackle

Tail Feather 3: Burnt orange grizzly saddle hackle

Tail Feather 4: White saddle hackle

Tail Feather 5: Olive saddle hackle

Thread 2: White 200-denier UTC G.S.P.

Top Feather: Olive marabou

Bottom Feather: Cream marabou

Hair 1: Light olive spinning deer hair

Hair 2: Cream deer belly hair

Hair 3: Brown deer belly hair

Hair 4: Black deer belly hair

Hair 5: Fluorescent chartreuse deer belly hair

Thread 3: Yellow olive 140-denier UTC Ultra Thread

Eye Resin: Loon UV Knot Sense

Eyes: Gold holographic eyes (³⁄₁₆")

Varnish: Hard as Hull head cement

Leg 1: Chartreuse grizzly barred rubber legs (medium)

Leg 2: Orange grizzly barred rubber legs (medium)

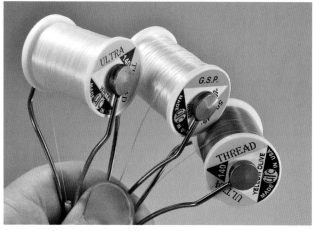

1. You will be using three different threads in the making of this fly. The white 140-denier thread will be used to tie in the weed guard, rear flash, and tail feathers. The white 200-denier G.S.P. will be used for most of the rest of the fly, to include the packing and spinning deer hair. The second, heavier thread is not used at the start in an attempt to reduce unnecessary bulk at the rear tie-down area. The third thread is yellow olive 140-denier. The white G.S.P. needs to be cut in preparation to shave down the deer hair, so you may as well switch to a thread color to match the final clump of hair before securing the weed guard at the nose. Having the spools of thread on separate bobbins saves time and hassle.

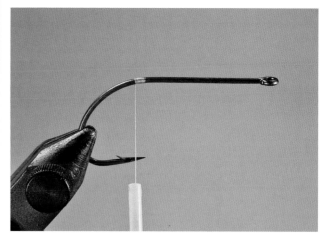

2. Secure the hook firmly into the jaws of the vise. Begin thread wraps (white 140-denier) at the rear end of the straight hook shank. Build a short thread base beginning at a point on the hook shank even with the hook point and extend it back about a hook-eye length. Let the bobbin hang.

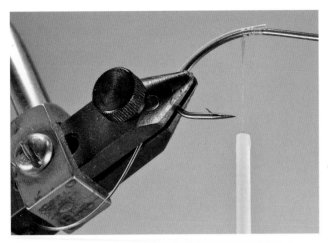

3. Cut a 3-inch (8 cm) length of Fluoroflex tippet to use as the weed guard. If you are not a fan of weed guards, you do not need to include this step, but this is an opportune place to demonstrate the technique. I use fluorocarbon because it is stiff, so one thin piece will do the job intended—I also use this specific fluorocarbon for another bass fly, so I have it readily available. Thread the length of fluorocarbon through the gap in the jaws of the vise immediately behind the hook and push it through until the end is even with the forward end of the short thread base. Tie the fluorocarbon down at this point—this enables you to leave the hook in the vise when pulling the weed guard forward at the end (look for any way to avoid having to remove the fly from the vise during the tying process). Thread the other end of the fluorocarbon into any available cranny you can find so it stays temporarily out of the way—this will vary depending on the vise.

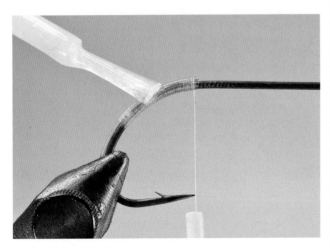

4. Create a solid thread base over the fluorocarbon weed guard that extends well down onto the bend of the hook. Return the thread to the forward end of the thread base. Be sure to keep the weed guard centered onto the back side of the hook bend as you are tying it down. The purpose of this extended tie-down is to keep the weed guard properly placed over the hook gape over time and use. Because this thread base will be mostly exposed when the fly is finished, coat it with Zap-A-Gap (or head cement) before continuing.

5. Select 12 complete strands of Krystal Flash for the tail: 6 strands of olive, 6 strands of rusty brown, and 2 strands of black.

6. Bundle all 12 strands of Krystal Flash and tie the bundle in at the forward end of the thread base. Each end of the Krystal Flash bundle should be folded down onto either side of the hook so that two bundles protrude separately off the rear of the fly.

7. Select 10 hackle feathers that are all at least 3½ inches (9 cm) long: 2 olive grizzly, 2 chartreuse, 2 burnt orange grizzly, 2 white, and 2 olive. Separate the feathers into two identical piles. Stack the feathers onto the edge of your tying bench concave side down and one on top of the other, one each in the order listed.

8. While stacking the two piles of feathers, be sure the tips are perfectly aligned. Wet each feather (I run them through my mouth) before adding it to the pile—this will temporarily adhere them to each other, making mounting them together onto the rear of the fly easier.

9. Mount the feather bundles onto the rear of the hook shank—one on either side. The concave side should be facing out, so they each flare off to either side. The feather tips should extend out about two hook-shank lengths behind the fly. Trim the bundles of Krystal Flash to this same length. Apply some Zap-A-Gap to the tie-down area before trimming away the butt ends of feather.

10. Trim away the butt ends of feather even with the forward end of the original thread base. Tie a whip-finish knot just in front of the material tie-down and trim the thread. You will be switching to a heavier thread for most of the rest of the fly.

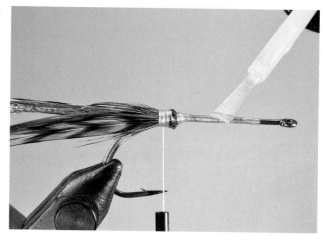

11. Switch threads to the white 200-denier G.S.P. Begin the thread wraps a bit more than a hook-eye length back onto the hook shank and build a solid thread base all the way back to the tail feather tie-down. Coat the entire thread base with Zap-A-Gap. The thread base will make packing deer hair more difficult (than if it were a bare shank), but will help keep individual colored clumps of deer hair in their place. The bare spot of shank up front is where the very last clump of hair will be placed, and that one will be allowed to spin around the hook shank (which is easier on a bare shank).

12. Select four marabou feathers: two olive and two cream. The olive feathers need to be robust, but the cream-colored feathers can be small, as less of them will be used.

13. Wet the two olive marabou feathers and tie them down on top of the tail feather tie-down. Even these feathers will have a slight arc that is more noticeable once the feather is wet—match this arc with the curve of the tail feathers. The tips of the olive feathers should extend about one hook-shank length (half the length of the tail feathers) off the back end of the fly. Do *not* trim the butt ends of marabou . . . yet.

14. Rotate the hook over and tie in the two cream marabou feathers. Wet these feathers as you did with the olive ones to make mounting them in the correct place easier. These two feathers should be tied in only half as long as the top olive feathers, and they should be mounted on either side of the hook bend so they extend straight back from the tie-down area—not following the curve of the rest of the feathers. Again, do *not* trim the butt ends of marabou.

15. Select five patches of hair: light olive spinning deer hair, cream deer belly hair, brown deer belly hair, black deer belly hair, and fluorescent chartreuse deer belly hair. I prefer to use back/body hair when I am keeping some of the hair tips and want a mottled look, but use deer belly hair for most everything else because that hair starts out white and is brighter once dyed.

16. Cut a large clump of light olive deer hair off the hide (cut as close to the hide as possible).

17. Hold the clump of deer hair firmly by the tips and use a hair comb to rake out all of the underfur and any loose or broken hairs. Underfur seriously hampers the ability to pack or compress deer hair once it is on the hook shank. Do this with every clump of hair for the duration of the tying process.

18. Insert the clump of deer hair tip first into a large brass hair stacker. The first four clumps of hair need to be stacked, as these are the only tips that will not be trimmed (for the most part).

19. Several firm taps of the hair stacker will line all the hair tips up evenly. Grab these tips firmly and avoid switching hands or rolling the hair around between your fingers, as this will misalign the tips.

20. Mount the clump of light olive deer hair on top of the tail feather tie-down area. The tips of hair should be about even with the tips of cream marabou on the underside of the fly. Pinch the clump of hair from the sides as you make two tight wraps of thread over the hair. The pressure applied will make the hair flare.

21. Rotate the vise so the fly is upside down. Cut a clump of cream deer belly hair and prepare it by combing out the underfur and stacking the tips even. Use two tight thread wraps to flare and secure the hair. The tips of cream deer hair should align with the tips of cream marabou.

22. Rotate the vise so the fly is right side up. Prepare and tie in a clump of brown deer hair right on top of the tie-down for the light olive hair. The olive hair will be splayed and flared, so you will have to press down with your thumb between the tips end and the butts end to make way for the brown clump of hair. Once that is secured, do the same with a clump of black deer belly hair. Each successive clump of hair should be slightly smaller than the last and centered on top of the previous clump. Be sure to lay each clump of hair down with the tips oriented toward the rear of the fly.

24. Tie in two more clumps of deer hair: a clump of cream hair on the bottom and a clump of light olive hair on the top. These two clumps of hair need to be combed out, but (as with any of the deer hair from here on out) there is no need to stack the tips even. This is about the spot on this fly where the head will end and the top collar will begin . . . but that comes later.

23. Now it is OK to trim the four butt ends of marabou feather. They were left in place temporarily to keep any of the multiple clumps of deer hair from slipping down off the bulky tie-down area and onto the hook shank—once there they can never be pushed back no matter how hard you pack.

25. Prepare and tie down another clump of light olive hair on top, another clump of cream on the bottom, then a clump of chartreuse deer hair in the middle of the light olive, followed by a smaller clump of black hair in the middle of the chartreuse.

26. Use a small brass hair packer to compress the last four clumps of deer hair back against the butt ends of the tail feather tie-down. This makes room on the hook shank for more material and creates a denser packed hair mass that will be more durable and easier to shave into the desired shape.

27. Repeat the process of four hair clumps (olive on top, cream on bottom, chartreuse on top and in the middle of the olive, and then black on top and in the middle of the chartreuse) and packing two more times, to make a total of three cycles. This should leave you hardly any room for material on the hook shank, but pack the hair back hard to make way for one last clump of light olive deer hair.

28. Prepare and tie in one last clump of light olive deer hair. Because the hook shank is bare this close to the hook eye, the hair will easily spin around the shank, covering all the way around. Wrap tightly until the hair stops spinning.

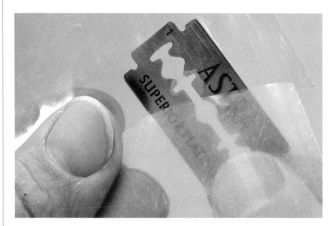

29. If you have packed as much deer hair as possible onto the hook shank, the hair will be flaring well out over the hook eye, making tying the final whip-finish knot difficult. A trick I picked up from Charlie Craven utilizes a piece of plastic (one of the material bags perhaps) with a slit cut in it.

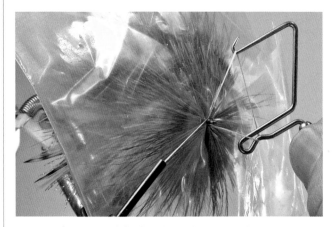

30. Use the cut to slide the plastic bag onto the thread all the way up to the hook eye. Use the plastic bag to hold back all the deer hair while you tie the whip-finish knot. Trim the thread and add a small drop of Zap-A-Gap to the finished knot. Remove the plastic bag.

31. Begin shaping the deer hair head of the fly by first shaving down the belly. Rotate the vise so the fly is upside down. Take a double-sided razor blade and make two sweeping cuts tight to the hook shank from the hook eye all the way back to the cream-colored marabou tied in at the rear of the fly. Each of these two cuts should be angled slightly to either side, leaving a raised crest down the center of the belly.

32. Rotate the vise so the fly is right side up again. Squeeze the razor blade so it forms an arch, then push the blade over the top of the fly to carve a rounded top. Stop cutting once you have cleared all of the black and chartreuse deer hair.

33. Take some time and care to shave the head of the fly into a symmetrical shape. The bottom should be cut tight to the hook shank and have two flat surfaces that form something like the hull of a boat. The top side should be rounded and loaf-like.

34. Once the head of the fly has been shaved down to the desired shape, switch to the third and final thread (yellow olive 140-denier). Even with the deer hair head shaved, there is little room left behind the hook eye to start a new thread base, so poke the thread through the hook eye, grab the end of thread with your non-wrapping hand, and hold tight as you make several wraps of thread immediately behind the hook eye. Pull the fluorocarbon weed guard forward and thread it through the hook eye from below. Once the weed guard is positioned so it forms a gentle loop out in front of the hook point, secure it in place with several tight wraps of thread. The thread wraps should bend the fluorocarbon back over the rear of the hook eye and kink it enough to prevent it from being pulled free. Trim the excess fluorocarbon, tie a whip-finish knot, trim the thread, and add a small drop of Zap-A-Gap to the finish knot.

35. Mount eyes onto the head of the fly with a clear UV-cured resin. I prefer the Loon UV Knot Sense for this because it comes in a small squeeze tube with a nozzle that lends itself perfectly to this application. Apply a small amount of the clear resin to the spot where you will place the eye. Let the resin soak into the deer hair.

36. Place the eyes onto the small puddles of UV resin. Squeeze some more of the resin onto the top of each eye and let it slide down over the sides of the eye until it joins the original wet resin and is completely encompassing the eye. Zap the resin-coated eyes with a UV lamp until cured—this should only take a second or two.

37. Remove the fly from the vise and apply a heavy dose of head cement to the forward edge of the untrimmed collar. Set the fly aside for a half hour or so to allow the cement to dry before trimming the collar—this is plenty of time to begin another fly. Once the next fly has reached this point in the tying process, this fly will be ready to trim. Brush some head cement onto the eyes as well (to ensure the UV resin remains clear).

38. Trim the collar to ⁵⁄₁₆ inch (8 mm) high and uniform all the way around. The hardened head cement will keep the front of the collar rigid and easier to trim evenly. Trim the rear of the collar at a slightly sloping angle back to the rear of the fly. Stop trimming once you reach the natural tips of deer hair.

39. Several common tools can be used to thread rubber legs into deer hair bass bugs. The cheapest and easiest may be simply using a wire bobbin threader. A typical wire bobbin threader bows out too much, so clip one end of the wire near the base and twist it around the other end of the wire. Secure the loose end with a bit of UV resin. This will leave you with a straight and fairly rigid threader with just enough opening at the tip to insert a pair of rubber legs. Poke a rigid bodkin through first, just above the hook shank, then the improvised wire threader.

40. Pull the pair of rubber legs through the body of packed deer hair and trim them to the desired length—1½ inches (38 mm) on either side is about right.

PATTERN VARIATION

DAHLBERG DIVER (ORIGINAL)

Hook: #2 Gamakatsu B10S

Thread 1: White 140-denier UTC Ultra Thread

Weed Guard: RIO Fluoroflex tippet (.017"/25 lb.)

Adhesive: Zap-A-Gap

Tail Flash: Gold Flashabou (3 dozen strands folded to make 6 dozen)

Bottom Tail Feather: White marabou (2 plumes)

Top Tail Feather: Dark brown marabou (2 plumes)

Thread 2: White 200-denier UTC G.S.P.

Body: Natural spinning deer hair

Thread 3: Tan 140-denier UTC Ultra Thread

BASS BUG

Hook: #4 Gamakatsu B10S

Thread 1: Black 140-denier UTC Ultra Thread

Weed Guard: RIO Fluoroflex tippet (.017"/25 lb.)

Adhesive: Zap-A-Gap

Outside Tail Feather: Sand grizzly hen saddle

Inside Tail Feather: Grizzly dyed yellow bugger saddle tips

Hackle: Grizzly dyed yellow bugger saddle

Main Body: Black deer belly hair

Body Bands: Yellow deer belly hair

Leg 1: Yellow round rubber (medium)

Leg 2: Black round rubber (medium)

Over the course of 140 years, the deer hair bass bug became, and remains, the quintessential bass fly. Florida's Seminole Indians were first recorded angling for largemouth bass with a wooden rod and deer hair and feather "bob" from the bows of canoes. It may have been James Henshall who first clipped the deer hair on his bass flies as early as the 1880s. However, it would be remiss not to mention a slew of other anglers and tiers who over the years have added their touch to the design, or at least carried the torch for a time: Orley Tuttle back in the early 1920s; Joe Messenger in the 1930s; William Sturgis, Horace Tapply, and Joe Brooks in the 1940s; and William Blades in the 1950s. Each of these men contributed in some way or another to what we all now generally refer to as a "bass bug."

I have tied a hundred different size and color variations of the deer hair bass bug, but my favorite is a black and yellow bug tied small and simple. This color scheme reminds me of a cork-bodied popper my dad let me have when I was about 13 years old. It was one of the first flies I ever caught bass on, and that confidence stuck with me. If I need larger topwater flies, I usually tie a Dahlberg Diving Frog or a more modern foam-bodied fly, but these small black and yellow bugs have always been a standby. They have a striking contrast so can be easily seen by both bass and angler and can be thrown with any weight fly rod.

All the fly-tying techniques used in the making of the Dahlberg Diving Frog can be utilized here in this simpler fly, but this particular version of the deer hair bass bug is tied on only a #4 hook, so some considerations must be taken—mainly with how the rubber legs are mounted. A tier can get away with inserting the legs through the body of a larger deer hair bug after the desired shape has been clipped or shaved out of the unruly mass of hair, but there is not enough packed hair in a small version to hold the legs in place on its own. At some point between the placing of clumps of deer hair you will need to lay the pair of rubber legs down. I like to place them under the hook shank, as this will allow them to "droop" below the fly and help it right itself properly in the water. Use just two semi-loose wraps of thread over the legs and continue on with the hair packing. Pull the legs out of the way as you are trimming the fly to shape.

Once the fly is done, hold it over a steaming kettle for a moment or two. This will further compress the packed deer hair, relax the wound hackle (which most likely got matted down during the hair-packing process), and give the tail feathers a wicked curl, which adds an exaggerated kicking action when the fly is retrieved.

5

GARTSIDE GURGLER

J ack Gartside was 10 years old when he learned to tie flies from the legendary Boston Red Sox slugger, left fielder, and Baseball Hall of Famer Ted Williams. Jack's illustrious fly-tying career began in 1956 and would cover more than a half century. He was profiled in *Sports Illustrated* (October 12, 1982) as well as in most major fly-fishing magazines, and wrote seven books including *The Fly Fisherman's Guide to Boston Harbor*, *Scratching the Surface*, and *Striper Flies*—the first "bible" of striped bass fly patterns. In 2010, a year after his death, Jack Gartside was selected into the Fly Fishing Hall of Fame.

The Gartside Gurgler in an older fly pattern that has never lost its effectiveness on bass water.

The Gartside Gurgler is Jack's most known and recognizable contribution to the world of fly design. The fly's conception began in 1988 while Jack was fishing in the Bahamas, but he soon developed it into an East Coast blue and striper streamer that mimicked a wounded baitfish struggling on the surface. The original marabou tail evolved into a longer, slimmer one made of deer tail hair, and the front foam lip was added to give a sputtering or gurgling effect to the fly as it is retrieved. The design was inspired by an old but famous conventional bass lure created by Fred Arbogast from Akron, Ohio, in 1937 called the Jitterbug. The upward-arching foam lip makes the pattern skim over the surface of the water in a subtle and unobtrusive manner that is less likely to spook skittish fish (as some topwater poppers can do) yet still elicit aggressive strikes from below. Since the late 1980s there have been many productive variations of Jack Gartside's fly, some made for tarpon and other saltwater species and others catering more to freshwater fish, such as northern pike and

bass. It has turned out to be one of those rare benchmark fly patterns that help define a particular way of angling.

I am not the first fly tier to adapt the Gurgler for service as a bass fly (the inventor himself had his own bass variations on the theme), but over the years I have spent on the water and at my own vise, I have become particular about what I like in a fly. By no means did I reinvent Jack's Gurgler, I just added things and tweaked others to suit my own preferences—much like a hundred other tiers have done to this and every other great fly ever made. The version of the Gartside Gurgler that I tie for bass and is featured in this tutorial has a slightly longer and more substantial tail than the rather wispy original. The thicker clump of bucktail off the rear of the fly, combined with a shorter-shanked hook, makes this version lie flatter on the surface of the water (as opposed to sitting back in the water, like the original), allowing it to have a better darting action when jerked . . . which I *really* like in a bass fly.

Big bass lurk in thick cover and along heavy weed lines that act as a sanctuary for bass forage. *Erin Block* photo.

Much like the tail, I have bulked up the body of my Gurglers. I never strip one side of the hackle feather, and I wrap the feather through a dense base of long-fibered and flashy dubbing. The dubbing not only adds substance to the fly and protects the quill of the hackle feather, but the Ice Dub I prefer adds the perfect pearly flash that mimics the underbelly of a baitfish—which, after all, is what the Gurgler is intended to be.

The quintessential Gartside Gurgler is white, and this is the color that has always worked best for me as well. However, I always add a second, darker color to the top of my Gurglers. The bottom of the fly (the part the fish sees) remains white and pearl, but the deer hair tail and foam back are two-tone. The top color has little to do with the fish, but everything to do with the water, lighting, and anything else that may affect my ability to see the fly—or, more times than not, the choice of color is determined purely by my current mood. One unintentional benefit to using two layers of foam over the top of this fly is that the Zap-A-Gap (used to adhere them at the front) creates a very stiff lip that is much less likely to be bent backwards when being yanked through a bass pond.

The Gartside Gurgler is best fished on a floating line, as it is meant to be a topwater fly. It does swim well below the surface, too, so do not shy away from tying one on if you are on the water with a full sinking or sink-tip line. Gurglers can be easily tied with hard-mono weed guards if the surface cover in the areas you haunt are thick and snag-riddled. One of my favorite ways to fish a Gurgler is in tandem with a lightweight subsurface fly such as a Finesse Worm. The Gurgler stays on the surface, making a bit of commotion and attracting attention, while the worm hovers over beds of underwater vegetation. The Gurgler will get smashed by any aggressive fish, and the trailing fly makes a safe and easy meal alternative that few of even the wariest bass can resist.

GARTSIDE GURGLER (OLIVE & WHITE)

Hook: #2 Tiemco 811S

Thread: Red 280-denier UTC Ultra Thread

Adhesive: Zap-A-Gap

Tail Hair 1: White bucktail

Tail Hair 2: Light olive bucktail

Tail Flash: Pearl Krystal Flash

Back 1: Olive sheet foam (2 mm)

Back 2: White sheet foam (2mm)

Hackle: White Whiting Bugger Hackle

Wax: BT's Tacky Dubbing Wax

Body: Pearl Ice Dub

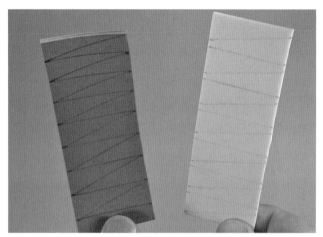

1. Do some prep work before beginning a batch of Gurglers—it is a fast fly to tie, so take the time to cut foam for several dozen. The 2 mm foam from Wapsi usually comes in 3-inch (76 mm) wide sheets, so begin by cutting that in half, giving you two 1½-inch (38 mm) sheets. Next, measure out ½-inch (13 mm) increments on either side of the olive sheet foam (or whichever dark foam is being used on the top), use a straight edge and sharp pencil to connect the marks to create triangles, and then cut them out. Do the same with the white (or bottom) foam, but stagger the marks between ½ inch (13 mm) and ⅛ inch (3 mm) so the apex of the sharpest angle in the triangular piece of foam is not a sharp point, but fatter than the same corner of the olive foam. This ensures the outside edges of the two pieces of foam will not line up evenly once they are tied in on top of each other.

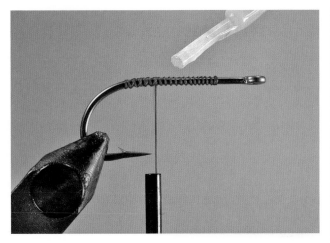

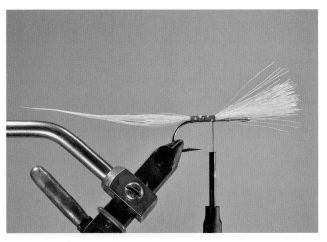

2. Once the triangular foam pieces have been cut, begin the first fly of the batch. Mount the hook firmly into the vise and begin the thread wraps a hook eye and a half back from the hook eye. Once the first few wraps of the thread base are in place, spin the bobbin until the thread is made tight and round—this will give the thread base a better grip on the first clump of deer hair being used for the tail. The 280-denier UTC thread is ideal for lashing foam down because it is flat and wide and will be less likely to cut into the foam when pressure is applied. Spinning the bobbin will only twist the thread from the spool to where it meets the hook shank, or just enough to create the thread base. Build a spiral-wrapped thread base (so the hook shank is partially exposed) all the way back to the rear end of the straight hook shank. Wrap the thread forward and let the bobbin hang so the thread is even with the hook point. Apply a light coat of Zap-A-Gap to the entire thread base (the spiral wrapping allows some of the adhesive to make contact with the hook shank).

4. Tie the clump of white bucktail down onto the top of the hook shank. The tips of hair should extend back about two and a half to three hook-shank lengths. Most tutorials for the Gurgler ask that the tail be only two shank lengths long and somewhat wispy. When made for bass, I prefer a longer, more substantial tail. Make the thread wraps near the rear of the tie-down a bit loose—this will keep the hair fibers from flaring.

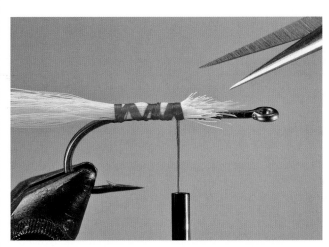

5. When tying down the first clump of hair, do not extend the thread tie-down onto the front third of the original thread base. Trim away the butt ends of white deer hair at an angle—this creates an even foundation for follow-on materials.

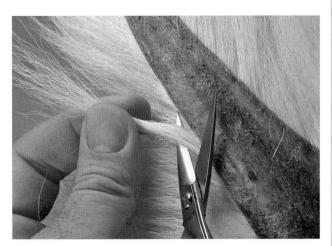

3. Select and cut a clump of white bucktail. The clump should be slightly smaller than the diameter of a pencil. Hold the clump of hair toward the tip end and use your other hand to pull out any stray or broken hairs. Be quick, as you want to get this first clump of deer hair mounted onto the thread base while the Zap-A-Gap is still wet.

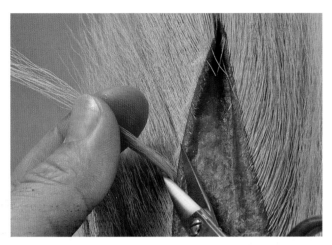

6. Select and cut a clump of light olive (or chosen top color) bucktail. This clump should be slightly smaller than the white clump of deer hair. Hold the clump of hair toward the tip end and use your other hand to pull out any stray or broken hairs.

7. Tie the top color of bucktail in the same way, but on top of the previous, white clump of deer hair. Be sure to make the rear thread wraps a bit loose to prevent hair flare. Trim the butt ends of hair, also at an angle.

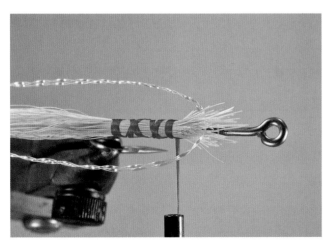

8. Select two strands of pearl Krystal Flash and trap the middle of the strands under the still-loose butt ends of

bucktail. Fold the two strands of flash back to make four strands, two on either side of the hair tail. Tie it all down. Continue to keep the very rear thread wraps a bit loose. Trim the four ends of Krystal Flash so they extend out even with the longest fibers of bucktail.

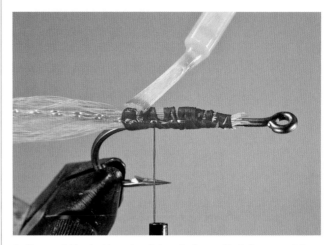

9. Once all the butt ends of deer hair are tied down and the Krystal Flash is secured on either side of the tail, bring the bobbin forward and let it hang so the thread is at a point between the hook point and the barb. Apply Zap-A-Gap to just the rear end of the thread tie-down. Allow the adhesive to seep down into the deer hair tail—this will help keep the tail firm and straight.

10. Take one of the olive triangles of foam and trim down the edges of the sharpest angle. Do not alter the shape of the silhouette, just do what you can to reduce the material bulk at what will be tied down and at the rear of the fly. This strategic trimming will add a subtle tapering effect to the top rear of the fly once finished. Trim off the edges from just one side.

11. Before tying down the first piece of foam, be sure the Zap-A-Gap on the thread base is completely dry. If it is still wet, the foam will partially stick to the tail and then tear when folded forward, so force the adhesive to dry by rolling your fingertips over the wet area. Tie the pointy end of the olive foam triangle down at the top rear of the thread base—be sure the side with the trimmed-down edges is facing up. The tip of the corner of foam being tied down should be even with the hook point.

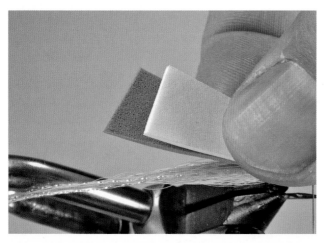

12. Lay the second piece of foam (the white triangle) on top of the hook so the shorter, back side of the triangle is about a hook eye and a half shorter than the darker, original piece of foam.

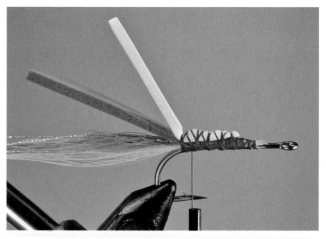

13. Tie the white foam down in place. The tip of the white foam will extend farther out over the hook shank than the olive. Return the bobbin to the rear of the fly.

14. Select a hackle feather that is long and full.

15. Tie the tip end of the hackle feather in at the rear of the fly. Avoid tying the feather down by the fine, terminal part of the quill at the very end of the feather—it should be long enough to be able to spare the weak tip and still have enough length to get at least six palmered wraps up to the hook eye. Lick your fingers and slick back the fibers on either side of the quill to help keep them out of the way. Trim away the excess tip of feather.

16. Create a long thread loop at the rear of the fly, then wrap the thread forward and leave the bobbin hanging so the thread is at the very forward end of the original thread base. Wax the thread loop in preparation for the dubbing. Wax temporarily keeps the loose dubbing in place between the two strands of thread.

17. Load the waxed thread loop with pearl Ice Dub.

18. Twist the thread loop into a tight dubbing rope, then use a wire dubbing brush to brush out any loose dubbing fibers and "fluff up" the remainder.

19. Wrap the dubbing rope forward over the hook shank. Make each wrap snug against the previous wrap, but be sure to sweep back any of the long dubbing fibers between wraps to avoid trapping them against the hook shank. Once you wrap the dubbing rope forward enough to reach the thread resting at the end of the thread base, tie the dubbing rope down there and trim away any excess.

20. Use a wire dubbing brush to loosen any long dubbing fibers that may have gotten trapped as the dubbing rope was wrapped forward on the hook shank. Brush across the hook shank, as this will leave the long dubbing fibers standing up in a way that will allow the hackle feather to be wrapped forward and buried neatly into the mass of dubbing without matting too much of it down.

21. Wrap the white hackle feather forward through the thick Ice Dub body—this should take about six evenly spaced wraps to reach the forward end of the dubbed body. Tie the butt end of the feather down and trim away the excess. The original Gurgler did not use dubbing on the body and was wrapped with a feather that had been stripped clean of fibers on one side of the quill, but this is a sturdier, more full-bodied version. As you are wrapping the hackle feather over the dubbed body, avoid twisting the feather. Wrap the feather not on its edge (like one would normally) but on one of its flat sides—this keeps fibers from getting trapped under the quill. As the feather quill gets pulled into the soft cushion of dubbing, the fibers from both sides of the quill will be pushed out and be forced to stand up off the belly of the fly. The quill will be somewhat protected once buried in the dubbing.

22. The act of tying down the butt end of the hackle feather should leave a short thread base covering the hook shank from the forward end of the dubbed body to the rear of the hook eye. This "thread head" will continue to grow fatter and will eventually be what helps prop the two pieces of foam up at the front of the finished fly. This will also be the only place on the fly where the thread will be visible, hence the use of red thread (to simulate bleeding gills of a wounded baitfish). Use the wire dubbing brush to brush out any trapped fibers, as well as pull most of the longer dubbing and hackle fibers off the top of the fly. Lick your fingers and slick back any remaining fibers off the top of the fly, parting the material down the middle like a '50s hairstyle. Be sure to leave the thread at the very rear of the thread head.

23. Fold the white foam down over the top of the fly and put two wraps of thread over it to hold it in place. Do not immediately make these thread wraps tight, as you will need to flip the fly over to be sure the foam is centered perfectly and then gradually tighten the thread.

24. Viewing the fly from below is the best way to ensure the foam is centered, by using the hook eye as a gauge. Make sure the foam stays centered as the two thread wraps are tightened. Once the foam is on tight, make two more wraps of thread over the tie-down and prepare to fold the second piece of foam down onto the body of the fly.

25. Fold the olive foam down on top of the white foam and mount it in place with two or three tight wraps of thread. Use the white foam as a centering gauge this time. You will now see the results of the tedious attention to detail earlier in the tying process. The reason the two pieces of foam were cut into slightly different-shaped triangles can be seen in the way the olive foam is much narrower at the rear (than the lower white foam) but evens out at the head. Also notice how thin the olive foam is as it wraps up onto the white foam—that is (in part) the result of the underside edge trimming that reduced the mass of that corner of the foam.

26. Once the top piece of foam is secured in place, use the thumb of your non-tying hand to force both pieces of foam back and away from the hook eye. As you are doing this, build up the thread head under the foam enough to permanently keep the foam "lip" up at an angle. As you are building up bulk with many thread wraps, be sure to keep a slight taper in this thread head that comes down to the hook eye. Once the thread head has reached the desired size, tie a whip-finish knot and trim the thread.

27. Apply a heavy coat of Zap-A-Gap to the underside of the thread head and between the two ends of foam that stick out over the hook eye. Use a clothespin to clamp the two ends of foam down onto each other (be sure they are lined up evenly) and remove the fly from the vise—clothespin still attached. Set the fly aside. It will be plenty dry and ready to finish by the time the next fly in the batch reaches this point.

28. Remove the clothespin from the front of the previously tied fly and trim down the double layer of foam so it extends just slightly over the outer edge of the hook eye. Trim the foam into a slight curve, about that of your big toe nail—a pair of curved-blade scissors will help here, but are not necessary.

COLOR VARIATIONS

I tie Gurglers for bass in many different colors besides the olive shown in the step-by-step tutorial here, including dark gray, blue, chartreuse, yellow, and red. However, the only alterations between these variations is the color of the top bucktail in the tail and the color of the top piece of foam—everything else stays the same.

GRIM REAPER

I first saw Pat Ehlers on the cover of something. It may have been a fly-fishing magazine, or maybe it was a fly-tying catalog. I can't remember exactly what the cover was on, but I remember the photo vividly. Pat is standing on a boat pointing a big northern pike at the camera like it was a deadly weapon. All you could see of the fish was two beady eyes, two outstretched pectoral fins, and a gaping mouth full of teeth and the hair and Flashabou remains of a pike fly. In the photo Pat is wearing sunglasses, a sweet horseshoe 'stash, and a grin that makes you like the guy because you feel as though you have just met him in person.

The Grim Reaper is one of my favorite big, subsurface baits when I am on large bodies of water that are slightly off-color.

Cliff Watts and sidekick with a belly boat bass. Cliff is a retired ER doctor and fly designer best known for his salmon and steelhead pattern the Kilowatt—the first jig-hook fly Umpqua Feather Merchants ever sold commercially. *Cliff Watts* photo.

Years later I would talk to him via cellphone as we both drove home from our respective fly shops—me from the one I work out of in Arvada, Colorado, and him, the one he founded in Milwaukee, Wisconsin. He was exactly who I thought he was . . . a Midwestern pragmatist who has no time for ego or nonsense and would rather talk about fish and flies than himself.

Pat grew up fishing in Wisconsin with his father and uncle and was indoctrinated into the worlds of both trout and warmwater species as well as fly-fishing and conventional gear—all worlds equally. In fact, he never drew a distinction between any of them, and that has carried over into his life and profession as an adult. You can see the strong conventional gear influence in the many flies he has designed. Pat began tying flies at an early age and even began selling his creations to sports shops in northern Wisconsin when he

was still in his early teens. He has gone on to design flies for Rainy's Flies and his own fly rod models for Echo. In 1988 Pat opened The Fly Fishers fly shop in Milwaukee.

The Grim Reaper is one of Pat's bass flies, and it is one of my favorite big, subsurface baits when I am on large bodies of water that are slightly off-color. The weight of the fly gets it down into deep submerged structure, yet the design of the fly around a 60-degree jig hook allows it to slide over branches and bounce off of rocks easily. Between the full rubber skirt and the long dancing tail, there is more jittery, lifelike movement on the Grim Reaper than any other fly I know, and the internal rattle makes this fly easy for a bass to locate at night or in deep, dirty water. Many fly patterns claim to be the fly rodder's answer to the classic jig 'n pig (a heavy conventional jig with a full rubber skirt and a long piece of pickled pork rind attached to the hook bend), but

Pat Ehlers's Grim Reaper is as close as any tier has ever got, in both action and appearance. That is a big deal, as a skirted jig may have won more bass tournaments than any other lure.

I prefer a color scheme that mimics a large adult crayfish, so I am using a brown Ultrasuede tail with an olive and brown body (with just a hint of blue) and brown speckled rubber legs (with just a hint of orange) to make the skirt. The subtleties in color surely mean more to me than the bass, as this is more of a suggestive or "abstract" fish-attracting fly. I also tie a more solidly olive version, as well as all black, pearl, and a crazy chartreuse and orange version for really muddy water. With the influx of new synthetic tying materials available, there is an almost limitless number of Grim Reaper color variations you can tie—you will be hard-pressed to find one that will not work.

GRIM REAPER (CRAYFISH)

Hook: #3/0 Gamakatsu Jig 60

Thread: Brown 140-denier UTC Ultra Thread

Eyes: Red painted lead dumbbell eyes (large)

Head Resin: Clear UV resin

Rattle: Standard 4 mm, 2-bead rattle

Tail: Clove brown Ultrasuede

Body: Olive copper UV Polar Chenille

Adhesive: Zap-A-Gap

Skirt: Pumpkin/orange fire tip Sili Legs

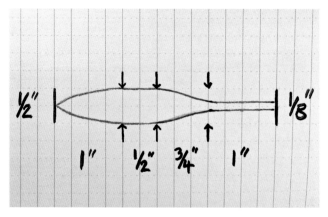

1. Create a template for the Grim Reaper tail. You can purchase premade tails from Cascade Crest Tools for about 80 cents apiece, but they are fast to make once you have your template. You can customize the shape if you cut your own, too. I prefer a tail that tapers down fairly narrow at the point where it first comes off the rear of the hook shank—this allows the tail a more active side-to-side wobble that is important because the Ultrasuede material is thin and hard to see when viewed from the side (as bass are often viewing

it). I also cut my tails with an extended butt section that I use to build a material ramp onto the fly rattle. Use a waterproof notepad that has ¼-inch graph paper. The tail should be a ½ inch (13 mm) wide and 3¼ inches (83 mm) long. The terminal taper should be 1 inch long (25 mm) and the rear taper should be ¾ inch long (19 mm). The butt section should be 1 inch long (25 mm) and ⅛ inch (3 mm) wide.

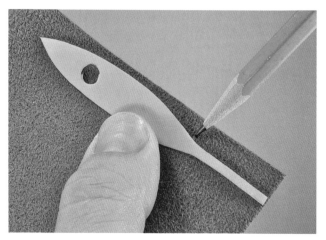

2. I use a waterproof paper to make a temporary template because it is thick and durable enough to work as the template for at least a dozen tails—which is more than enough to decide if you have the shape you like. Once you have dialed in the perfectly shaped tail, use clear shipping tape to mount the temporary paper template onto the heavy plastic back cover of the waterproof notebook and use it to guide the cutting of your permanent template. I punch a hole in the fat part of the template so I can hang it on a hook and not lose it. Use this heavy plastic template to make all the Grim Reaper tails you need. Use a pencil to draw the outline, as it will easily fade.

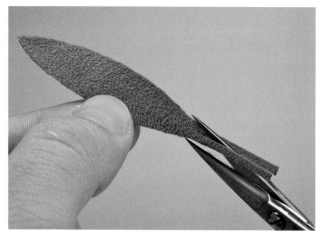

3. Once a tail has been cut to shape from the Ultrasuede, cut a slit up the center of the narrow butt section.

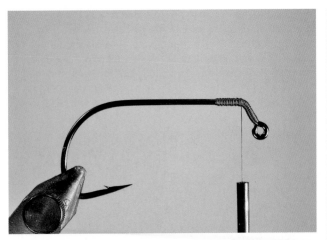

4. Mount the hook firmly into the vise and create a heavy thread base that covers the entire "jigged" section of the hook shank and an equal amount of the main, straight shank of the hook. Bring the thread to the forward end of the straight shank and let the bobbin hang in place.

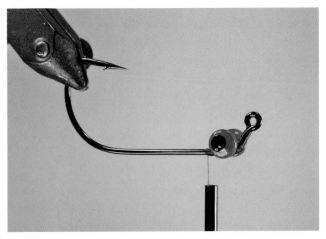

6. Once the dumbbell eyes are properly mounted, bring the bobbin back to the very rear of the thread base and let it hang in place.

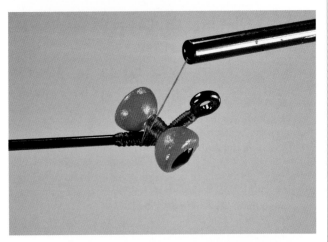

5. Rotate the vise so the hook point and the hook eye are facing up. Mount the large lead dumbbell eyes in the crux, or "armpit," of the jigged hook shank. Use as many tight thread wraps as it takes to completely cover the middle "arbor" of the eyes—none of the red paint should be visible. The dumbbell will be left cocked to one side, so use the thumbnail of your non-thread-wrapping hand to pull the near side of the dumbbell to the rear and use more tight thread wraps (crossing the middle from the other direction) to lock the eyes permanently in place and perpendicular to the hook shank.

7. Goop a liberal amount of clear UV-cured resin onto the head and dumbbell eyes, then use a bodkin to push some resin all the way around both sides of the eyes. Be sure all surfaces, both painted lead and thread, are covered. Avoid getting any buildup on the thread base or hook shank directly behind the eyes, as this area needs to remain clear so there is plenty of room to lash in the rubber skirt later on in the tying process.

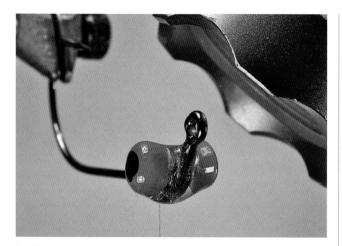

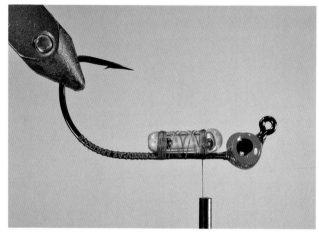

this has to do with the buoyancy caused by the air trapped in the rattle or the volume of the lightweight Polar Chenille body wrap pushed farther to what will be the bottom of the finished fly. Either way, mounting the rattle on the top eliminates the fly's tendency to list onto its side when retrieved quickly, and there is still over a half inch of gape clearance when tied on a 3/0 hook.

8. When the resin head is shaped correctly, zap it with a UV lamp. The more powerful the lamp, the faster the resin will set up and cure all the way through. The power of the light used has more to do with the tackiness (or lack thereof) when the resin is hard than the type or brand of resin being used. On the head of my Grim Reapers I like to have the resin slightly concave on the top, creating a bit of a scoop, and bulging downward on the bottom. The bulge of resin at the bottom will help deflect snags on the bottom of a lake and better protect the painted lead eyes from getting dinged up. It is very difficult to get a perfectly shaped resin head unless you are using a true rotary tying vise because the fly needs to be rotated around while the resin is wet—this process is akin to blowing glass using a furnace and blowpipe.

10. Tie the fly rattle down onto the bare hook shank using a solid band of thread wraps at each end of the rattle. Even with two thread tie-down points (and the two turns of thread connecting them), the rattle will still want to move around and twist; just keep it in place the best you can—it will take Zap-A-Gap adhesive to lock it down solid, but that comes later. Once the rattle is mounted, create a sparse thread base that extends to the rear of the straight hook shank and well onto the beginning of the hook bend. Stop the thread base at a point about even with the middle of the rattle (if you imagined a line horizontal to the straight hook shank). Wrap the thread forward and stop at the forward of the two rattle tie-downs and let the bobbin hang.

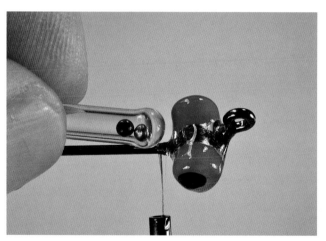

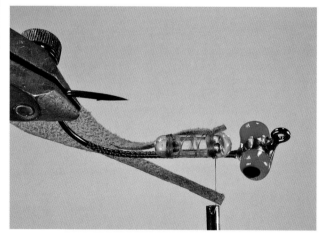

9. Place the fly rattle on the bare hook shank directly behind the lead eyes. It is important to mount the rattle with direct contact to the hook, as the entire hook will now act as a tuning fork and quickly send out any reverberations caused by the rattle (even once the rattle is thoroughly swaddled in tying materials). Be sure to leave a slight gap between the forward end of the rattle and the rear of the lead eyes—this gap will be where the rubber skirt is tied down. Examine the fly rattle before mounting it. One end of the rattle will be slightly larger than the other—put this fatter end toward the lead eyes to increase the working hook gape. The original Grim Reaper is tied with the rattle mounted on the bottom of the fly, but I have always found the fly to ride better in the water when it is mounted on the top. I am not sure if

11. Begin tying in the Ultrasuede tail by using two thread wraps to secure one side of the split butt section on top of (but slightly off to the side of) the fly rattle. Be sure to leave a slight tag of material popping up right at the forward end of the rattle—this will act as a lip to catch the Polar Chenille body wrap and keep it from sliding over the end of the rattle.

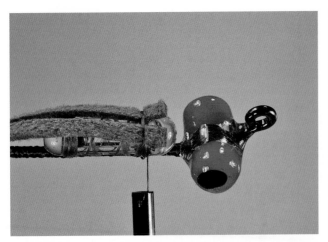

12. Swing the other side of the split butt section of the tail piece around the back side of the hook bend and tie it down on top of the fly rattle next to its mate.

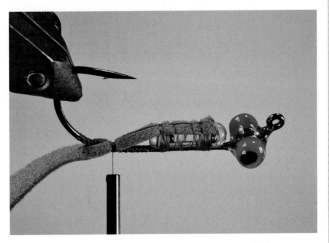

13. Once the two split ends of the butt of the tail piece are secured at the top front of the fly rattle, wrap the thread to the rear of the rattle and then jump the thread back onto the rear thread base without getting a thread wrap over the suede material ramp that has been created from the hook shank up to the top of the rattle. The reason you made the rear thread base sparse was to create better traction to catch the thread as you made the leap off the fly rattle all the way back to what is now the rear of the Ultrasuede material ramp. Use several tight thread wraps to lock the tail down in place.

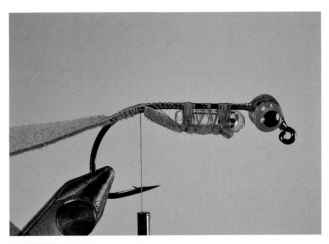

14. Rotate the fly to the hook-down position. Continue tying the tail down to the hook shank. Use the end of the rear thread base as a marker to let you know when the tail is tied back far enough. (The act of tying the tail in well back onto the hook bend is called "tail creeping" and is a technique used to help the fly swim hook point up.) Wrap the thread forward and stop at the base of the suede material ramp.

15. Tie down an end of the Polar Chenille body wrap at the rear of the fly. To avoid material waste, do not cut a length of the chenille to use for an individual fly; rather, keep it all loosely balled up in your hand when you wrap it forward. Take a close look at both ends of the Polar Chenille before choosing which end to tie down. The flash and synthetic hair comes off the cord slightly favoring one direction of lean. Choose the end that all the material is leaning away from—this will make wrapping the body easier because the "hair" will not be as likely to get trapped under each wrap. Once the Polar Chenille is tied down, wrap the thread all the way forward (don't forget to jump over the Ultrasuede material ramp) and leave the bobbin hanging so the thread rests between the forward end of the fly rattle and the lead eyes.

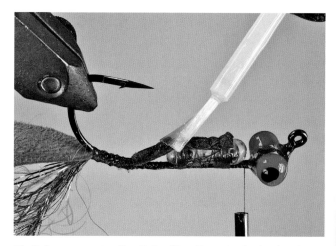

16. Before wrapping the Polar Chenille onto the body of the fly, thoroughly coat the entire area between the butt of the tail and the forward end of the fly rattle with Zap-A-Gap adhesive. Be sure the fly rattle is perfectly straight on the hook shank before coating the thread used to tie it down. Also be sure to completely soak all the Ultrasuede used in the material ramp and over the top of the fly rattle. Begin wrapping the Polar Chenille before the adhesive has a chance to completely dry.

18. Use an entire bundle of Sili Legs material for the rubber skirt. Wapsi sells packs of these rubber legs that come with five bundles per pack—each bundle is connected at a solid tab at either end. Hold the bundle of rubber legs stretched out horizontally, then slide them under the fly and under the last wrap of thread. The weight of the hanging bobbin will hold the bundle in place on top of the fly. Adjust the bundle so that slightly more than half of it is on the side draping over the body of the fly. (This ensures both sides will be even when the fly is finished.) Once the bundle of Sili Legs has been properly adjusted, make another *loose* wrap of thread over the top and let the bobbin hang once more. Use a fingernail to spread out and evenly disperse the rubber legs out over the entire top of the tie-down area.

17. Wrap the Polar Chenille forward over the fly rattle, then tie it off and trim the excess after the last wrap (or half wrap) is made between the rattle and the lead eyes. The suede material ramp will make getting the body wrap up onto the rattle much easier and tidier than the alternative, which is bunching as much material at the base of the rattle as it takes to build up level to the top of the rattle. Make each wrap neatly next to the last, but try to accomplish complete body coverage in 24 wraps. Trim away the excess once the end is tied down.

19. Once the Sili Legs have been spread out over the top of the fly, cut off the back half fairly close to the thread tie-down. Now make several more *tight* wraps of thread to lock the remaining half of bundled Sili Legs in place. The tight wraps of thread will pull most of the butt ends of severed rubber down into the gap between the body wrap and the lead eyes.

20. Rotate the fly and tie down (with two *loose* thread wraps) the other half of the Sili Legs bundle on what will be the top side of the fly. The severed end of rubber legs should be the side toward the body of the fly. Tie the bundle down so that the color change at the tabbed end of the bundles are roughly even—this should mean the butt ends sticking out over the body of the fly are relatively short. Use your fingernail to spread out the legs as you did with the first side. Trim away the butt ends and use several more *tight* wraps of thread to secure them in place. The tight wraps of thread will pull most of the butt ends of severed rubber down into the gap between the body wrap and the lead eyes.

21. Bring the thread forward of all the rubber legs and sweep all the rubber back over the body of the fly, exposing the head and lead eyes. Tie a whip-finish knot between the rubber and the head. Because the knot will be buried into a material crevice and out of sight, it will be difficult to apply head cement to it, so tie a second whip-finish knot over the first for durability in redundancy and forgo the head cement. Trim the thread.

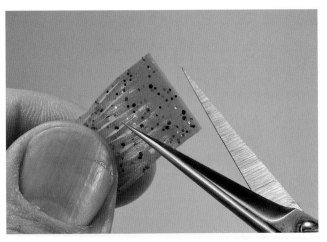

22. Hold up each tabbed end of the Sili Legs bundle and cut away the solid tabs, freeing all the individual rubber legs.

23. Remove the fly from the vise and hold it up so all the Sili Legs fall down alongside the body. The tips of all the legs should be roughly even, but if a couple are a tad too long, trim them accordingly.

PATTERN VARIATIONS

GRIM REAPER (MIDNIGHT)

Hook: #3/0 Gamakatsu Jig 60

Thread: Black 140-denier UTC Ultra Thread

Eyes: Red painted lead dumbbell eyes (large)

Head Resin: Clear UV resin

Rattle: Standard 4 mm, 2-bead rattle

Tail: Black Ultrasuede

Body: Black UV Polar Chenille

Adhesive: Zap-A-Gap

Skirt: Black/purple fire tip Sili Legs

GRIM REAPER (PEARL)

Hook: #3/0 Gamakatsu Jig 60

Thread: White 140-denier UTC Ultra Thread

Eyes: Pearl-white painted lead dumbbell eyes (large)

Head Resin: Clear UV resin

Rattle: Standard 4 mm, 2-bead rattle

Tail: White Ultrasuede

Body: Pearl UV Polar Chenille

Adhesive: Zap-A-Gap

Skirt: Clear/fire orange fire tip Sili Legs

GRIM REAPER (POND OLIVE)

Hook: #3/0 Gamakatsu Jig 60

Thread: Olive 140-denier UTC Ultra Thread

Eyes: Yellow painted lead dumbbell eyes (large)

Head Resin: Clear UV resin

Rattle: Standard 4 mm, 2-bead rattle

Tail: Pea green Ultrasuede

Body: Olive dyed UV Polar Chenille

Adhesive: Zap-A-Gap

Skirt: Olive/orange fire tip Sili Legs

GRIM REAPER (FIRE TIGER)

Hook: #3/0 Gamakatsu Jig 60

Thread: Fluorescent green 140-denier UTC Ultra Thread

Eyes: Chartreuse painted lead dumbbell eyes (large)

Head Resin: Clear UV resin

Rattle: Standard 4 mm, 2-bead rattle

Tail: Chartreuse Ultrasuede

Body: Chartreuse dyed UV Polar Chenille

Adhesive: Zap-A-Gap

Skirt: Chartreuse/fire orange fire tip Sili Legs

KRYSTOWSKI MINNOW

The Krystowski Minnow got its name by pure happenstance. In the spring of 2002 I was temporarily living back in my home state of Ohio and primarily fishing for (and tying flies for) Great Lakes–run steelhead, river smallmouth, and farm-pond largemouth bass. At that point in my life I was already several years removed from the army, recently back from a commercial fishing stint in Alaska, and restlessly anticipating a move to Colorado.

I have landed thousands of bass on this simple streamer.

Small bass ponds are fun to fish with lightweight rods and small flies, but sometimes large bass can crash your ultralight party! Eva Zimmerman instantly regretted using a 5-weight fly rod and 5X tippet when this beast ate her fly.

It was a tumultuous period for me both personally and financially, but I survived it by spending time fishing local waters with an old high school friend and creating flies that were simple, durable, and inexpensive to tie. I was running around with a young schoolteacher from a nearby Catholic high school at the time (it never worked out, me being a heathen with serious wanderlust who cursed like a sailor). One weekend afternoon she lured me to dinner at another teacher-couple's house because they had a bass pond on their property—at that time, I guess I would have subjected myself to almost anything to gain access to private water. The couple was Mary and Rick Krystowski, and their spread was a mile outside the small, rural town of New London. The pond behind their house would be the first place I would ever fish the streamer pattern I would later call the Krystowski Minnow.

I remember exchanging only brief pleasantries on the Krystowskis' expansive back deck before excusing myself

to "go see a man about a bass." The pond was small, about an acre, and shaped roughly like a kidney bean. I guessed the pond to be about 10 to 12 feet deep, and it had all the trappings of a modern backyard swimming hole—there was a small floating dock for kids and paddleboats, a windmill aerator in the middle, and even a cable stretched from one side to the other for a makeshift zip line. The banks seemed a bit too manicured for my liking, but there were healthy growths of cattails on the east and west ends that Rick had apparently been struggling to kill for as long as they had owned the property. I was also told that a neighbor (or relative, I cannot remember which) frequently fished the pond with conventional tackle. All these variables (the small size of the pond, it's overgrooming, and the fishing pressure) were previously unknown to me, and I was seriously regretting my decision to be social that evening. I could not gather whether or not the neighbor/relative who had access to the pond kept or released his fish. It was not looking promising, and the first half hour that I fished the pond resulted in nary a strike. Then, to make matters worse, a rainstorm moved in.

The rain did not last long, just a solitary May storm, and I took cover in a small, dilapidated outbuilding beside the pond. The windows were broken out, so I hunkered down in the back, astride a pile of old lawn chairs and softball bats. While waiting out the rain, I rifled through my many fly boxes looking for something that could alter my luck, and came up with a recently tied prototype streamer that I had never fished before. I had two of them stashed in a corner of a fly box, and as soon as the rain lightened up, I slipped back out to the bank of the pond and tried again. This time things were different—I was moving fish on almost every retrieve, and before I was eventually called back up to the house for dinner, I had landed and released several good-size largemouth bass as well as some of the largest bluegill and redear sunfish I had ever seen in the state. I have no idea what was served for dinner, or what the table conversation was . . . all I could think about was getting more of these new streamers tied!

I tied and fished the Krystowski Minnow almost exclusively during the rest of that year and the next. I landed hundreds and hundreds of bass from all the nearby reservoirs and farm ponds that I had permission to fish, and had days where I landed more bass on a fly rod than I ever had previously. I also used it to fool spring steelhead in the Lake Erie tributaries, as well as big smallmouth bass and northern pike during fishing trips into Ontario, Canada. Eventually I would leave Ohio and move West, where my reliable Krystowski worked for the bass and pike in Colorado and Wyoming, as well as some good-size brown trout.

One of those original two prototype streamers is secured away in a plastic bag in a drawer near my fly-tying bench. (The other fly was lost to a bass that first day.) When I dug out that old fly, before writing this bit, I noticed how rough the fly was and how sloppy a fly tier I was back then . . . and

Bass fishin' with your best mate is as good as it gets! *Erin Block* photo.

how far along the pattern has come. That first Krystowski Minnow was tied on a size 8 Mustad 80300-BR hook and had medium silver bead chain for eyes. The hair was still the same—black, olive, and white Icelandic sheep hair. The immediate change I made with the pattern was to replace the bead-chain eyes with painted lead eyes. The bead chain was just not heavy enough to flip the fly over and make it ride hook point up, as it was supposed to.

That change created another problem, however. The lead eyes I tied on were so heavy that the action of the fly changed completely. Instead of a smooth but undulating swimming action, it became a jig. There is a time and place for a fly or lure with a distinctly jig-like action, but not in the smaller ponds with heavy weed growth near their bottoms that I was regularly fishing. I needed the fly to have a little weight but still be light enough to glide over the old tractor tires, ex–Christmas trees, and other farm pond "cover" without easily hanging up. The extra-small lead barbell eyes were the ideal weight but still were not quite enough to make the fly ride correctly—it would sort of just slump over onto its side when retrieved. This was my first lesson in streamer hydrodynamics and how I learned to create what years later I would begin calling a "natural lift kit." By tying in the first two clumps of hair (and putting the white belly hair on the other side of the hook) before tying on the lead eyes, it put a significant amount of separation between the weight and the hook shank, which drastically affected the center mass of the fly. This enabled me to keep the streamer at the desired weight but also be sure it rode hook point up and stayed as weedless and snag-free as possible.

I now tie the Krystowski Minnow on a Gamakatsu B10S hook. I was forced to make this change when Mustad stopped making the 80300. Tiemco makes a better hook of almost the exact style (TMC 8089) but not in the size 8, my favorite. The Gamakatsu B10S hook in a size 2 has the same dimensions as the old Mustad stinger hook but is slightly heavier gauge, making it slightly heavier (.04 gram)—which does not noticeably affect the action of the fly. I now tie two sizes in this pattern; the one tied in this tutorial is the shorter, 2¾-inch (7 cm) version and the one I use mostly for bass. The longer version I tie on a Gamakatsu B10S hook in a size 1, or the Tiemco 8089 size 6, and I trim it to 3¼ inches (83 mm).

The Krystowski Minnow is a very simple fly and very fast to tie. Over the years, I have resisted the urge to make the pattern more complicated and "sexy," which would make it more commercially viable. It is perfect in its simplicity because it is a suggestive baitfish pattern that plays off the general color schemes of living minnows and baitfish.

KRYSTOWSKI MINNOW (CHARTREUSE)

Hook: #2 Gamakatsu B10S

Thread: Black 6/0 UNI-Thread

Adhesive: Zap-A-Gap

Hair 1: White Icelandic sheep hair

Hair 2: Fluorescent chartreuse Icelandic sheep hair

Eyes: Pearl painted lead barbell eyes (x-small)

Hair 3: Black Icelandic sheep hair

Head Cement: Hard as Hull

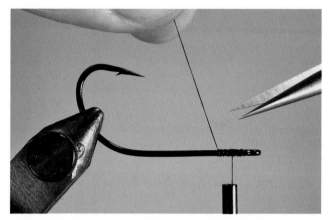

1. Clamp the hook securely into the jaws of the vise. Mount the large stinger-style hook upside down. You will be flipping the hook back and forth from this position, to the hook-down position repeatedly throughout the process of tying this fly, so using a rotary vise is recommended. Begin the thread wraps immediately behind the hook eye and create a thread base that extends ³⁄₁₆ inch (5 mm) or one and a half hook-eye lengths behind the hook eye. Leave the bobbin hanging so that the thread is in the middle of the thread base. Trim the excess thread tag from the rear of the thread base.

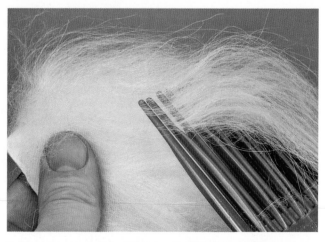

2. The main material making up the Krystowski Minnow is Icelandic sheep hair. I use three different colors of the sheep hair in most of the variations I tie, and I always comb out all the patches of hair before I begin tying. A large hair pick will get all the gnarls and nappy funk out of the hair.

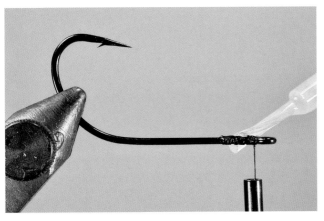

3. Apply a small amount of Zap-A-Gap to the short thread base. You will want to prepare and tie in the first clump of sheep hair before this adhesive dries.

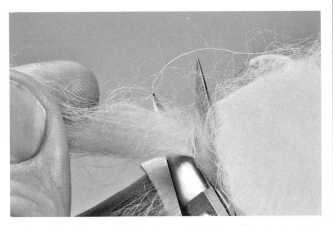

4. Cut off a clump of white sheep hair. You will get a feel of how much hair you want after you have tied a few of these flies, but begin with a clump roughly the diameter of a pencil. Cut the hair close to the hide.

5. There will be lots of underfur buried in the butt end of the clump of sheep hair that you have cut. This fur must be removed before you mount the hair onto the hook. Grasp the clump of hair with one hand and use a bodkin to rake out all the fuzz. This underfur can be used as dubbing for other flies later down the line, but if kept will most likely take up space for decades and later be tossed with the rest of your tying stuff by your next of kin.

6. Rotate the hook so that the point is down. Tie down the clump of white sheep hair. Leave a small amount of the butt ends of the hair protruding out past the hook eye. Also, be sure to only tie the hair down on the rear half of the short thread base, and don't extend the tie-down past the rear of the thread base, as you want to keep the head of this fly as compact as possible.

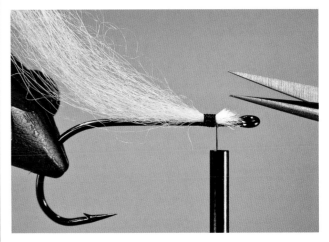

7. Trim the butt end of the clump of sheep hair. The reason you only tied the hair down over the rear half of the thread base was to allow room to trim the hair tight to the hook and at an angle—this will allow you to completely cover the trimmed ends of hair with thread. The angled cut will make a more naturally shaped head on the finished fly and make the later mounting of the lead eyes easier.

8. Apply a small dab of Zap-A-Gap to the remaining butt ends of hair exposed over the thread base. I do this to ensure none of the hair gets pulled out later, as the tie-down area is quite small. Before the adhesive dries, finish the thread tie-down to completely cover the butt ends of sheep hair. Leave the bobbin hanging so that the thread is in the middle of the thread base (in preparation for the next clump of hair).

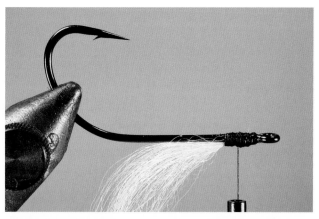

9. Rotate the hook back to the hook-point-up position.

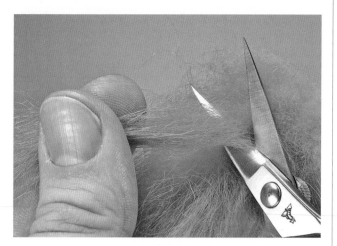

10. Cut off another clump of sheep hair—the middle color, chartreuse in this case. The middle color of hair should always be a slightly larger clump—even as much as twice that of the white bottom or black top.

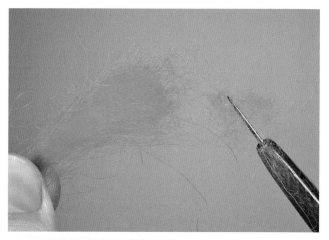

11. Clean out the underfur with a bodkin.

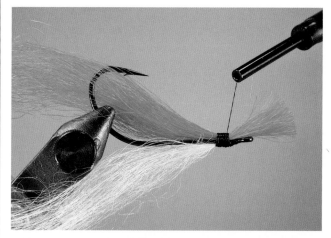

12. Tie down this clump of sheep hair on the other side of the hook shank as the first clump. Apart from the side of the hook shank the clump is tied to, every other aspect of this tie-down is the same as the first: Leave some sticking out past the hook eye, tie it down over the rear half of the thread base only, and be sure not to wrap thread back past the rear of the original thread base.

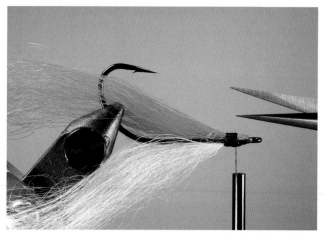

13. Trim the butt ends of the chartreuse sheep hair at an angle.

14. Apply a small dab of Zap-A-Gap to the remaining butt ends of hair exposed over the thread base. Before the adhesive dries, finish the thread tie-down to completely cover the butt ends of sheep hair. Leave the bobbin hanging so that the thread is once again in the middle of the thread base.

15. Rotate the hook so that the hook point is down. Mount the lead barbell eyes on the top side, in the middle of the thread tie-down. Notice how high up off the hook shank the eyes are—this is the effect of a pronounced "natural lift kit." The reason you have waited until now to mount the eyes is to allow the act of tying in the first two clumps of sheep hair to build up enough material to provide separation between the dense lead eyes and the less-dense mass of hair, which will make the fly flip hook point up even with the extra-small barbell eyes.

16. Position the bobbin so that the thread hangs behind the lead barbell eyes. Brush some Zap-A-Gap over the thread tie-down. The adhesive will ensure the eyes do not move around, even after many days of fishing use. Avoid getting any Zap-A-Gap on the eyes, as it could smear the paint.

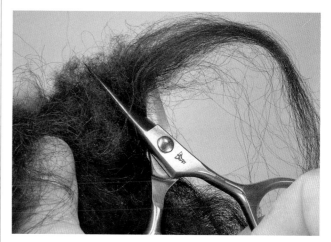

17. Cut off a clump of black Icelandic sheep hair.

18. Clean out the underfur with a bodkin.

19. Flip the hook again, back to the hook-point-up position. Tie down the clump of black sheep hair. This time you can tie the hair down over the entire head of the fly. Leave a much longer length of the black hair sticking out past the hook eye, as you will be using this material to bulk up the head of the fly. Leave roughly 1¼ inches (3 cm) protruding out past the hook eye.

20. Divide the clump of black sheep hair into two equal sections.

21. Select one of the two segregated lengths of sheep hair and wrap it directly over the thread tie-down over the arbor

of the lead barbell eyes (between the two eyes). Continue the wrap so that it goes around the hook shank once, and then tie it off behind the eyes. Trim the excess as tight to the tie-down as you can, leaving none of the excess material to mingle with the long body material. The extra length of this hair you left yourself when first tying down the black sheep hair makes holding onto it while wrapping it back over the head much easier.

22. Repeat the process using the second clump of sheep hair, only wrap it in the other direction—this will add bulk evenly to the head of the fly. Trim the excess material from the back of the head.

23. Brush some Zap-A-Gap over the top of the fly's head. The adhesive will soak into the hair and thread and make a very solid head.

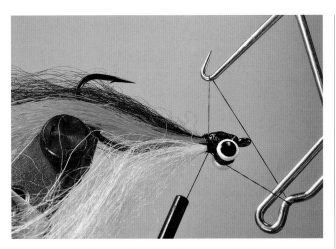

24. Before the Zap-A-Gap dries, tie a whip-finish knot behind the lead eyes. You should not need an extended-reach whip-finish tool; the standard size will do fine. Trim the thread.

25. Remove the fly from the vise and trim the sheep hair to the desired length. I tie the Krystowski Minnow in two sizes: 2¾ inches (7 cm) or 3¼ inches (83 mm). Besides length, the only difference between the short and the long version is the hook size. This version is the shorter of the two, and the one I fish the most.

26. Once the fly has been trimmed to the proper length, take a coarse wire dubbing brush and brush out the body, or wing, of the fly. This is easiest done by holding the fly by the head and laying the hair over the top of your leg as you sit, brushing out any tangles or underfur that was missed while preparing the individual clumps of hair. Finally, give the very end of the streamer a natural, tapered look by turning your scissors so that the blades run the same direction as the hair and making many short snips—in a sense, "feathering" the terminal ends of the sheep hair.

27. Bury the hook point into a cork or block of hard foam and coat the entire head and eyes with a brushable head cement such as Hard as Hull. I use wine corks because there are a lot of them rolling around under my tying bench (I blame the cats), and they make it easy to turn the fly around to get at all the nooks and crannies around the lead eyes. I always coat the eyes with head cement because this saves them from chipping for a bit longer, but you must be careful not to smudge the pearl and black paint. I usually have multiple partially used bottles of head cement at any given time, so I choose the oldest one—the one that is more than half empty, thick, and in need of a shot of head cement thinner. Snce the older head cement is thicker, it will be the equivalent of two or three coats of the fresh stuff, and because it is less potent, will be less likely to smudge the paint. Set the cork somewhere safe to dry (again, the cats).

PATTERN VARIATIONS

KRYSTOWSKI MINNOW (OLIVE)

Hook: #2 Gamakatsu B10S

Thread: Black 6/0 UNI-Thread

Adhesive: Zap-A-Gap

First Body Hair: White Icelandic sheep hair

Second Body Hair: Light olive Icelandic sheep hair

Eyes: Pearl painted lead barbell eyes (x-small)

Third Body Hair: Black Icelandic sheep hair

Head Cement: Hard as Hull

KRYSTOWSKI MINNOW (RED)

Hook: #2 Gamakatsu B10S

Thread: Black 6/0 UNI-Thread

Adhesive: Zap-A-Gap

Hair 1: White Icelandic sheep hair

Hair 2: Red Icelandic sheep hair

Eyes: Pearl painted lead barbell eyes (x-small)

Hair 3: Black Icelandic sheep hair

Head Cement: Hard as Hull

KRYSTOWSKI MINNOW (PURPLE)

Hook: #2 Gamakatsu B10S

Thread: Black 6/0 UNI-Thread

Adhesive: Zap-A-Gap

Hair 1: White Icelandic sheep hair

Hair 2: Purple Icelandic sheep hair

Eyes: Pearl painted lead barbell eyes (x-small)

Hair 3: Black Icelandic sheep hair

Head Cement: Hard as Hull

KRYSTOWSKI MINNOW (ORANGE)

Hook: #2 Gamakatsu B10S

Thread: Black 6/0 UNI-Thread

Adhesive: Zap-A-Gap

Hair 1: White Icelandic sheep hair

Hair 2: Orange Icelandic sheep hair

Eyes: Pearl painted lead barbell eyes (x-small)

Hair 3: Black Icelandic sheep hair

Head Cement: Hard as Hull

MEAT WHISTLE

John Barr has come far . . . to say the least. Once an eight-year-old boy in Seattle, Washington, strapping torn strips of bedsheet onto bent nails in an attempt to mimic the act of fly tying he had witnessed in a neighbor's garage, then poring through a spiral-bound copy of *Pacific Northwest Fly Patterns* purchased from Roy Patrick at the local fly shop.

The Meat Whistle uses a lot of rabbit hide and marabou—two of the easiest to find, cheapest to buy, and most movement-oriented tying materials out there.

Erik Johnson and his boatswain's mate Whiskey patrol the high seas with Meat Whistles on one of John Barr's favorite Colorado bass lakes. *Cliff Watts* photo.

The Dead Chicken fly from that book (a gaudy size 6 soft hackle with a red tail and yellow chenille body) was the first actual pattern he ever tied. It did not take long for John to begin tinkering with his own fly designs for the rainbow trout in the little creek that flowed by his family's vacation cabin, or for the crappie and bluegill in the gravel pits near the house he later moved to in San Jose, California.

That was a while ago. John is now a retired dentist living in Boulder, Colorado, and the creator of some of the best-selling trout flies to ever grace the color pages of a wholesale catalog or the wooden bins at a fly shop. If you have ever been recommended a few hot nymphs at your favorite fly shop anytime in the last 20 years, chances are you were given a Copper John or Barr Emerger. However, it is not trout flies alone that have made John Barr a household name (in fly-fishing households anyways), as he has designed many other fly patterns for warmwater species such as carp, pike, and bass. In fact, bass and bass flies are usually the main topic

of our phone conversations, or when I bump into him at the fly shop. Looking back, I believe the lengthiest of these chats always happen in late winter, when business is slow at the shop and John is bored and restless. We idly poke at bins of size 26 midge pupae and take turns speculating on when the Front Range bass ponds will ice off.

John is known for kicking out into bass water with both a fly rod and a conventional casting rod and switching out between fish, or moods, or both. He tied the first Meat Whistle in the summer of 2002, for the large and small-mouth bass in the lakes and ponds near his home in Colorado. Some of the more effective conventional lures John was using then were weighted bass jigs, so that summer he set out to make a version he could cast and fish easily on a light fly rod. The Meat Whistle is tied on a large jig hook and uses a brass cone up front for weight (or tungsten if you need the fly to be as heavy as possible). John uses a cone at the front instead of lead barbell eyes because he finds the cone slides over snags and picks up less grass and muck. These are attributes more important to bass anglers than most others because the warm water and long growing seasons in typical bass fisheries often leave them choking in vegetation both living and dead. The Meat Whistle was designed to be a suggestive, swimming crayfish fly pattern and it serves this purpose well, but I am convinced it doubles as a lifelike sculpin imitation.

What I like best about John's fly is the unabashed use of rabbit hide and marabou—two of the easiest to find, cheapest to buy, and most movement-oriented tying materials out there. Of course, the jig hook and cone are what *make* the Meat Whistle, but those are the utilitarian aspects of the fly that make it work—the soft materials are what make fish want to eat it. Whereas some bass flies rely on what I categorize as "action" (darting, erratic behavior) to induce a strike, this fly goes *all in* on "movement"—that soft, subtle, undulating behavior that works so well on those occasions when we are confronted with wary bass in clear, pressured areas or in water slightly colder than what is ideal for encouraging energetic behavior in a warmwater fish.

The Meat Whistle is now sold commercially by Umpqua Feather Merchants in two sizes (2 and 1/0) and six colors (black, chartreuse, rust, olive, white, and tan). I have experimented with all of these size and color combinations, and they all work. That is an understatement—they all work *very well.* You can customize your own size/color Meat Whistle for whatever obscure fishing trip you may be planning—a giant one with white rabbit strip, silver Flashabou, and bright red marabou for northern pike, or a smaller version for steelhead with purple rabbit and black marabou. The Meat Whistle is such a great, universal streamer that the options are almost limitless. However, the versions of John's fly that I tie for bass fall into a fairly mundane/drab category of size and color.

The Meat Whistles I like to tie for bass are almost always on a size 2/0 Gamakatsu hook. I tie mine on a larger jig hook because the extra hook gap allows me room to use the thickest rabbit hide I can find and the space to wrap lead wire under the Sparkle Braid body of the ones I want extra heavy. (I do prefer to use a wider body flash such as Flat Diamond Braid whenever I am covering a lead wire body.) You may notice the commercially tied Meat Whistles have cones that are seemingly color-coordinated with the rabbit and marabou, such as a brass cone used with the rusty brown or a gold cone used with the olive, but I believe this has more to do with fly marketing than anything else. The flies I tie are either rusty brown, dark olive, or black, and every variation is tied with a black cone. To follow this line of subtlety, all my own Meat Whistles are tied with minimal Flashabou—much less than the original. Maybe this is just further proof that this is one of those great streamers that will stand the test of not only time, but also relentless tampering.

MEAT WHISTLE (BLACK 'N BLUE)

Hook: #2/0 Gamakatsu Jig 90

Cone: Black Spirit River conehead (6.3 mm)

Filler: Loon UV Knot Sense

Thread: Black 3/0 Danville's Waxed Monocord

Top: Black rabbit strip (magnum)

Wire Rib: Blue UTC Ultra Wire (brassie)

Body Wrap: Royal blue Sparkle Braid

Adhesive: Zap-A-Gap

Flash: Blue Holographic Flashabou

Legs: Blue/silver flake Sili Legs

Front: Black marabou blood quills

Wax: BT's Tacky Dubbing Wax

1. For ease and economy of movement, do not begin this fly by placing the hook in the vise. Instead, prepare the rabbit hide and the cone before mounting the hook. The magnum rabbit strips sold by the material wholesaler Hareline Dubbin come in a 10-inch (25 cm) piece cut into three equal strips. Prepare the rabbit by cutting all the strips into 2½-inch (64 mm) lengths—this can be easily done by folding the entire patch of rabbit and cutting at the middle, then repeating the process with the two remaining halves. This will leave you with material for a dozen Meat Whistles. Be sure to cut just the hide, *not the hair,* anytime you are cutting rabbit strips to length.

2. Continue preparing the rabbit by trimming the rear end of each of the 12 short strips. The rear end is the one with hair extending out past the cut. Trim this end into a gradual point. This is done purely for cosmetic reasons, as leaving rabbit strips squared off looks unnaturally "blocky" and is the tying equivalent to an unedited adverb in literature.

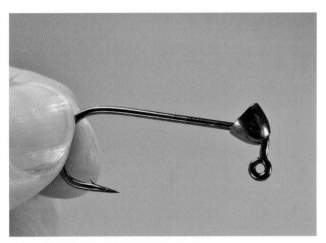

3. Slide the cone onto the jig hook. While you are at it, cone-up an entire dozen. The barb on the hook will usually not let the cone slide easily over, so either crimp all the barbs at the start or simply apply a bit of pressure to the cone, forcing the very tip of the barb backwards far enough to let the cone pass over it. Once in place at the forward end of the straight hook shank, you will notice the cone wants to creep onto the "jigged" section of the hook—this is not desired. Traditionally, a small thread dam is created on the hook shank to keep the cone from moving forward, but a faster method is to fill the hollowed area of the cone with UV-cured resin.

4. Hold the hook and cone up to expose the hollow side of the cone, and fill it with UV-cured resin. Do not overfill the cone—add just enough to fill most of the hollow, but leave the back end of the cone slightly concave once the resin is cured. I prefer Loon UV Knot Sense in this application because it is inexpensive and comes in a squeeze tube with a nozzle, which makes filling the cone fast and easy.

5. Cure the UV resin inside the cone with a handheld UV lamp (the sun also works). Be sure the cone is centered on the hook shank and the nose of the cone is nestled right up against the 45-degree bend of the jig hook. The curing process should only take a few seconds if you are using a powerful UV lamp. Go ahead and prepare 12 hook and cone combinations before getting started.

6. Pick up one of the 12 prepared pieces of rabbit strip and skewer it with one of the hook and cone combos. Stick the rabbit strip from the hide side and be sure to go in at the very center of the 2½-inch (64 mm) strip.

7. Place the hook in the vise and clamp it down tight. Pull the skewered strip of rabbit as far back onto the hook bend as you can, as it needs to be temporarily out of the way. Lick your fingers and slick back the rabbit hair as well—this will keep the hair from irritating you through the power of static electricity. Begin your first thread wraps immediately behind the cone and build a solid thread base back about a cone length on the hook shank. Let the bobbin hang in place.

8. Tie in both a length of wire and Sparkle Braid at this spot on the hook shank. If you have subscribed to the "tie-a-dozen" theme I am attempting to develop with this fly pattern, go ahead and cut 12 6-inch (15 cm) lengths of Sparkle Braid and 12 4-inch (10 cm) lengths of wire.

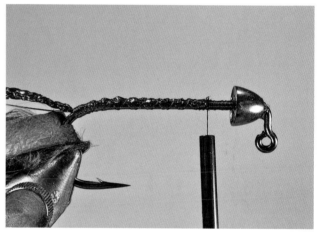

9. Use wide, spiraling thread wraps (to conserve time and material) to secure the wire and Sparkle Braid onto the entire hook shank. The one part of the tie-down that should be made solid is at the very rear. Build a short section of solid thread base right at the very end of the tie-down, where the straight shank dips down into the beginning of the hook bend. This provides security in the material tie-down and creates a bit of "tail creep" to get a good swim from a hook-point-up-style fly. Spiral wrap the thread forward and let the bobbin hang with the thread at rest at the beginning of the material tie-down.

10. Wrap the Sparkle Braid forward, covering most of the hook shank. Tie the braid down a cone length back behind the cone—where the thread should be waiting for you. Trim the excess.

11. Flip the hook over to the hook-point-up position (this is easy if you are using a rotary vise). Lay the rabbit strip over the length of the hook shank and tie it down with one tight wrap of thread. Before wrapping the thread, wet your fingers and pull back all the hair forward of the exact tie-down spot, as you do not want to trap and then cut any of the hair forward of this point. Also, be sure to start the single tie-down thread wrap at the forward end of the Sparkle Braid body and end at a point immediately behind the cone. This will ensure that the forward pressure of the thread wrap will pull any stretch out of the strip of rabbit hide. Add two tight thread wraps between the rabbit strip and the cone to lock everything in place.

12. Grasp the tip ends of the rabbit hair protruding from the short section of hide forward of the rear edge of the cone, and trim the rabbit strip at that point. Do not set this small patch of rabbit hair and hide down! Hold it up and cut off the tab of hide. You will need this small clump of hair to use as dubbing at the front end of the fly.

13. Hand blend the small clump of rabbit hair you trimmed from the strip and set it aside for later use.

14. Apply a small dab of Zap-A-Gap to the severed end of rabbit strip that should be poking up over the rear edge of the cone. Use several more tight wraps of thread to lock this wet end of rabbit strip down onto the hook shank and snug up to the rear of the cone. The dry hide should absorb the adhesive quickly, so do not dally.

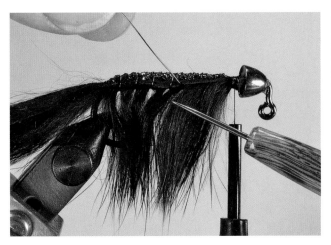

15. Rotate the fly back to a hook-point-down position. Wrap the wire forward, securing the rabbit strip in place. It should take about seven wide wraps of wire to reach the gap between the end of the rabbit strip and the rear of the cone, where the end of the wire will be tied down and trimmed with wire cutters. Before beginning the wire wraps, pull at the rabbit hair with wet fingers to encourage it to all point downward—this makes wrapping the wire through the hair easier to do without trapping any hair. Use a bodkin to assist with hair control as you wrap the wire forward.

16. Select six long strands of Flashabou.

17. Tie the six strands of Flashabou in at their middle. Sometimes Flashabou is unruly, so I like to grasp the strands at one end and run them through my mouth—the dampness temporarily binds all the strands together and eliminates static. Bring the clump of Flashabou in low and from the front of the fly. Once the material hits the hanging thread, pull both ends up over the top of the fly, then grasp both ends of the flash in one hand and make several thread wraps with the other hand—this action will quickly secure the flash in place.

18. Trim all 12 strands of Flashabou at a point roughly halfway between the end of the Sparkle Braid body and the tip of the tapered rabbit hide.

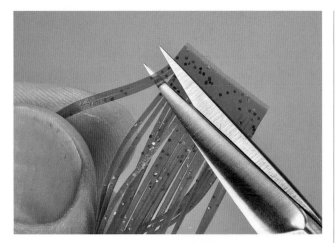

19. Select (and cut out) a pair of Sili Legs.

20. Mount and tie down the two Sili Legs in the same manner as you did with the Flashabou. Gently hold all four legs back toward the rear of the fly and trim them so they are all even in length—this should be roughly even with the trimmed tip of rabbit hide. It is more important to mount the two strands of leg material at their exact middle because most of their length is needed (as opposed to the Flashabou, which is much longer).

21. Select two marabou feathers.

22. Tie one of the two marabou feathers down behind the cone. As with much of the material used in the creation of this fly, the marabou is easier to control when damp. The tips of the marabou feather should extend back just past the outside bend of the hook. Trim the butt end of the feather using the rim of the cone as a guide.

23. Rotate the fly to the hook-point-up position and tie down the second marabou feather on top, or opposite, the first.

24. Trim the butt end of the second marabou feather using the rim of the cone as a guide. Leave some of the bushy butt ends of marabou . . . it's OK.

25. Create a short thread loop and wax it to help contain the rabbit fur dubbing you are about to insert into the loop.

26. Take the rabbit dubbing you trimmed from the strip and hand-blended earlier and use it to fill the dubbing loop.

27. Twist the end of the dubbing loop to form a tight dubbing rope, then use a wire brush to rake out the long dubbing fibers. The purpose of using a dubbing loop is to accentuate the long, bushy fibers of dubbing, so brushing out the dubbing before wrapping it onto the fly should go without saying.

28. Wrap the rabbit fur dubbing loop onto the neck of the fly and end with a whip-finish knot. The dubbing rope should nestle well into the concave rear of the UV-resin-filled cone, eliminating any gap between the cone and the start of the fly's soft materials. I always add a touch of Zap-A-Gap just before the whip-finish knot for durability's sake, but this is difficult to do without fouling the bushy rabbit dubbing. Brush the rabbit fur back with a damp finger and add a small amount of adhesive to the thread, then wrap that thread into the small gap between the cone and the dubbing.

PATTERN VARIATIONS

MEAT WHISTLE (CRAWFISH ORANGE)

Hook: #2/0 Gamakatsu Jig 90

Cone: Black Spirit River conehead (6.3 mm)

Filler: Loon UV Knot Sense

Thread: Dark brown 3/0 Danville's Waxed Monocord

Top: Crawfish orange rabbit strip (magnum)

Wire Rib: Copper brown UTC Ultra Wire (brassie)

Body Wrap: Copper Sparkle Braid

Adhesive: Zap-A-Gap

Flash: Copper Flashabou

Legs: Orange/orange-black flake Sili Legs

Front: Rusty brown marabou blood quills

Wax: BT's Tacky Dubbing Wax

MEAT WHISTLE (OLIVE VARIANT)

Hook: #2/0 Gamakatsu Jig 90

Cone: Black Spirit River conehead (6.3 mm)

Filler: Loon UV Knot Sense

Thread: Olive 3/0 Danville's Waxed Monocord

Top: Olive variant rabbit strip (magnum)

Wire Rib: Gold UTC Ultra Wire (brassie)

Body Wrap: Olive/pearl Sparkle Braid

Adhesive: Zap-A-Gap

Flash: Gold Holographic Flashabou

Legs: Olive/black flake Sili Legs

Front: Dark olive marabou blood quills

Wax: BT's Tacky Dubbing Wax

SUPER BUGGER

Cathy Beck's Super Bugger is a simple streamer fly, but a giant leap forward in the evolution of the original Woolly Bugger. Russell Blessing is most often credited with inventing the Woolly Bugger to mimic the hellgrammites (dobsonfly larvae) for the smallmouth bass in his home rivers in eastern Pennsylvania. Russ tied his first Buggers in the late 1960s, but his pattern was admittedly strongly influenced by an earlier western trout fly called the Woolly Worm.

The Super Bugger has heavy lead dumbbell eyes that add the needed weight to sink the fly quickly, as well as offset the balance of the hook and make it swim hook point up.

In the mid-1930s a fly shop owner in West Yellowstone, Montana, named Don Martinez was given a fly by a friend, Walter Bales from Kansas City, Missouri. Don took this fly, tweaked it, and played with it—as fly tinkerers tend to do—until it turned into what he called a Woolly Worm. It is hard to say what that fly Walter gave Don back then looked like, but it surely was a creative relative of one of the much older Tadpole or Palmer flies that have been influencing fly design for as long as it has been written about.

The lineage of the Woolly Bugger may be complicated, and even argued about, but what is neither is the fact it is one of only a handful of fly patterns that have become staples in fly boxes and hat brims across the globe. Even more important than being well-known and fished, the Woolly Bugger has become a creative standard or starting point for the vast majority of modern streamers. Look at the rear end of almost any new-age articulated trout streamer and you will see what is essentially a Woolly Bugger. What Cathy Beck (also from eastern Pennsylvania) did was take the basic gist of what a Woolly Bugger is (a bushy marabou tail behind a chenille body, with saddle hackle palmer-wrapped over it) and beef it up to make the perfect, modern, subsurface bass fly.

There have been many slight changes and adaptations to the Woolly Bugger over the years—adding flash to the tail, replacing the subtle rayon chenille with gaudy Estaz, adding brass beads or cones to the front—and all these modifications add a desired freshness to a long-standing pattern. What makes the Super Bugger modifications so ideal to bass anglers are the heavy lead dumbbell eyes that add the needed weight to sink the fly quickly, as well as offset the balance of the hook and make it swim hook point up. Also, there is no true "body" material, such as chenille, wrapped up the hook shank of the Super Bugger, just long-fibered saddle hackle wrapped closely together to make a full, bushy body that undulates naturally and appears to come to life when in the water. This streamer takes full advantage of the entire length of a saddle hackle feather, even the base "afterfeather" that is soft and fluffy and very marabou-like but is so often discarded by the fly tier.

Whereas the original Woolly Bugger was tied to imitate a large nymph, Cathy's Super Bugger is tied larger and can be fished to mimic a variety of different creatures that live and move around at the very bottom of lakes and rivers, such as crayfish and sculpins. I carry several of these flies in tan, olive, brown, and black, and it is one of my go-to river smallmouth patterns.

SUPER BUGGER (TAN)

Hook: #8 Tiemco 5262
Thread: Tan 3/0 Danville's Waxed Monocord
Eyes: Yellow painted lead eyes (medium)
Adhesive 1: Zap-A-Gap
Tail: Tan grizzly marabou
Tail Flash: Root beer Krystal Flash
Body: Sand grizzly hen saddle
Adhesive 2: Zap Goo
Legs: Pumpkin/green-orange barred Sili Legs
Wax: BT's Tacky Dubbing Wax
Dubbing: Damsel nymph tan Dave Whitlock SLF

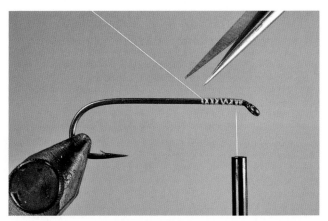

1. Clamp the hook securely into the jaws of the tying vise. Begin the thread wraps immediately behind the hook eye and wrap the thread a little more than one-third of the way down the length of the hook shank. Wrap the thread forward again and leave the bobbin hanging so that the thread rests a hook-eye length behind the hook eye. Trim away any excess thread from the rear of the thread base.

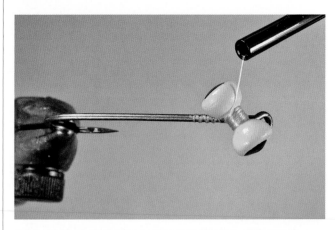

2. Mount the painted lead eyes onto the top of the hook shank. Rest the eyes on the hook shank at an angle and secure them in place with many tight thread wraps, then force the eyes into their proper position perpendicular to the hook shank and secure them in place with more tight thread wrapped in the opposite direction of the first set of wraps.

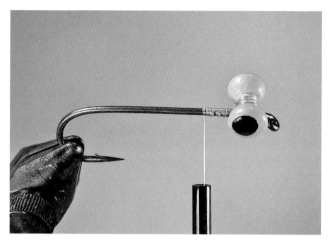

3. Once the painted lead eyes are in their proper place and snug, wrap the thread to the rear of the thread base and let the bobbin hang.

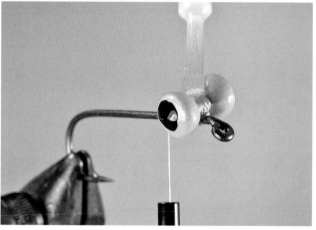

4. Apply a light coat of Zap-A-Gap to the entire thread base, to include both the top and bottom of the tie-down point for the lead eyes. This step is important if you want the eyes to stay in their proper place through long days on the water.

5. Select three grizzly marabou feathers. Choose full and fluffy feathers that have similar and distinct barring.

6. Take one of the marabou feathers and wet it and slick the fibers back—this makes tying the feather down in an exact position and lining up the barring on each consecutive feather easier.

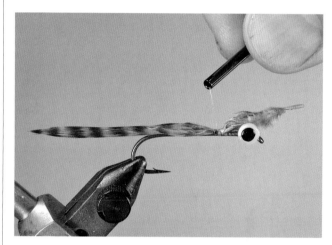

7. Use two tight thread wraps to tie down the first of the three marabou feathers. The tail should extend a hook-shank length out past the bend of the hook.

8. Tie down the remaining two marabou feathers one at a time in the same manner you tied in the first. Keep the tips of each feather lined up evenly first, but also try to keep the barring lined up, as this will help make the three-feather tail appear as one.

9. Tie the cluster of three marabou feathers all the way back to the rear of the hook shank, then wrap the thread forward and let the bobbin hang so the thread is even with the hook point. Trim the butt ends of the three feathers.

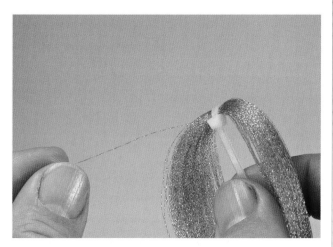

10. Pull one strand of Krystal Flash from the bundle. The individual strands are usually close to 15 inches (38 cm) long, which is more than enough length even when folded over twice—once before mounting and once after it is tied in. Krystal Flash is held together by a plastic zip tie, and it is easy to extract the strands individually. I recommend doing this instead of cutting clumps of material, as this keeps the bundle neat and manageable.

11. Fold the long strand of Krystal Flash in half. Twist the folded end between your thumb and forefinger to put a permanent kink in the material—this will take the big loop out of it and allow the doubled-over strand to lie down easier on the hook shank. Tie this double strand down on top of the hook shank.

12. Pull back both ends of the double strand of Krystal Flash and tie it down so that it joins with the marabou of the tail. As you are bringing the thread wraps back to the butt of the tail, spread the Krystal Flash so that two strands fall to either side of the tail. Wrap the thread forward again and leave the bobbin hanging so the thread is even with the hook point.

13. Select a 5- to 6-inch (12 to 15 cm) long saddle feather. This particular feather is a sand grizzly hen saddle, although I have used anything from Whiting Woolly Bugger saddle to cheap Chinese strung saddle. The color and markings should match that of the marabou tail, but the most important traits of the feather you choose should be the length (it has to be long enough to cover the entire hook shank) and the presence of plenty of full, fluffy, marabou-like "afterfeather" at the butt end of the quill. I look for feathers where at least half the feather is bushy.

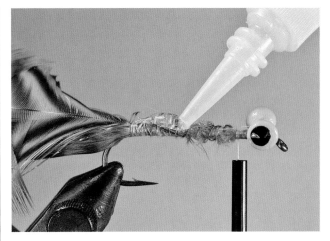

15. Wrap the thread forward and let the bobbin hang just slightly behind the painted lead eyes. Apply a small amount of Zap Goo over the material buildup created on the hook shank. This is not a necessary tying step, but will result in a much more durable fly. The weak point in this pattern is the quill of the feather wrapped up the hook shank to form the bushy body—as it is not reinforced with a cross-wrapped wire (this tends to mat down the fibers on such a densely palmer-wrapped feather body), it is left vulnerable to breakage when being fished.

14. Tie the saddle feather down on top of the hook shank. Position the tip of the feather directly behind the painted lead eyes—this keeps the fine and most brittle part of the quill (the very tip) buried and allows the slightly thicker and stronger part of the quill to be wrapped around the hook shank. Be sure to lay the feather down onto the hook shank so that the convex, or "top," is facing up—this way the individual feather fibers will arch to the rear of the fly once you wrap the feather forward.

16. Wrap the saddle feather forward on the hook shank. Each wrap of feather should be fairly close to each other—this is not like a normal Woolly Bugger fly where the hackle is palmer-wrapped with wide gaps between wraps to expose the chenille underneath. Use the entire feather, including the fluffy afterfeather. In fact, if you have chosen the perfect saddle feather, the fluffy part should be wound onto the entire front half of the body. Because I have smeared Zap Goo onto the area that I am wrapping the feather, I like to pull back the feather fibers on the side of the quill that is being wrapped against the hook shank—this keeps most of the fibers from getting gooped up in the Goo.

17. Wrap the saddle feather right up to the painted lead eyes and tie it in place with the thread that is waiting there. Trim away what remains of the butt end of the feather.

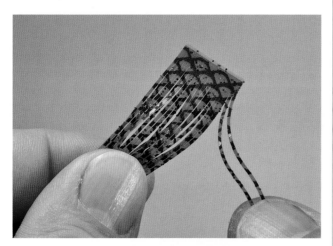

18. Select two strands of the rubber Sili Legs material.

19. Tie down the double strand of Sili Legs on the side of the hook shank immediately behind one side of the painted lead eyes. Tie the material down at its middle, so there is enough to make a pair of legs on either side of the fly.

20. Once all four legs are secured in place behind the near side of the painted lead eyes, bring two of the legs around to the other side of the fly and lock them in place with a few tight wraps of thread. This set of legs has a tendency to move around and slightly change position once the fly is completed—this is caused by the rubber sliding ever so slightly against the thread tie-down. The result is a Super Bugger with one side of its legs sticking out on the bottom and not the side where it should be. To avoid this, wrap this set of legs around the arbor of the painted lead eyes and then tie it down in place on the other side of the eyes. This allows you to easily cross-wrap the thread around the legs and prevent them from slipping out of place.

21. Pull your bobbin down, exposing a short length of thread. Apply wax to the exposed thread in preparation for creating a short dubbing rope. Get some wax on the thumb and forefinger of the hand you will use to roll the dubbing.

22. Roll the dubbing onto the exposed and now-waxed length of thread to create a short dubbing rope.

23. Wrap the dubbing rope around the painted lead eyes, creating a dubbing head for the fly. Turn the fly over as you are doing this to be sure you are creating a uniform head and not leaving gaps exposed. Tie a whip-finish knot behind the hook eye and trim the thread. Finish the knot with a small dab of Zap-A-Gap.

24. Remove the fly from the vise and hold it by the hook bend so the legs and tail flash hang down. Trim these materials so they are just slightly longer than the tip of the marabou tail.

PATTERN VARIATIONS

SUPER BUGGER (OLIVE)

Hook: #8 Tiemco 5262

Thread: Olive 3/0 Danville's Waxed Monocord

Eyes: Yellow painted lead eyes (medium)

Adhesive 1: Zap-A-Gap

Tail: Olive grizzly marabou

Tail Flash: Peacock Krystal Flash

Body: Grizzly olive bugger hackle

Adhesive 2: Zap Goo

Legs: Green/black chrome Sili Legs

Wax: BT's Tacky Dubbing Wax

Dubbing: Nearnuff sculpin olive Dave Whitlock SLF

SUPER BUGGER (BLACK)

Hook: #8 Tiemco 5262

Thread: Black 3/0 Danville's Waxed Monocord

Eyes: Yellow painted lead eyes (medium)

Adhesive 1: Zap-A-Gap

Tail: Black marabou

Tail Flash: Black Krystal Flash

Body: Black bugger hackle

Adhesive 2: Zap Goo

Legs: Black/red flake Sili Legs

Wax: BT's Tacky Dubbing Wax

Dubbing: Dark stone nymph Dave Whitlock SLF

SUPER BUGGER (BROWN)

Hook: #8 Tiemco 5262

Thread: Dark brown 3/0 Danville's Waxed Monocord

Eyes: Yellow painted lead eyes (medium)

Adhesive 1: Zap-A-Gap

Tail: Brown grizzly marabou

Tail Flash: Rusty brown Krystal Flash

Body: Grizzly brown bugger hackle

Adhesive 2: Zap Goo

Legs: Copper/black chrome Sili Legs

Wax: BT's Tacky Dubbing Wax

Dubbing: Brown stone nymph Dave Whitlock SLF

BOOBY FROG

I could tell you the exact day in June 2010 that I tied the first Booby Frog. I had just left one small bass pond and was headed to another to fish with a friend until dark. I frantically needed more flies before continuing with my fishing day and had an idea that was too fresh and too good to back-burner for even a day. What I could *not* tell you is the actual name of the body of water I had fished that morning, or the name of the place I was eager to fish that evening. This is not a case of forgetfulness or even secrecy—these places, like so many favorite bass waters, have no official names.

The Booby Frog casts smoothly with a common trout-weight fly rod and crawls easily and seductively over even the thickest weed beds, logs, and lily pads.

Frogs and largemouth bass almost always like the same places, and this shared existence often ends poorly for the frogs. Fish a Booby Frog close to grassy shorelines and through openings in weed beds.

The pond or lake may only appear on maps as a vague blob of blue tucked away between crosshatched roads and winding contour lines, but those of us who know where it is and have fished it more than a handful of times will eventually give it our own name. These kinds of places get one of those accidental names that somehow stick, like the names given young barn cats that surely will not survive summer traffic on the highway or the next encounter with misplaced antifreeze.

The pond I fished in the morning on that day in June is one I call "Patrick's Pond" and is just large enough to have a wooded island (a dozen trees at most) out in the middle that you cannot reach with even the longest cast. You can get somewhat close if you position yourself in an area along the outer bank with a clear lane for a proper backcast. But *somewhat close* to the far shore is not close enough to properly cover all the submerged logs, stumps, and other enticing cover that surely held the larger bass in

the area, so the temptation and "grass is greener" mentality persisted. One evening earlier that month, my friend Patrick (whom I named the pond after, but who himself calls the place "Doughnut Pond" . . . again, barn cats) and I became overwhelmed with this need to finally reach the far shore, so we stripped down naked and swam to the island. I nearly drowned with all the gear and clothing I was attempting to hold out of the water as I swam. And, yes, it was just as good as we thought it could be . . . bass on every cast 'til dark. We did lose a measurable amount of blood to mosquitoes and leeches, however—a small price to pay.

The pond I was planning to fish that evening with a different friend, and the one that I frantically needed more flies for, I call "4th of July Pond." The name stuck after I discovered the pond accidentally on the evening of July 4, 2005. That day I had been chased off one of my favorite trout streams by the ever-increasing number of holiday family gatherings with dogs, tubes, and kayaks. I retreated to a lesser-known and more out-of-the-way creek. The fishing there was incredible that day, mostly brown trout in the 10- to 12-inch range with the occasional rainbow. The prize of the day was a 20-inch brown that hammered a small black Woolly Bugger. As I briefly held the small-stream brute to unhinge the streamer, I could feel the crunchy belly of a trout that was full of crayfish. This would have been the highlight of the evening had it not been for the discovery of a new and amazing little bass pond. I had fished farther downstream than I ever had before and it was getting late, so I cut through the woods in an attempt to find a gravel bike path I knew somewhat paralleled the creek. What I stumbled on instead was a small, algae-covered body of water that just screamed *largemouth bass!* I was carrying only a 3-weight fly rod that night, and the largest, bass-iest fly I had was a yellow marabou Muddler Minnow, but I landed many 2- to 3-pound bass and some of the largest green sunfish I had ever seen. I did eventually find the bike path I was looking for, albeit well after sunset, and I had a long, dark walk back to my truck. I still remember the fireworks on the horizon . . . from Denver and every other direction, too.

On that day in June when I first tied the Booby Frog, I was living in—and paying through the nose for—a studio apartment in Boulder, Colorado, and besides the bed and futon, my fly-tying desk was the main piece of furniture. After fishing Patrick's Pond I had plans to hit 4th of July and needed a few more bass flies in a bad way. I raced into the apartment, sat down at the desk, and cranked out four or five new flies that surely a bass in a little frog-infested algae bowl would eat up like bar nuts. I had spent the first part of the day watching bass ambush assorted pond critters in the meager few inches of water between the tops of aquatic vegetation beds and the surface of the pond. The bass would slip through little openings in the weeds or patrol the edges looking for windows of edible opportunity. What I tied was a very simple version of what would end up being the Booby Frog.

Bass in shallow water primary feed during low-light periods of the day.

I think I landed over 40 largemouth bass and green sunfish on those prototype frogs that evening. I knew I was onto something good. During the course of that summer I perfected the pattern, designing it to look, move, and float the way a real frog does on a pond and remain completely snag-free. Like a real frog, the Booby Frog does not always float . . . and when it does, it sits in the surface film of the pond at a 45-degree angle with its legs splayed out and just the big foam eyes popping out of the water. The angler need only touch the fly line to get the front-facing rubber legs to twitch back—often being just the right trigger for the big bass lurking nearby.

This fly has so much great movement and action in the water because the natural materials are not bound to the entire length of the hook shank. The Booby Frog is tied on a large stinger-style hook, but all the materials are tied in at the same ³⁄₁₆ inch of the hook shank directly behind the eye of the hook—this allows the frog body no restrictions in movement. Also, this frog rides hook point up, completely eliminating the need for any cumbersome and distracting hard-mono weed guards that only partially work. The Booby Frog casts easily with a common trout-weight fly rod and crawls smoothly and seductively over even the thickest weed beds, logs, and lily pads.

BOOBY FROG

Hook: #2 Gamakatsu B10S

Thread: Dark brown 3/0 Danville's Waxed Monocord

Body Bottom: Cream marabou

Adhesive: Zap-A-Gap

Body Middle: Golden olive marabou

Body Sides: Olive mink Zonker strips

Body Top: Olive grizzly marabou

Foam Eyes: Olive Rainy's Boobie Round Eyes (x-large)

Legs: Speckled yellow Montana Fly Centipede Legs (medium)

Hard Eyes 1: Yellow Loon Outdoors UV Fly Paint

Hard Eyes 2: Black Sharpie marker

Hard Eyes 3: Loon Outdoors UV Knot Sense

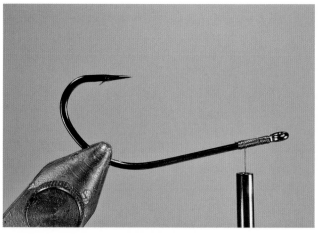

1. Mount the stinger-style hook firmly into the jaws of the vise. Mount the hook point up with the straight hook shank tilted up at a slight angle—this is close to how the hook will be positioned once the fly is finished and being fished. A rotary vise makes tying flies much easier, especially bass flies such as this that need to be flipped over multiple times during the tying process. Start the thread wraps immediately behind the hook eye and build a solid but short thread base. The thread base should be exactly ³⁄₁₆ inch (5 mm). The entire fly will be tied to this thread base only. Leave the bobbin hanging so the thread is positioned at the rear of the thread base, as this allows room to properly taper the butt end of the first clump of marabou to be tied down.

2. Select three full and fluffy marabou feathers: two golden olive and one cream.

3. Wet the marabou feathers by either licking them or with a damp rag. This allows you to better position them in their proper place on the hook and keeps the tie-down area tidy and precise.

4. Tie down the cream clump of marabou on what we will now call the "top" of the hook shank—the tips should extend slightly past the farthest part of the hook bend. Use just two tight thread wraps at the rear of the thread base to secure the marabou in place, allowing room to trim the butt end of the marabou clump at an angle—this makes a smooth platform for further materials to be added to the same place.

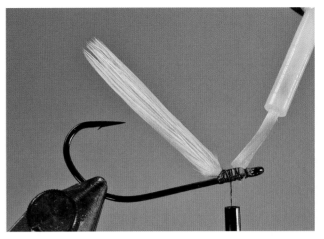

5. Once the butt end of the cream marabou clump is trimmed, finish the tie-down process with several more thread wraps over the top and a couple wraps behind the marabou to help kick the material up so that it is at a 45-degree angle off the hook shank. Once again, leave the bobbin hanging so that the thread is toward the rear of the thread base. Brush on a liberal amount of Zap-A-Gap—some should be allowed to soak into the clump of marabou, as this will make it rigid in the base and help keep the rest of the fly well off the hook shank. The deliberate separation of the hook shank and the lighter materials are what make this fly ride in the water hook point up.

6. Tie down the first of the two golden olive marabou clumps. Tie this clump on top of the cream marabou but significantly off to one side, as you will be tying the second one down next to it. The tip of this clump of marabou should extend 2 inches (5 cm) back behind the lead edge of the hook eye. The front (or lead) side of the hook eye will be the point on this fly at which we will be measuring all materials—this will hopefully eliminate some confusion.

7. Tie down the second clump of golden olive marabou next to the last one you tied down so that the two tips are even and both are on top of the cream clump of marabou. Keep the thread wraps back away from the hook eye to allow room to trim both butt sections at an angle.

8. Trim the two butt ends of marabou at an angle from behind the hook eye to the first thread wrap, then finish tying them down. The rigid base of the cream marabou clump should keep even the golden olive marabou standing up at a 45-degree angle.

9. By now the thread-covered tie-down area should be significantly fatter than when you started, and this should allow space for the olive mink Zonker strips to be tied in on the sides. Tie in the end of the mink strip so that the hair is swept back to the rear of the fly. Trim the leather of the strip so it is just short enough not to touch the tip of the hook point. Be careful to only cut the leather and not any of the actual hair.

10. Tie down the mink Zonker strip on the other side of the fly as well. Trim to match.

11. Select two small olive grizzly marabou feathers. I like to sort through the bag and find two like-size feathers with similar distinct barring, as they will be tied down next to each other and I want the markings to blend naturally.

12. Wet the grizzly marabou feathers by either licking them or with a damp rag. This allows you to better position them in their proper place and keeps the tie-down area tidy and precise.

13. Tie down both grizzly marabou feathers (one at a time) onto the top of the fly. Do your best to get the two feathers in beside each other with minimal overlap—this will be much

easier if the feathers are damp and slicked back and made narrow. The tips of the marabou should extend back 1¾ inches (44 mm) from the lead edge of the hook eye. Trim away the butt ends of the marabou feathers.

14. Brush some Zap-A-Gap onto the material tie-down area. Adding a bit of adhesive at this point in the tying process is important, as everything is only tied down by a very short length of material and is susceptible to being pulled free during the abuse the fly will surely see one evening at your favorite bass pond.

15. Tie down the foam Boobie Eyes onto the top of the now quite fat material tie-down area at the front of the fly. Mount these eyes just as you would a metal barbell eye—set it on top at an angle at first and secure it with a couple tight thread wraps.

16. Turn the foam eyes so they are positioned properly perpendicular to the hook shank and use two more tight thread wraps crossing the original two in order to secure them in this position. By mounting the eyes at an angle and then turning them, you tighten down the first thread wraps, which will further compress the foam arbor (middle) of the eyes, making them more secure.

17. Rotate the fly over to expose the belly of the frog. Tie in a set of two rubber legs behind the foam eyes on either side of the hook shank. Make the band of multiple thread wraps as wide as possible, but without extending the tie-down area farther than the rear of the original thread base. Centipede Legs usually come in 6-inch (15 cm) strands, so you can cut them all in half and position them in place, avoiding the need to trim them to length, not to mention conserving a lot of material. I rarely do this, however, as it is often fiddly and time-consuming to line everything up just right—sometimes time is worth more than material.

18. Once you are confident there is enough thread over the two sets of rubber legs to hold them in place, bring the thread forward and tie a whip-finish knot between the foam eyes and the tie-down for the rubber legs. An extended-reach whip-finish tool will make it easier to get the knot done over the foam eyes. You will have to pull back the forward four legs when you tie this knot, and that can test your tying coordination, as you will need to maintain a grasp on the bobbin with the same hand.

19. While the fly is still turned over, apply a very small dab of Zap-A-Gap to the underside of the thread base. This is important to keep the rubber legs in place over many days on the water. Be very careful not to get even the smallest amount of this adhesive on the actual rubber legs, as it will "rot" the rubber and the legs will fall off. Put a small amount on the thread base and rub it slightly with your fingertip until it is dry.

20. If you are conserving the rubber leg material and have precut all the legs to 3 inches (76 mm), the front legs should extend out 1 inch (25 mm) and the rear legs should extend back 2 inches (5 cm). If not, trim them to these lengths.

21. Prepare the Boobie Eyes for the UV resin eyes by creating a socket for the resin to collect. These foam eyes have a small hole running right through their middle (most likely part of the manufacturing process), and it is this small hole that you need to accentuate to provide a place for the UV resin to collect—this also provides more surface area for the resin to adhere to the foam, making it more secure. I have found the butt end of my whip-finish tool works perfectly for this task.

22. Fill the socket with just enough yellow Loon Outdoors UV Fly Paint so it bulges out slightly. Fill the socket quickly after enlarging the hole in the foam, as it will want to close up if left too long. Cure the resin with a UV lamp before rotating the fly over and doing the same to the other eye. Hold the lamp on the eye for at least 15 seconds.

23. Use a black Sharpie marker to draw the pupils. I like to draw them slightly elongated to look more like those of an actual frog—this makes no difference to a fish, but it does to me.

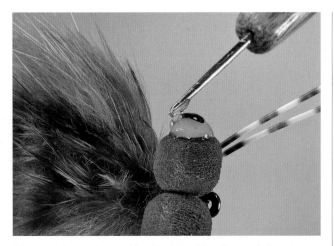

24. Coat the entirety of both eyes with a layer of clear Loon Outdoors UV Knot Sense. Cure the first eye before rotating the fly over and doing the second eye. Apply a small dollop of the resin on the apex of the eye and use a bodkin to encourage it to slide down the sides of the eye evenly. Be sure this clear coat comes down and makes slight contact with the bare foam all the way around the eye. The UV Knot Sense will make the eye appear larger and will protect the black pupil from smearing off (head cement will ruin the pupil almost immediately).

25. Hold the UV lamp on the eyes for at least 15 seconds each to ensure a solid cure. I will often brush some Hard as Hull head cement onto the finished eyes to ensure a clear, tack-free finish.

PATTERN VARIATION

BOOBY MOUSE

Hook: #2 Gamakatsu B10S

Thread: Dark brown 3/0 Danville's Waxed Monocord

Body Bottom: Cream marabou

Adhesive: Zap-A-Gap

Tail: Brown Leech Leather

Body Middle: Tan marabou

Body Sides: Charcoal rabbit strip

Body Top: Dark brown marabou

Foam Eyes: Black Rainy's Boobie Round Eyes (x-large)

Legs: Brown round rubber (medium)

Hard Eyes 1: Red Loon Outdoors UV Fly Paint

Hard Eyes 2: Black Sharpie marker

Hard Eyes 3: Loon Outdoors UV Knot Sense

FINESSE WORM

When I was a kid growing up in rural Ohio, I did not realize that the general fishing community expected me to declare myself one type of angler or another. I began fly fishing and tying my own flies at a young age, but never knew there were purists— those who would turn their noses up at bait and bass plugs. I fished anywhere and by any method I had gear for and for any species of fish my dad said was OK to eat. I was strictly a meat hunter then, and my summer chore was to fill the freezer with fish.

Fish the Finesse Worm with a loop knot if you want an erratic, "walk-the-dog"-type action.

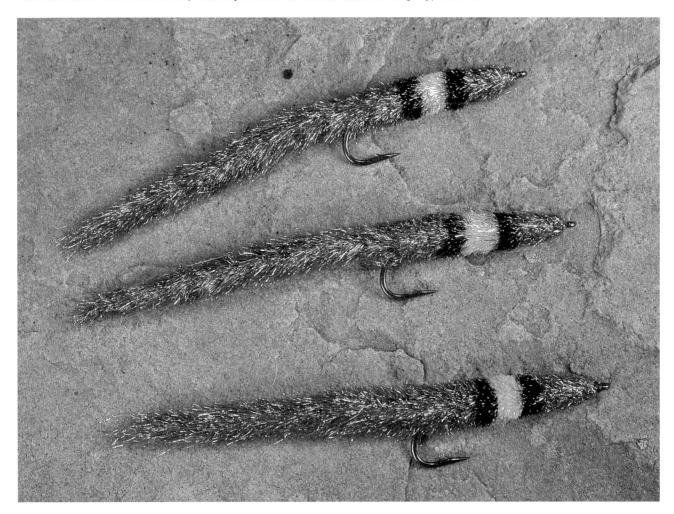

My fishing season would abruptly end in September when squirrel season opened. I gathered night crawlers after spring thunderstorms and kept them in a worm farm in the root cellar, and I tied my own flies on snelled bait hooks stolen from Dad's tackle box. Any money earned from orchard work (I was a cherry picker) was spent on .22 hollow points or walleye trolling lures—anything else was considered too extravagant.

My first experience with soft plastic bass lures ("rubber worms") was a serious eye-opener. I remember the first one I ever fished was about 6 inches long, purple, and had three different hooks protruding at different places through the soft plastic. I have no idea where I acquired this creature, but it was already a bit beat up and chewed on. The first place I fished it was in Dick Koegle's pond in Huron, Ohio. Dick was the local barber, and he and his brother Jack were chums with my dad and uncle back in school, so I had permission to fish. Dick loved that pond and the bass and bluegill in it,

so I was never allowed to keep anything. (This was my first experience with catch-and-release fishing, too.) I could not believe how aggressively the largemouth in that pond would attack that purple worm. I was astounded. And I fished that lure until it finished falling apart.

It was not until I left home and joined the army that I had the money to experiment further with rubber worms. I was with the 82nd Airborne Division stationed at Fort Bragg, North Carolina, for a few years, and between training operations and overseas deployments, I fished. I still spent a good deal of time chasing bass with a fly rod, but got discouraged with the disparity between the effectiveness of bass flies and bass lures. It was this frustration and the memory of how well that old purple worm worked that got me hooked on conventional-gear bass fishing.

My two favorite bass spots on post were Kiest Lake and Wyatt Lake, both accessible by the maze of dirt roads that also surrounded the nearby Small Arms Range 19 (other-

The Finesse Worm can be tied with eyes at the front and a "hot" tip at the tail, and the front trimmed into a subtle baitfish shape.

wise known as the Delta Force compound). Both lakes had healthy largemouth bass populations, but were subject to a lot of fishing pressure. I was not the only joe who liked to unwind on the water, as it turned out. I familiarized myself with all the latest bass plugs and spinner baits and the absolute sea of soft plastics. For these pressured Fort Bragg bass I found that a short, slim, soft jerk worm was the best medicine. The worm I liked best was sort of a smaller, finesse version of the then-popular Slug-Go worm. I would fish it with no added weight to the line, so I would have to use a light spinning rod to enable a decent cast. The worm was just dense enough to sink slowly and could be made to swim very erratically just below the surface of the water if retrieved with a jerky, almost spastic rod motion.

My conventional-gear fishing tapered off after I got out of the army, gradually being completely replaced by fly fishing. I believe it has been almost 20 years since I could remember where I last put my good spinning rods or any other remembrances of my conventional past. I did not ditch all that gear because I was ashamed of it—I just found myself living in places such as Alaska and Colorado where salmon, char, trout, and other perfect fly-rod prey were abundant. After a while, I realized my relationship with fishing had become a single-minded love affair with the fly rod. The problems did not arise until I started to get back into bass fishing and no longer had the fallback plan waiting around in plastic bags in an old tackle box. I was determined to solve my bass problems at the tying vise.

I was already using the ferruled dubbing loop technique to create a durable wormlike appearance for the Geezus Lizard and Texas Ringworm before I perfected the Finesse Worm. Neither of those two early flies swam with the same jerky, erratic action as the soft plastics I grew fond of in North Carolina, however—they had too much else going on in front of the "worm" part of the fly. What I was lacking was pure simplicity. The Finesse Worm works because it is very sleek and narrow, which allows it to dart quickly through the water.

The most difficult part of tying this fly is not wading through a sea of dubbing and twisting dubbing loops until you are dizzy, it is resisting the urge to leave the fly bushy. Be harsh and trim that baby like it was headed to boot camp—it is the only way to get it to do what you want. Do not be tempted to make this fly weedless with hard mono or try to get it to swim hook point up. As much as I would like every fly I cast to swim hook point up, this one just never will . . . trust me, I have spent years trying. Any attempt to mess with the streamer hydrodynamics of this pattern only

Public places that receive a fair amount of fishing pressure often require finesse flies and tactics.

hinders the action. I have found that because the Tiemco 9395 is a 3X heavy hook and this fly is almost always fished on a heavy leader (2X to 0X), it can be ripped through most vegetation it comes in contact with. This particular hook is perfectly suited for this sort of pattern, and not just because it is sturdy. The 9395 is long (4X), with a straight shank and a large straight eye—there are not many hooks styles out there that meet these specifications, and they are all crucial.

It took me a long time to find exactly the right dubbing to use for the Finesse Worm. As almost any long-fibered blend will suffice, and even look good, it was difficult to narrow it down to the Wapsi SLF Prism dubbing. I like this blend because it has long, flashy fibers that are more consistent and straighter than some other similar dubbing. I have tied and fished a ton of variations of this fly, and almost all of them have worked wonderfully—some were all one color, others had bands of every color of dubbing I had on hand. Over time, I became partial to the solid color with accent near the front, like an eye. I think this mimics nature in a way and draws the attention to the head of the fly. The narrow band of black on either end of the accent color acts like eyeliner, or further accents the accent. This is important because this fly is meant to move quickly on a lateral plane, and it is this drastic variation in color that can get the attention of a bass when silhouetted against a variety of backgrounds and lighting conditions.

Fish the Finesse Worm with a loop knot if you want an erratic, "walk-the-dog"-type action. Tie a snug knot to the hook eye if you want the fly to track straight and fast.

FINESSE WORM (OLIVE)

Hook: #4 Tiemco 9395

Thread: Black 3/0 Danville's Waxed Monocord

Wax: BT's Tacky Dubbing Wax

Primary Dubbing: Olive SLF Prism dubbing

Adhesive: Zap-A-Gap

Accent Dubbing: Black SLF Prism dubbing

Secondary Dubbing: Fluorescent chartreuse SLF Prism dubbing

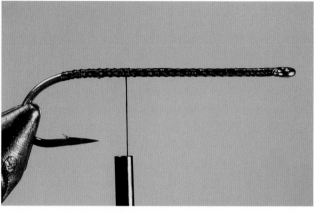

1. Clamp the hook firmly into the jaws of the vise. The Tiemco 9395 is a 4X-long streamer hook, and it will sometimes move in the jaws if they are not clamped tight or the hook is anchored incorrectly. Start the thread wraps immediately behind the hook eye and wrap all the way back to the very end of the straight hook shank. The thread base should encroach a *tiny* bit onto the beginning of the hook bend. Then wrap the thread forward to a point ahead of the hook point, about a third of the way back up the thread base. We will call this spot where the thread is in the photo the "quarter point."

2. Flip the hook upside down. From the quarter point, create a 10-inch (25 cm) double-strand thread loop. This will be the thread used in the ferruled dubbing loop that will make the rear, or "tail," of this fly, and it will only be stiff enough to work correctly if it is made with two strands of 3/0 thread. Wrap the thread forward and leave the bobbin hanging so the thread is resting behind the hook eye (this keeps it temporarily out of the way). Wax the thread.

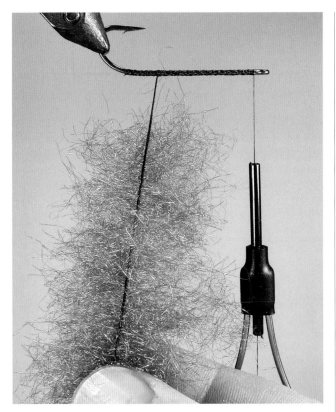

3. Stack the primary dubbing into the thread loop. When building such a long dubbing loop, the wax on the thread really helps keep everything in place. Stack the dubbing in as snug as possible, but keep it all evenly distributed and be sure not to leave any clumps—dense consistency is what you are after. Although the thread loop you made is 10 inches (25 cm) long, only stack 8 inches (20 cm) with dubbing. Leave some of the loop empty at both ends—this will keep dubbing from binding up with the hook (or, in later steps, with existing dubbing) and allow you space to twist the dubbing loop by hand or use a dubbing twirl.

4. Twist the dubbing loop into a rope. There should be a lot of dubbing in the loop, so it will quickly twist into a very thick rope. Before it gets too tight, brush out as much of the loose fibers as you can. Then continue twisting until the rope has shrunk to about 6 inches (15 cm) long. You will need to brush out the rope about three times before you are done. A coarse wire dubbing brush is needed, as you will be removing large amounts of the loose dubbing. Dubbing is inexpensive as tying materials go, but this fly will consume a ton and become a much more costly tie if you do not do your best to conserve dubbing. Use a bodkin to pick the brush clean before brushing out another dubbing color. Keep little piles of the recycled dubbing segregated by color so they can be reused.

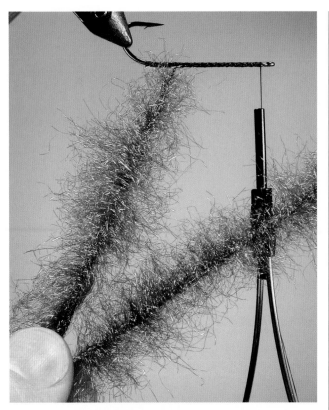 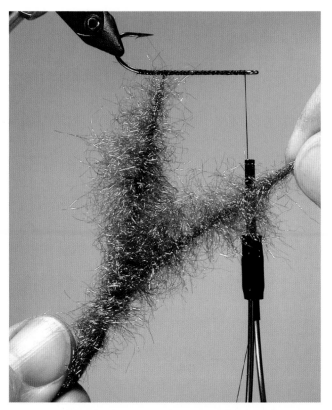

5. Once the dubbing rope is properly twisted and brushed, prepare to ferrule the rope. Hold onto the terminal end of the rope with one hand, and then pinch the rope with the thumb and index finger of your other hand. Grab the rope near the middle, but slightly closer to the hook than your other hand. Sweep the longer dubbing fibers back and into your grasp when you pinch down on the rope—do this by creating a circle with your fingers (the dubbing rope should be inside the circle) and then pull your hand back, forcing the rope into your pinch. This technique is similar to how you may already be folding hackle feathers.

6. The dubbing rope will have a lot of twist built up like a spring and will try to ferrule back on its own, which is nice, but you want to maintain control of the situation and create a tail shaped the right way. To do this, you will need to keep everything pulled tight, relax the tension slightly, and roll the tip of the tail between your thumb and index finger (in the same direction that it wants to ferrule)—this makes the ferruling process smooth and tidy. Keep the first part of the tail (the tip one-third) thinner than the butt (the rear two-thirds) by spacing the spiral wraps at first, then making them tight (almost on top of each other) for the remainder of the tail. Keep the twist going all the way to the very end, even once you have reached the end of what will be usable dubbing rope—this should create a short taper at the rear of the tail section that will become the tie-down point.

7. Cut the ferruled dubbing tail off the hook shank. You do not need to brush it at this point, but if you do, you can see if it is the proper shape. The tail should have a long taper from the tip forward and an abrupt taper at the butt end. It should be sleek and feel a bit stiff.

8. Rotate the hook so that it is right side up and tie the ferruled dubbing tail down on the top of the hook shank. Position the tail so that the fattest part of the butt is nestled right up on the top of the hook bend. The overall length of this fly (from tip of tail to lead edge of hook eye) needs to be 3¾ inches (95 mm) long, but the exact length of the fly is less important than getting the tail mounted properly—use your discretion. If you are trying to get the fly to the exact length called for, keep in mind that the long dubbing fibers extending out from the very tip of the tail will be trimmed shortly before the fly is finished, so adjust accordingly. I try to tie all the thread tag ends of the tail down onto the hook shank, as I am trying to build up some body bulk anyway.

9. Rotate the hook once again and apply some Zap-A-Gap to the underside of the tie-down for the ferruled dubbing tail. Applying the adhesive from this side allows it to do its job better (keep everything locked up tight).

10. Create a second, one-strand thread loop at the very butt of the tail, then wrap the thread forward and let the bobbin hang at the quarter point. This thread loop should be 5 inches (13 cm) long. Wax the thread.

11. Stack the loop with the same primary dubbing used to make the ferruled dubbing tail. Although the thread loop is 5 inches (13 cm) long, only stack 3 inches (76 mm) of dubbing.

12. Twist the dubbing loop until it forms a rope and brush out any loose dubbing fibers. You will not be ferruling this rope, so you do not need to twist it nearly as much as the last dubbing loop. Also, your wire dubbing brush should remove a lot of dubbing, so remember to keep saving the excess.

13. Wrap the dubbing loop forward onto the hook shank. If you have brushed out the dubbing properly before wrapping and lay each wrap tight next to the last wrap, you should exhaust the dubbing rope right at the quarter point and have your thread waiting handily. Tie down the thread tag end of the dubbing rope.

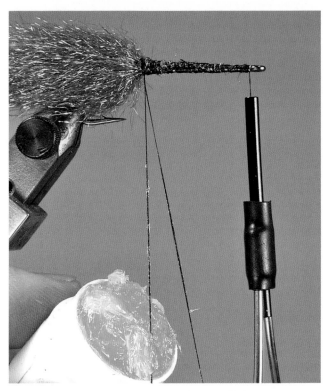

14. Create a third (and final) single-strand thread loop right at the quarter point (end of the existing dubbing). This thread loop should be at least 8 inches (20 cm) long but can be slightly longer if you like. Wrap the thread forward and leave the bobbin hanging immediately behind the hook eye. Wax the thread loop.

15. Although this thread loop is 8 inches (20 cm) long, stack only 6 inches (15 cm) of dubbing. This dubbing rope will consist of three different colors of dubbing. The first 1 inch (25 mm) is the accent dubbing (usually black), the second 1½ inches (38 mm) is the secondary dubbing color (usually much lighter than the primary color), and the next 1 inch (25 mm) is the accent color once again. The final 2½ inches (64 mm) is back to the primary dubbing color that matches the tail.

16. Twist the dubbing loop into a rope. Brush out all the loose dubbing fibers the same way you have done in the previous steps, but this time take extra care in keeping the three different colors separated. Brush out the primary color first, clean out the brush with a bodkin, then move on to the secondary color and do the same. Lastly, brush out the accent colors.

17. Wrap the brushed-out dubbing rope forward onto the hook shank. There should be just enough rope to bring you right up to the hook eye if each wrap is tight to the last. You do not want to trap the dubbing, so be sure to sweep the long fibers back as you are wrapping the rope forward, as this will ensure the worm is good and bushy.

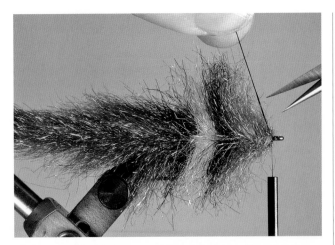

18. Wrap the dubbing rope right up to the hook eye and trim the excess thread.

19. Add a whip-finish knot or two and trim the thread. The tying part of the fly is over—on to the grooming!

20. Give the entire fly a vigorous brushing. You want all the loose dubbing fibers gone, any trapped fibers pulled loose, and everything swept to the rear.

21. Remove the fly from the vise in order to properly trim. Your instinct is to want to leave the fly nice and bushy, but you must resist! This fly works so well because of its erratic, darting movements in the water, which it gets from being slim and sleek. Trim aggressively.

22. The front of the worm will need the most aggressive haircut, but be sure to trim the entire fly down to a compact wormlike shape. On a #4 hook the finished fly should be 3¾ inches (95 mm) long. Add a small drop of Zap-A-Gap to the finish knot.

PATTERN VARIATIONS

FINESSE WORM (PURPLE)

Hook: #4 Tiemco 9395

Thread: Dark brown 3/0 Danville's Waxed Monocord

Wax: BT's Tacky Dubbing Wax

Primary Dubbing: Hot purple SLF Prism dubbing

Adhesive: Zap-A-Gap

Accent Dubbing: Black SLF Prism dubbing

Secondary Dubbing: Light gray SLF Prism dubbing

FINESSE WORM (BROWN)

Hook: #4 Tiemco 9395

Thread: Dark brown 3/0 Danville's Waxed Monocord

Wax: BT's Tacky Dubbing Wax

Primary Dubbing: Hare's ear SLF Prism dubbing

Adhesive: Zap-A-Gap

Accent Dubbing: Black SLF Prism dubbing

Secondary Dubbing: Fluorescent orange SLF Prism dubbing

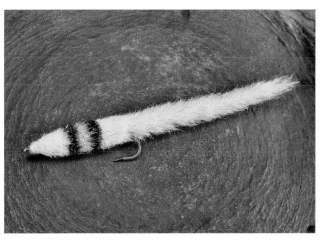

FINESSE WORM (PEARL)

Hook: #4 Tiemco 9395

Thread: White 3/0 Danville's Waxed Monocord

Wax: BT's Tacky Dubbing Wax

Primary Dubbing: Ice pearl SLF Prism dubbing

Adhesive: Zap-A-Gap

Accent Dubbing: Black SLF Prism dubbing

Secondary Dubbing: Fluorescent yellow SLF Prism dubbing

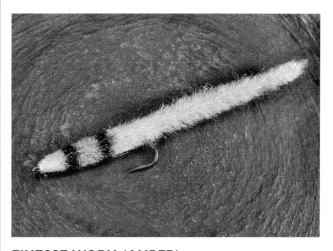

FINESSE WORM (AMBER)

Hook: #4 Tiemco 9395

Thread: White 3/0 Danville's Waxed Monocord

Wax: BT's Tacky Dubbing Wax

Primary Dubbing: Amber SLF Prism dubbing

Adhesive: Zap-A-Gap

Accent Dubbing: Black SLF Prism dubbing

Secondary Dubbing: Fluorescent fire orange SLF Prism dubbing

FINESSE WORM (BROWN OLIVE)

Hook: #4 Tiemco 9395

Thread: Dark brown 3/0 Danville's Waxed Monocord

Wax: BT's Tacky Dubbing Wax

Primary Dubbing: Brown olive SLF Prism dubbing

Adhesive: Zap-A-Gap

Accent Dubbing: Black SLF Prism dubbing

Secondary Dubbing: Sand SLF Prism dubbing

FINESSE WORM (OLIVE/WEIGHTED)

Hook: #4 Tiemco 5263

Thread: Dark brown 3/0 Danville's Waxed Monocord

Lead Barbell Eyes: Wapsi Presentation Lead Eyes
    (x-small, 5/32")

Wax: BT's Tacky Dubbing Wax

Primary Dubbing: Olive SLF Prism dubbing

Adhesive: Zap-A-Gap

Accent Dubbing: Black SLF Prism dubbing

Secondary Dubbing: Fluorescent chartreuse SLF Prism
    dubbing

When I tie a weighted version of the Finesse Worm, I use a black lead eye at the front and tie it on a different hook. The Tiemco 5263 is slightly shorter than the 9395 (3X long vs. 4X long) and of a slightly lighter-gauge wire (2X heavy vs. 3X heavy), and it is a down-eyed hook. All of these variables make the 5263 easier to flip and make it ride hook point up, which is important with heavier flies that need to remain as snag-free as possible.

STEALTH BOMBER

K ent Edmonds invented the Stealth Bomber nearly 30 years ago, and he is no weekend warrior. Kent is a fly-fishing guide in LaGrange, Georgia, specializing in warm- and saltwater species. He is also a regional manufacturer's representative for Rainy's Flies and other fishing products. His Stealth Bomber pattern and several others are sold commercially though Rainy's.

The turbulence the Stealth Bomber creates, along with the shape of its wing, causes the fly to wiggle side-to-side.

Topwater bass flies like the Stealth Bomber that make a lot of commotion can elicit explosive strikes. Cheney Geeslin with a bass from one of the water hazards on the golf course where he works.

Kent was inspired by Guy Turck's Tarantula, the fly that George Anderson put on the map by using it to win the 1990 Jackson Hole One Fly contest. Turck's trout fly quickly became one of Kent's favorites for bass and bream in Georgia. He designed the Stealth Bomber to duplicate the diving motion and the resulting bubble trail made when the Tarantula is given a hard strip. The looped rear portion of foam captures air, which bubbles and pops on the dive. The turbulence it creates, along with the shape of the wing, causes the fly to wiggle side-to-side. The first Stealth Bomber was tied with black foam and only a wisp of tail and resembled the flying wing silhouette of the B-2 stealth bomber that was all over the news (around the time of the first Gulf War).

The Stealth Bomber pattern is simple and fast to tie once you have made a template to get just the right shape of foam cut, yet the fly has a certain graceful complexity that held my gaze when I was first sent photos. I sat down that night to tie a couple of my friend's favorite fly with the intention of testing them on a bass pond on the way to the shop the next morning. I may have tied two dozen instead, partially because they looked good and I wanted to have some in another color, then another, but also because the fly was fast to tie—and fun to tie. I played around with them the next morning and continued to fish the pattern the rest of the summer. I was a convert. The fly is so different from what I have tied and fished for years, but still oddly familiar—sort of reminding me of a Dahlberg Diver crossbred with a Gartside Gurgler. But the action on a Stealth Bomber is different—it dives and makes noise like the Dahlberg, but it is more exaggerated. The dive is deeper with a shorter strip, and the pop it makes as it is pulled under the water is loud.

My favorite two scenarios for fishing a Stealth Bomber are on opposite sides of the bass-fishing situational Rolodex. Use this fly as a true topwater popper/diver on small, clear bass ponds. It lands softly and can look unbelievably enticing as it sits motionless in a small pocket of open water between weed beds or in the calm water in a back cove. Give the fly a subtle twitch from time to time with an occasional big jerk to plunge the Bomber deep under the surface, bubbles trailing the fly, then let it float back to the surface as gentle and pretty as you please. On bigger water where visibility and ambient noise are considerations, fish the Bomber on a long leader and sinking-tip fly line. The fly will still rest on the surface (if the leader is long enough) but will dive much deeper when pulled hard. Tuck your fly rod under your casting arm and use both hands to move the fly with a steady, hand-over-hand retrieve. This constant retrieve will keep the fly underwater where it will wiggle more than some articulated streamers and move more water than a crankbait.

STEALTH BOMBER (CHARTREUSE)
Hook: #4 Gamakatsu B10S
Thread: White 210-denier UTC Ultra Thread
Tail: Lime green bucktail
Adhesive: Zap-A-Gap
Flash: Chartreuse Dyed Pearl Flashabou
Foam: Chartreuse closed-cell foam (2 mm)
Body: Pearl Cactus Chenille (medium)
Legs: Chartreuse neon green grizzly barred rubber legs (medium)

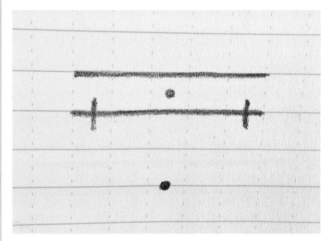

1. A properly tied Bomber includes a simple yet precise piece of foam, and to get just the right shape of foam every time, you need to take the time to create a template. Use a pad of waterproof graph paper to make a temporary template; the paper is thick and durable enough to be used a few times—which is enough to decide if you have the shape you like. Create this odd figure on the graph paper to act as a guideline for the template shape. This is a ¼-inch graph, so use a pencil to draw two parallel horizontal lines five "boxes" long (1¼ inches). Make a vertical mark at either end of the lower line, right at the center of both end boxes. Draw a dot in the center of the middle box between the two lines. Draw a second dot on the graph line on the third graph line below the first dot. Now draw a perfectly symmetrical Valentine-worthy heart using these marks as a guide.

2. Use the pencil marks as a guide to draw the heart 1 inch wide (25 mm) and ¾ inch (19 mm) tall. Then sketch a ¼-inch-wide "stick" extending nine graph blocks, or 2¼ inches (57 mm) below the heart shape. The overall template length should be 3 inches (76 mm). When cutting out this template, cut a gentle, sweeping transition at the two points where the "stick" meets the "heart" as well as the crux between the two lobes at the top of the heart.

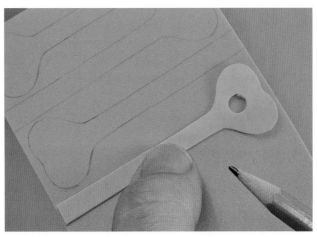

3. Once you have dialed in the perfect shape, use clear shipping tape to mount the temporary paper template onto the heavy plastic back cover of the waterproof notebook and use it to guide the cutting of your permanent template. I punch a hole in the fat part of the template so I can hang it on a hook and not lose it. Use a pencil to draw the outline, as it will easily fade.

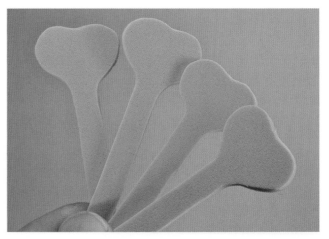

4. Use the heavy plastic template to make as many foam Bomber backs as you need in a given tying session. If this pattern turns into one of your favorites (and it may), it will be a great time-saving idea to go ahead and cut up a handy surplus of your best colors.

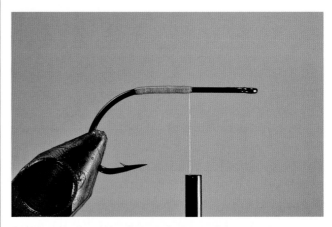

5. Mount the hook firmly into the jaws of the vise. Begin thread wraps at the center of the straight hook shank. Create a solid thread base from that and extend it to the rear of the straight shank. Finish with the thread hanging at the forward end of the thread base. Let the bobbin hang in place.

6. Cut off a clump of bucktail about as big around as your pinkie finger.

7. Comb any underfur, broken hairs, or short hairs out from the cut base of the clump of bucktail.

8. Tie the bucktail down on top of the thread base. Be sure the material tie-down does not extend out past the front of the thread base or creep down onto the bend of the hook. The tips of all the hair should be of varying lengths (as the hair was not stacked), and the longest hairs in the clump should be about two hook-shank lengths out behind the rear of the fly. Leave the bobbin hanging so the thread is in the middle of the tie-down area.

9. Pull the butt ends of hair back and trim them. Leave a bit of hair sticking out of the tie-down, as it will act as a material dam of sorts later on in the tying process. Rotate the hook upside down and brush on some Zap-A-Gap.

Applying the adhesive to the underside of the hair tie-down ensures contact with the hook shank—this is important, as it will prevent the entire body from rotating around freely on the hook shank once the fly is finished.

10. Select eight strands of Flashabou to use on the tail of the fly. You will need a second eight-strand bundle later in the tying process, so it is not a bad idea to pull both bundles now and be done. Run the spare bundle of Flashabou through your mouth to get it wet so it will stay together while left unattended on the tying bench.

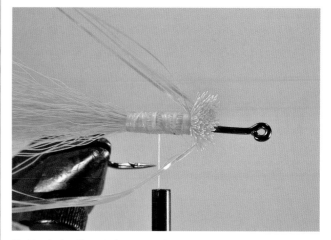

11. Hook the first eight-strand bundle of Flashabou around the butt ends of deer hair and fold the strands back on either side of the bucktail.

12. Make about four thread wraps toward the rear of the fly, ending right at the base of the deer hair tail—this will secure the Flashabou in place and position the thread for the next move. There will now be eight strands of flash on either side of the tail. Trim all 16 strands just slightly longer than the longest hair.

13. Use two thread wraps to tie down the precut foam Bomber back. Before mounting the foam, fold it exactly in half to see where the center point is and use that slight crease to gauge where the tie-down should be.

14. Tie in an end of the Cactus Chenille body wrap material. Tuck it between the forward end of the foam and the hook shank—this will hold the chenille in place just long enough

for you to secure it properly with thread wraps. Finish with the thread just onto the bare hook shank forward of the thread base.

15. Make the first wrap of Cactus Chenille between the two ends of foam (at the foam tie-down point), then continue wrapping the material forward (under the forward end of foam) until you reach the material dam created with the butt ends of bucktail. Zap-A-Gap adhesive should have leached into this end of the hair and dried, so the dam should be fairly rigid and keep the last wrap of Cactus Chenille from slipping off the now-bulky material tie-down.

16. Fold the forward end of foam down over the body wrapped in Cactus Chenille and secure it in place right at the lead edge of the body material. Be careful not to make these thread wraps too tight, as the thread can easily cut through the foam if there is no padding between the foam and the hook shank.

17. Fold the rear half of foam over the body of the fly and tie it down at the same point as the forward half. The end of the rear (now the "top") piece of foam should be even with the lead edge of the hook eye. The top foam will create an arch over the body of the fly.

19. Create a long thread loop at the foam tie-down point. This thread loop will be the thread that finishes tying the fly without having to bring the bobbin back to this spot. The thread loop should be at least 12 to 14 inches (30 to 35 cm) long for ease of holding onto later on. No need to wax this thread loop, as it will not be used to hold dubbing. Hook the thread loop back in a material clip or let it hang freely . . . as long as it is out of the way.

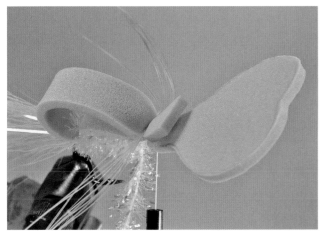

18. Take the second bundle of eight Flashabou strands and slide it between the two forward-facing ends of foam. Shimmy the Flashabou down as far as it will go (it should go all the way until it hits the thread used to tie down the top piece of foam), then cross the two ends of the Flashabou bundle over each other at the crease where both ends of foam are tied down. Make two cross-wraps of thread over the Flashabou to keep it in place.

20. Advance the thread forward to behind the hook eye, then wrap the Cactus Chenille up to the thread and tie it off. The first wrap of chenille should be over the crease created by the forward foam tie-down area. Trim away the excess chenille.

21. Pull back both sides of the second bundle of Flashabou and trim them all even with a point about halfway back on the hair tail. Both ends of the Flashabou should be sticking out slightly over the back of the fly.

22. Trim away most of what remains of the end of the top side of foam protruding from the tie-down area.

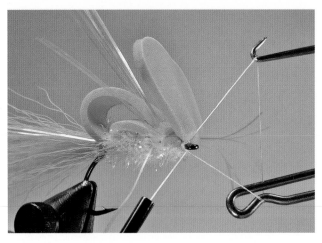

23. Tie the forward foam down directly behind the hook eye—this is the third and most forward foam tie-down area. Pull the foam "heart" (this should be about all that remains of the forward end of foam) back and tie a whip-finish knot behind the hook eye. Trim the thread.

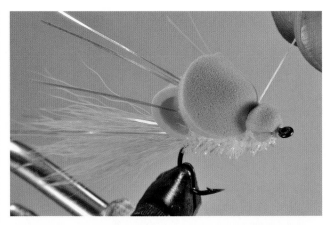

24. Fold the foam heart back over the body and use the thread loop left back at the second (or middle) foam tie-down spot to lash it back, forming both a round foam head between this tie-down and the hook eye and a foam "shield" of sorts over the body of the fly. You can pull tightly on the thread, as the foam is well padded and the doubled-over thread is thick (420 denier).

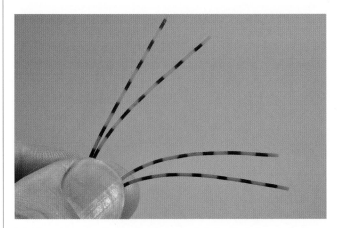

25. The thread will stay in place, as it is buried deeply in the crease created in the multiple layers of foam, allowing you to select four strands of barred rubber leg material. Separate them into pairs, each strand being 3 inches (76 mm) long.

26. Use the doubled-over thread to draw the first set of rubber legs into the side of the fly. The set of rubber should be about even on either side if the tie-down, making all four legs the same length. Repeat this process on the other side of the fly with the remaining set of rubber legs.

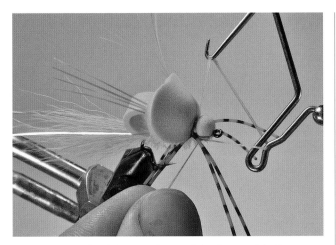

27. Tie a whip-finish knot in front of the forward-facing sets of rubber legs, but behind the round foam "head." Trim away the remaining thread.

PATTERN VARIATIONS

STEALTH BOMBER (BLACK)

Hook: #4 Gamakatsu B10S

Thread: Black 210-denier UTC Ultra Thread

Tail: Black bucktail

Adhesive: Zap-A-Gap

Flash 1: Black Holographic Flashabou (4 strands each)

Flash 2: Blue Holographic Flashabou (4 strands each)

Foam: Black closed-cell foam (2 mm)

Body: Purple Cactus Chenille (medium)

Legs 1: Black medium round rubber (1 each)

Legs 2: Purple medium round rubber (1 each)

STEALTH BOMBER (WHITE)

Hook: #4 Gamakatsu B10S

Thread: Fluorescent shell pink 210-denier UTC Ultra Thread

Tail: White bucktail

Adhesive: Zap-A-Gap

Flash: Pearl Flashabou

Foam: White closed-cell foam (2 mm)

Body: Shrimp pink Cactus Chenille (medium)

Legs: White grizzly barred rubber legs (medium)

STEALTH BOMBER (OLIVE)

Hook: #4 Gamakatsu B10S

Thread: Olive 210-denier UTC Ultra Thread

Tail: Light olive bucktail

Adhesive: Zap-A-Gap

Flash: Gold Holographic Flashabou

Foam: Olive closed-cell foam (2 mm)

Body: Olive Cactus Chenille (medium)

Legs: Fluorescent chartreuse grizzly barred rubber legs (medium)

GEEZUS LIZARD

I gave this bass fly the name Geezus Lizard after carrying one of the first prototypes around in my shirt pocket for several days and periodically pulling it out to look at it and stroke it like a pet hamster. I had not set out to create something that resembled a lizard, or even a salamander for that matter. In the end it just wound up looking like one. The idea for the pattern began with the tail and then became a matter of choosing which other tying materials or techniques could be added to the hook to make it as squirrelly, as lively, and as effective for bass as possible.

The Geezus Lizard quickly darts back to the bottom after being jerked by the angler. This mimics the action of a spooked crayfish perfectly.

The Geezus Lizard uses large lead dumbbell eyes on a jig hook, making this fly very heavy. It's best when fished slow and steady on the bottom, usually in deep water near submerged cover.

Once I realized my new fly looked more like a lizard than anything else living, I was reminded of an episode from my past involving the Jesus Christ lizard. There is actually such a thing. The common basilisk (*Basiliscus basiliscus*) is a small lizard that lives in the rain forests of Central and South America and is best known for its ability to run on its hind legs over water . . . hence the name. They look a bit comical when they do their frantic water dash, and it was this humor that struck a chord with a particularly sinister noncommissioned officer I once knew when I was a young man and in the US Army.

I was a private at the time (19 years old, fresh out of basic training and Airborne School) and on my first overseas deployment with the 2/505th Parachute Infantry Regiment. I and a handful of other recruits were sent to Panama as replacements a week after the unit had arrived "in country," and the reception was not welcoming. The battalion was living in green canvas tents (large enough to sleep about 20

men) in a clearing carved out of the jungle near the Panama Canal. It was stifling hot and muggy, and everyone there was bored and outranked me.

The first couple months were brutal. Not only was I learning a hard job, but I was also the new kid, so was used as a source of entertainment. The hazing involved forced "cock fights" with other privates, songs sung from the beds of deuce and a halves for the enjoyment of the older enlisted while they rode on the benches, and painful animal reenactments that would often last all day. Sometimes we were made to squat low to the ground and waddle around flapping our arms and quacking like a duck. All day. Other times it was a cow. Or a pig. But then, on a patrol, someone spooked a Jesus Christ lizard, and that too was added to the list. It was humiliating to be made to spastically run to and fro with my arms waving about and feet kicking off to the side, but it did mean I got to run away. By the time everyone stopped laughing and wiped away their tears, I was long gone. I learned many other ways to survive. I learned if you are forced to sing, serenade your torturers with something from Little River Band—it will hurt them worse, and you will never be made to do it again. I also learned how to win a fight and how to do my job. That time in my life made me tough and allowed me to prove something to myself, and I look back on it with great pride. But I will never forget how to run like a Jesus lizard.

Years later, at a fly shop in Longmont, Colorado, I watched a coworker twist and furl some blue yarn to create the extended body of an adult damselfly. This struck me as one of the coolest things I had seen in a long while, and I felt it was an underutilized trick in fly tying. In the summer of 2005 I set out to furl every material long enough to twist and wrap back over itself. I furled McFly Foam to make soft abdomens of grasshoppers, chenille and Estaz to make long bass worms (they looked horrible and fell apart), and even clumps of red and pink thread to make my own weird little San Juan Worms. It was when I built a long dubbing loop and twisted and furled it that I knew I had found something significant to offer the world of bass flies.

I certainly did not invent the furled dubbing loop. I thought I had for a glorious day or two (just like as a kid when I invented the double haul and the uni knot), but I soon discovered this was not so. Darrel Martin demonstrated this technique in his book *Fly-Tying Methods* (Lyons & Burford, 1987) and used the furled dubbing loop to create bodies of midge pupae, damselfly nymphs, and extended bodies on adult mayflies. Shane Stalcup, a late friend of mine, also used to tie a leech pattern using his well-known Sparkle Dubbing in a furled loop. What I saw was an opportunity to further advance the concept and turn it into a viable soft-plastic worm option for fly anglers.

Other fly tiers have tinkered with similar ideas to make bass worm flies, even going so far as furling chenille and tying in a tail tip at the end. More often than not these flies

The author with an early-season bass taken on a Geezus Lizard.

are too stiff or too evenly skinny to look good or work the way they were intended, and almost always fall apart quickly. Materials such as chenille and Bohemian Yarn were made to be incorporated into something larger and sturdier, and in fly tying are meant to be wrapped onto a hook shank, so do not have a strong enough core to stand alone through the rigors they are subjected to on bass waters. With a furled dubbing loop, the fly tier is in complete control of the size and strength of the thread used, as well as the color and consistency of the dubbing. This technique also allows the tier to make a variegated "worm" by adding two different-colored dubbings on either end of the dubbing loop and furling them together.

Once the concept for the tail was perfected, I was left to build the rest of the fly in a way that would best complement the awesome, wormlike appendage sticking out the back end. I had to create the Geezus Lizard backwards. I was fishing a lot of heavy, jig-like bass flies at the time, so this new fly took that turn without much consideration. Painted lead eyes and rubber legs were a given, as well as the use of a wrapped rabbit strip to give the body as much lifelike movement as possible. Even after all these bass-fly staples were added, the pattern did not quite swim like I wanted it to—it just sort of *moved* through the water without much *action*.

I was working in a fly shop in Boulder, Colorado, at the time with Patrick Knackendoffel, a young fly-fishing guide from Grand Junction. One of the many great fly patterns Patrick was tying back then was a big, heavy crayfish imitation he called the Mudslider. This fly had rabbit wrapped over the entire body, but used Scud Back over both the top and bottom to push all the fur off to either side of the fly. It also had wire ribbing to hold the Scud Back in place and give the fly a great segmented look similar to the exoskeleton over the abdomen of a real crayfish. I stole this idea and installed it at the bottom of my Geezus Lizard. This not only drastically improved the overall "bin appeal" of my new fly, but also gave the fly a more lively action in the water. Because all the rabbit fur was either left on the top or pushed off the sides (leaving the bottom bare), the Geezus Lizard would quickly dart back to the bottom after being jerked by the angler. This mimicked the action of a spooked crayfish perfectly.

The Geezus Lizard uses large lead dumbbell eyes on a jig hook, making this fly very heavy. I have found this fly works best when fished slow and steady on the bottom, usually in deep water near submerged cover (old pilings, tree stumps, sunken stuff, et cetera). This makes the fly extremely useful when fishing from a boat, but these fishing situations usually only arise for a shorebound angler when confronted with steep banks in ponds, or dams at the deep end of man-made reservoirs.

GEEZUS LIZARD (CRAYFISH)

Hook: #1/0 Gamakatsu Jig 90 Heavy Wire (Round Bend)

Thread: Dark brown 3/0 Danville's Waxed Monocord

Eyes: Yellow painted lead dumbbell eyes (large)

Wax: BT's Tacky Dubbing Wax

Tail Dubbing 1: Nearnuff crayfish orange Dave Whitlock SLF

Tail Tip: Golden yellow Montana Fly Frog's Hair

Tail Dubbing 2: Dark stone nymph Dave Whitlock SLF

Adhesive: Zap-A-Gap

Legs: Neon orange grizzly barred rubber legs (medium)

Ribbing: Black UTC Ultra Wire (medium)

Back: Clear Scud Back (¼")

Body 1: Rust rabbit strip

Body 2: Light rust rabbit strip

Head Cement: Hard-as-Hull

Top: Dark brown marabou blood quill

Head Dubbing: Dragonfly nymph dark Dave Whitlock SLF

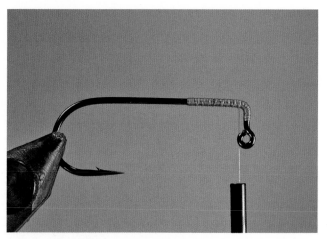

1. Clamp the hook firmly into the jaws of the vise. Create a solid thread base at the front end of the hook shank, beginning halfway between the hook eye and the 45-degree bend in the jig hook and extending back ⅜ inch (1 cm) onto the hook shank. Once the solid thread base is complete, wrap the thread forward and leave the bobbin hanging so the thread is just behind the shank bend—this is where the lead eyes will be mounted. The solid thread base extending down onto the shank bend of the hook is to give the lead eyes more stability once mounted, making them less likely to be forcibly spun around on the hook shank—as will often happen when the angler is attempting to pry the fly from the mouth of a fish. I have used white thread for the first two steps in this tutorial to better illustrate where the back end of this original thread base ends, as this is an important yardstick for measuring the correct proportions of the fly.

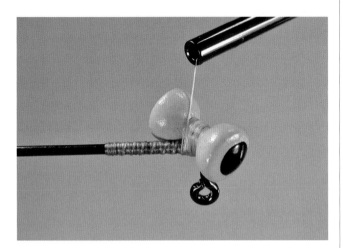

2. Mount the painted lead dumbbell eyes onto the very front end of the main hook shank. Use many tight thread wraps at the same angle—this will cock the eyes at an angle on the hook shank. Next, use your thumbnail to pull back the near side of the dumbbell eyes until the eyes are perfectly perpendicular to the hook shank, then use an equal number of tight thread wraps (wrapped at the other angle) to secure the eyes in their proper place.

3. Once the lead eyes are properly mounted, continue building a solid thread base all the way back to the rear of the hook shank. You will notice I have switched to brown thread. This would normally be the thread you begin with and use for the entirety of the fly. Again, the use of two different-colored threads in this tutorial is just to make the end of the original thread base easier to find. Leave the bobbin hanging a bit behind the transition point between the original thread base and the secondary thread base— this will be the spot you build the ferruled dubbing loop tail.

4. Before you create the thread loop, prepare all three ingredients that will make up the tail. The two wads of SLF dubbing should be loosened up by hand, and any clumps or other oddities removed. Section out a piece of golden yellow Frog's Hair a tad smaller (in both diameter and length) than your pinkie finger. Set these prepared ingredients aside, but within easy reach.

5. Create an 8- to 10-inch (20 to 25 cm), three-strand thread loop and wax the thread—the wax makes filling such a long thread loop with dubbing easier. You can use a dubbing twirl if you lack the necessary coordination, but it is really simple and less cumbersome to do by hand. Pull a long length of thread from the bobbin, wrap it around the tip of the index finger of your non-tying hand to the length you want the loop to be, then return the thread to the hook shank, wrap the thread around the shank, and repeat twice more. It is important to keep all three thread loops exactly the same size because you will only be able to pull tight the shortest loop, and you do not want any of the thread to be slack. To ensure all three loops of thread are the same and tight, I will wrap the thread twice around the hook shank before pulling out another long length of thread from the bobbin for the next loop—this keeps the thread tension from shrinking the size of the previous loops. Once the three-strand thread loop is complete, flip the bobbin over the base of the loop twice, cinching the start of all the thread in the loops together. This creates a pinch point that will allow you to better "close" the loop, trapping the already-placed dubbing in situ as you reach for the next pinch of loose dubbing.

6. Stack the three-strand waxed thread loop with the three ingredients you prepared and set aside earlier. Stack in the lighter color of the two dubbing materials first, then insert the piece of Frog's Hair and finish up with the darker of the two colors of dubbing. The two sections of dubbing should be at least 3 inches (8 cm) long and packed in as dense as possible.

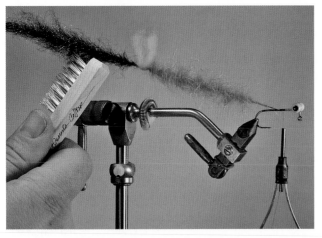

7. Twist the dubbing loop, turning it into a rope. After just a few twists, pull both ends of the Frog's Hair over onto the same side of the dubbing rope. After several more twists, rake out any loose dubbing. Do your best to keep the brush picked clean with the point of a bodkin, and brush out one end of the rope and clean out the dubbing from the brush before moving onto the other end. This allows you to salvage

excess dubbing and keep the two colors from mixing—this is important, as this pattern consumes a lot of dubbing.

8. Once you have as many twists in the dubbing rope as it can take (too many twists will break the rope off right at the hook shank), grasp the Frog's Hair and use it to pull back on the rope as you would draw a bowstring. Let the drawn dubbing rope have a small amount of slack, just enough for it to show you which way it wants to furl, then encourage that by gently twisting the Frog's Hair. Find just the right angle to hold the end of the dubbing rope as it furls back over itself to create the desired spacing in the variegated tail.

9. Once the entire dubbing rope has been furled (creating the tail), cut the tail from the hook shank (don't let go of the butt end or it will unwrap!) and tie it down to the hook shank at the desired length. The end of the furled section of the tail should extend 1⅜ inches (35 mm) out past the hook bend. You can't measure out to the tip of the tail because it still needs to be trimmed.

10. Trim the butt end of the furled tail right at the transition point between the original thread base and the secondary thread base—trim the butt at a slight angle, as this will increase ease and tidiness when wrapping later materials over this buildup. Tie the furled tail down all the way back to the rear of the hook shank and let the bobbin hang so the thread is at the rear of the shank. It will take many tight thread wraps to compress the dubbing, which is needed to properly secure the tail and reduce bulk in the body of the fly. Trim the Frog's Hair tail tip to ½ inch (13 mm)—this should make the overall length of this fly somewhere between 3 and 3¼ inches (76 to 83 mm).

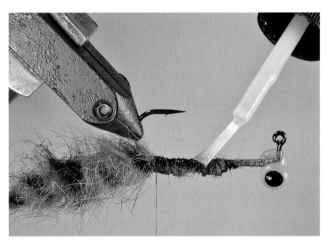

11. Lock everything in place with Zap-A-Gap. Coat the entire original thread base, to include the thread over the arbor of the lead eyes, with this adhesive. When applying Zap-A-Gap to the furled tail tie-down, brush it onto the hook-shank side (rotate the fly to do this), as this will ensure the butt of the tail is properly bonded to the secondary thread base.

12. Add a small dab of Zap-A-Gap to the junction of the Frog's Hair tail tip and the furled section of the tail. It is important for a tiny amount of the adhesive to soak into the tail tip, but too much will turn the entire tip into a hard ball—the desired outcome is to have a tail tip that does not shed even when pulled at, but that remains soft. Touch the junction spot lightly with the Zap-A-Gap brush, then roll it quickly between your fingers to immediately set the adhesive.

13. Once the tail tip is permanently fixed, it is now safe to shape and trim. Use a bodkin to "fluff up" the tail tip and pick out any loose fibers.

14. Once the Frog's Hair tail tip is picked out with a bodkin, trim it into a more natural, tapered shape (while maintaining the same length).

15. Select a single strand of the rubber legs and tie it in at the very rear of the hook shank (butting up against the base of the furled tail). Fold the rubber leg material in half around the thread between the fly and the end of the bobbin, then use the bobbin to draw the rubber leg down into its proper place on the side of the hook shank. Use three or four additional thread wraps to ensure one of the ends of rubber leg is fixed in place. Next, pull the other end of the rubber leg over the top of the hook shank and secure it in place with more thread wraps.

16. Once the rear pair of rubber legs are in place (extending out at either side of the hook shank at the base of the furled tail), snip off a 5½-inch (14 cm) length of wire from its spool and tie it down at the rear of the hook shank. This length of wire will be just long enough to use as the ribbing over the body of the fly and allow just enough to hold onto while wrapping. Be sure to tie the wire in so it extends off the back of the hook shank from the side (same as the rubber leg on that side)—this is to set up the first wire wrap at the proper interval away from the base of the tail.

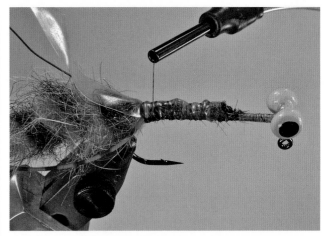

17. Tie the end of a length of clear ¼-inch Scud Back onto the top of the hook shank and all the way back to the base of the tail. Unlike the wire (which will be wrapped), the entire piece of Scud Back can be tied down straight out of the package. The Scud Back will just lie back out of the way until later when it is folded back over the body of the fly, so by not cutting off individual lengths and then trimming the excess, you conserve a lot of material.

18. Select a length of rabbit strip at least 3 inches (8 cm) long of the darker of the two colors you will be using on this fly. Trim the forward end into a point—this will reduce bulk under the rabbit in the initial wrap or two.

19. Tie in the rabbit strip at the rear of the fly by its forward (prepared) end. Be sure to tie it in off to the side of the hook shank (the same place the wire is tied). Once the rabbit is secured in place, wrap the thread forward and let the bobbin hang at the junction of the original thread base and the secondary thread base, or what is now the forward end of the material buildup from all the tied-down odds and ends hanging off the back of the hook.

20. Wrap the rabbit strip forward onto the hook shank. I will often brush a sparse streak of Zap-A-Gap over the top of the material buildup on the hook shank before wrapping the rabbit over it—this increases the durability of the fly.

21. Wrap the rabbit strip up to where the bobbin is hanging and tie it down. Trim away the excess rabbit.

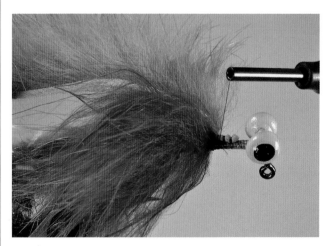

22. Prepare the forward end of a second strip of rabbit (of the lighter of the two colors) the same as the first piece of rabbit—trim the tip to a point. Tie the prepared end of the rabbit strip in right where you left off with the first strip. Once the end of the rabbit is secured, wrap the thread forward and let the bobbin hang directly behind the painted lead eyes.

23. Wrap the rabbit strip forward to the painted lead eyes and tie it down directly behind the eyes. Trim away the excess rabbit strip. Use the tips of your scissors to trim, and be careful not to accidentally cut any of the rabbit fur.

24. Prepare the body of the fly for the Scud Back by pulling all the fur off to either side of the hook shank. Wet your fingers to help control the rabbit fur—this also keeps the fur parted and in place long enough to fold the Scud Back over the body of the fly.

25. Fold the Scud Back over the part in the rabbit fur and tie it down behind the painted lead eyes. Do not immediately

trim away the excess. Pull the Scud Back toward the rear of the fly and use several more tight thread wraps to further secure the end of the Scud Back in place. Trim away the excess Scud Back, but be sure to leave a short tag end of the material. By folding the Scud Back over itself in the tie-down and leaving a tag end, you have greatly reduced the chances of the material pulling free (a hazard when tying down any stretchy material).

26. Wrap the wire forward over the Scud Back and through the rabbit fur. Be sure not to trap any of the fur with each wrap of wire—this is easier to avoid with the help of a bodkin. It should take about five or six turns to spiral the wire to the rear of the painted lead eyes. Tie the wire down behind the eyes and clip away the excess.

27. Select a second single strand of the rubber legs and tie it down between the rabbit fur body and the painted lead eyes. Use thread wraps to position the material so it creates a leg on either side of the fly, protruding out from behind each painted eye.

28. Wet your fingers and part the lighter-colored rabbit fur at the front of the fly and apply a very small dab of head cement (*not* Zap-A-Gap) to the hide exposed by the parting of the fur. This will encourage the lighter-colored rabbit fur to remain off to the sides where (once marabou is tied on top) it can always be seen.

29. Select two good straight-fibered marabou blood quills.

30. Wet one of the marabou feathers and slick it back so you can mount it precisely and see where the tips will line up. Tie the feather down directly behind the painted lead eyes, but just off to one or the other side of the hook

eye. The tips of the feather should be about even with the farthest rearward tips of rabbit fur.

31. Wet and slick back the second marabou feather and tie it down on the other side of the hook eye—both feather tips should be even. Trim the butt ends of the marabou feather.

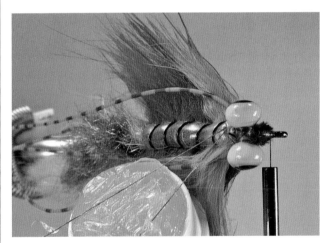

32. Create a 4-inch (10 cm) thread loop, then wrap the thread forward and let the bobbin hang so the thread is directly behind the hook eye—because this is a jig hook, you will have to turn the vise so the fly is on its side to keep the thread in place and out of the way. Wax the thread loop in preparation for the dubbing.

33. Fill the waxed thread loop with the chosen head dubbing.

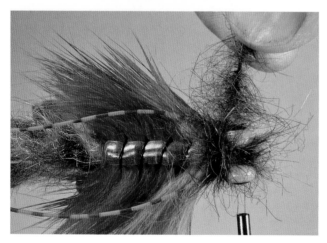

34. Once the thread loop is full of dubbing, twist it to form a dubbing rope, then brush it out with your dubbing brush. Once the dubbing is properly brushed out, wrap the dubbing rope between the painted eyes at least once from both angles as well as a full couple wraps entirely behind the set of eyes. Finish the wraps directly behind the hook eye.

35. Tie off the dubbing rope directly behind the hook eye. Do a whip-finish knot. Trim the excess dubbing rope and the thread. Apply a small dab of Zap-A-Gap to the finish knot.

36. Use a wire dubbing brush to brush out the head dubbing, then rotate the fly upside down (the start position) and trim the brushed-out dubbing so it is cropped short on the front and top (actually the bottom, as the fly is meant to swim).

37. Remove the fly from the vise and trim all four rubber legs to their proper length. The rear two legs should extend out past the tail tip about ¼ inch (6 mm) and the forward two legs should be trimmed even with the base of the tail tip, or at the very rear end of the furled section of the tail.

PATTERN VARIATION

GEEZUS LIZARD (BLACK & OLIVE)

Hook: #1/0 Gamakatsu Jig 90 Heavy Wire (Round Bend)

Thread: Black 3/0 Danville's Waxed Monocord

Eyes: Yellow painted lead dumbbell eyes (large)

Wax: BT's Tacky Dubbing Wax

Tail Dubbing 1: Red fox squirrel nymph-abdomen Dave Whitlock SLF

Tail Tip: Golden yellow Montana Fly Frog's Hair

Tail Dubbing 2: Dark stone nymph Dave Whitlock SLF

Adhesive: Zap-A-Gap

Legs: Natural grizzly barred rubber legs (medium)

Ribbing: Ginger (or fluorescent orange) UTC Ultra Wire (medium)

Back: Clear Scud Back (¼")

Body 1: Black rabbit strip

Body 2: Olive rabbit strip

Head Cement: Hard-as-Hull

Top: Black marabou blood quill

Head Dubbing: Hellgrammite Dave Whitlock SLF

MUDSLIDER

Hook: #4 Tiemco 5263

Thread: Rusty brown 140-denier UTC Ultra Thread

Rear Dubbing: Nearnuff crayfish natural brown Dave Whitlock SLF

Antennae: Rusty brown Krystal Flash

Rubber Legs: Brown Perfectly Barred Sili Legs

Eyes: Plain lead dumbbell eyes (small)

Claws: Rust rabbit strip

Rib: Gold UTC Ultra Wire (brassie)

Exoskeleton: Tan Scud Back (¼")

Body: Crawfish orange rabbit strip

Head Cement: Zap-A-Gap

The Mudslider is a crayfish pattern created by Patrick Knackendoffel, originally of Grand Junction, Colorado. Patrick was guiding out of the same fly shop I was while he attended the University of Colorado Boulder. The Scud Back and wire ribbing of the Mudslider was the inspiration behind the body of my Geezus Lizard pattern. Patrick's pattern is one of my favorite crayfish flies for both large-mouth and smallmouth bass, and I would have included an extensive tying tutorial here if I had not already done a small version of it in an earlier book, *The Best Carp Flies* (Headwater Books, 2015).

BALL PEEN CRAW

T he Ball Peen is a suggestive crawfish pattern originally designed to be a carp fly and is a direct descendant of Ian Anderson's Hammerhead. The name of the fly itself is an ode to the pattern that influenced it, as a ball-peen hammer is a smaller, lightweight version of what could be argued (because of its size and weight) is the sledgehammer of carp flies. Ian first tied his Hammerhead fly in 2009 while on a carp expedition to Beaver Island in Lake Michigan.

The Ball Peen Craw is a simple and suggestive crayfish imitation.

Ben Rogers nets a beauty smallmouth on a cloudy day. *Jon Luke* photo.

Many fly anglers have been introduced to the big cray-fish attractor pattern while on similar fishing trips to that island or other destinations around the Great Lakes. The fly certainly wins the hearts and minds of the big (20- to even 30-pound) common carp hunting the flats of the Great Lakes, thus equally gaining esteem among the anglers.

The fallout happens afterward, as the fly's size and weight limits it to being a regionally successful carp fly. Many trav-eling fly anglers have found that the Hammerhead scares the daylights out of carp once they return to the smaller, less aggressive fish in their home states. The Ball Peen Craw was invented as an answer to this problem—creating a carp fly in a size, weight, and color combination suitable for more universal carp situations. The irony of this particular fly's evolution is that so many of the first (greatest?) carp flies ever tied started out as bass flies—Bob Clouser's Swimming Nymph comes to mind. This may be one of the first, or only, *carp* fly that is now being tied regularly as a bass fly. Turnabout is fair play, I suppose.

My initial reaction after tying the very first Ball Peen was, "Dang . . . that would make a great smallmouth fly!" My imagination transported me like a cheesy movie flashback to the hot summer days I spent fishing the Huron River in Ohio as a child. My mother would drop me off in the Milan town square and I would slip past the Wonder Bar, down a side street leading past the old steel plant and on down to the river. I would get picked back up just before dark, two and a half miles upriver, by the Lovers Lane Bridge. The river there was low and clear during the summer months, but still held a decent mix of fish. I could find rock bass, creek chubs, longnose gar, quillback . . . and the occasional prized smallmouth bass. I was armed with a slow-action fiberglass fly rod borrowed from my father and a cheap plastic box of wet flies. I was too young to drive, had no television at home and no local fly shop, and the only fly-tying resource I had available to me was a copy of *Trout and Salmon Flies* by

Douglas Sutherland and Jack Chance. How this fishing fly book published in Great Britain found its way onto my fam-ily's bookshelf is still a mystery, but being the only influence at the time, caused me to tie and fish nothing but Bloody Butchers, Wickham's Fancys, and other classic wet flies to bass, thinking this was how one did such things.

It did not take me too long, even as a learning disabled youth, to figure out it was the crawfish that got the atten-tion of some of the larger bass in that river. I would see the little crustaceans darting away from my feet at I waded upstream, and I would sometimes steal a wire deep-fryer cage from the kitchen to aid in their capture. They fasci-nated me. Being the budding fly designer that I was and having a wide-open summer vacation schedule, I set about tying the most realistic crawfish imitations I could muster. I put some great stuff on hooks back then, but never did any of these creations fish even close to as well as just a plain brown Woolly Bugger. It took me a long time to figure out that fish are not impressed with what we think they will be impressed with . . . not even close. All that mattered was if the fly moved like it was alive and swam like a real crayfish. Many years later I would read research done in Berkeley laboratories that concluded bass actually preferred crayfish that had lost both their pincers. So much for my awesome fake crawfish hands.

It was the memory of these childhood fly-tying tribula-tions that triggered the red flag in my mind (like an ice fisher's tip up). The fly I scaled down for spooky Colorado carp was just the right size, color, and shape to be a poten-tial smallie slayer. Most importantly, the Ball Peen Craw moved through the water just like a real crayfish. The fly would undulate slightly while being rested and dart up when retrieved, only to dart straight back to the perceived sanctu-ary of the muddy bottom afterward—the length of bead chain making the slightest of crayfish-like clicking noises against rocks. The fly is simple, lively, and suggestive. Perfect.

BALL PEEN CRAW (RUST)

Hook: #6 Tiemco 3769

Thread: Dark brown 140-denier UTC Ultra Thread

Tail Flash: Rusty brown Krystal Flash

Tail Rubber: Brown Perfectly Barred Sili Legs

Eyes: Black bead chain (medium)

Adhesive: Zap-A-Gap

Wax: BT's Tacky Dubbing Wax

Body, Rear 1/3: Nearnuff crayfish brown Dave
Whitlock SLF Dubbing

Body, Forward 2/3: Rusty brown Crawdub

Head Cement: Zap-A-Gap

2. Select four strands of Krystal Flash. You can pull the entire strands out from the plastic zip tie they are bundled with or cut them from one side or the other. If you choose to cut them, be sure they are all over 4 inches (10 cm) long.

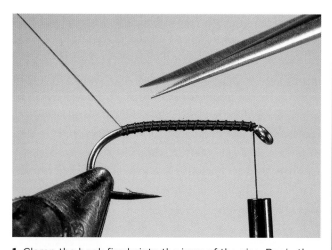

1. Clamp the hook firmly into the jaws of the vise. Begin the thread wraps behind the hook eye and wrap the thread to the rear of the hook shank—creating a solid but thin thread base. The UTC thread lies flat, so let the bobbin hang free and spin it until the thread twists up enough to become round. Spiral wrap the now-rounded thread forward and let the bobbin hang free with the thread resting immediately behind the hook eye. The round thread over the flat thread creates a base with a greater ability to grip material and, like knots in a garrote, does not let objects spin around on you. Trim the thread tag at the rear of the thread base.

3. Fold the four strands of Krystal Flash around the exposed thread between the hook shank and the tip of the bobbin and draw the material down onto the hook shank. The flash material needs to be tied in immediately behind the hook eye, and the forward four strands then need to be swept back over the hook shank and tied down all the way to the rear of the thread base—creating eight strands of flash sticking out the back. This fly will be later trimmed to an overall length of 2 inches (5 cm), so be sure to have enough length on both ends of the initial material tie-down.

the usual thread wraps—this keeps the cluster of rubber legs from flaring too much. Flared legs would not normally be such a bad thing, but in this case they could alter the way this delicately balanced fly swims. Bring the thread forward again and let the bobbin hang free a hook-eye length behind the hook eye. When tying down the rubber legs, I like to leave two small gaps in the thread wrapping just behind the hook eye, leaving two bits of exposed rubber that bulge up slightly—this creates a subtle "saddle" in which I rest the bead-chain eyes once they are ready to tie down.

4. Select four strands of the Sili Legs rubber.

5. Tie the rubber legs down the same way and in the same place as the Krystal Flash. It is crucial that this material is tied in immediately behind the hook eye, as the material buildup here is needed to lift the bead-chain eyes (that will be tied on shortly) up off the hook shank, creating what I call a "natural lift kit." This slight lift will ensure the fly is balanced properly—which makes it swim hook point up.

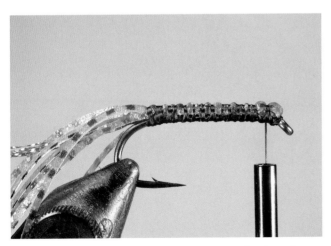

6. Tie down the clump of Sili Legs all the way back to the rear of the hook. The tension in the last few wraps at the very rear of this tie-down should be kept a bit lighter than

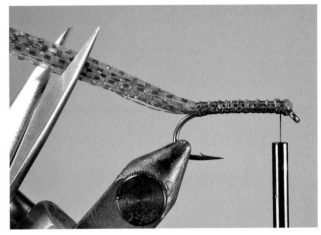

7. Trim the entire tail (the eight strands of Krystal Flash and eight strands of Sili Legs) so that the entire fly is 2 inches (5 cm) long.

8. Snip off a four-bead section from a length of bead chain. Use wire cutters. Often there will be a short length of the severed link protruding from one of the end beads—be sure to clip it off, as it is both unsightly and can throw off the balance of the fly.

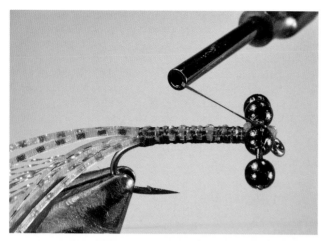

9. Set the bead chain into the little rubber saddle created earlier and tie it down by the middle link in the chain.

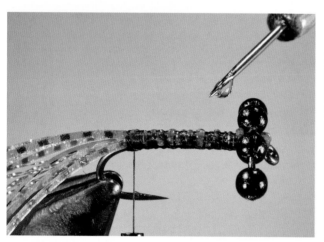

10. Wind the thread to the rear of the thread base/butt of the tail. Apply a drop of Zap-A-Gap to the thread tie-down for the bead chain and the area on the hook shank directly behind the bead chain. This fly is designed to be lightweight but ride hook point up, so it is delicately balanced. The length of bead chain is abnormally long and susceptible to being leveraged off to one side or the other—this will drastically alter the way the fly swims. The glue will give the eyes a better chance at staying straight, thus keeping the fly riding true. Be careful not to let any of the glue seep into the length of bead chain—you want the chain to roll around freely while being fished.

11. Create a short thread dubbing loop (3 inches; 8 cm) at the rear of the fly. Bring the bobbin forward and let it hang free so that the thread comes down even with the hook point. Wax the thread loop using tacky dubbing wax. The wax keeps the dubbing stuck in the loop while you are "loading" it.

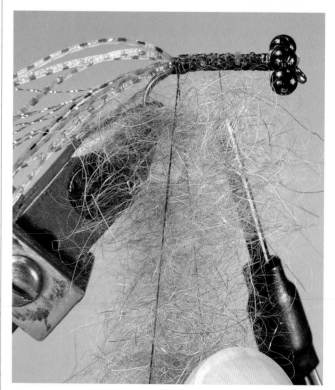

12. Load the thread loop with the SLF dubbing. All dubbing material will become tightly clumped up while enclosed in the little plastic bags they are sold in, so it is necessary to hand-blend or loosen up the dubbing before inserting it into the thread loop.

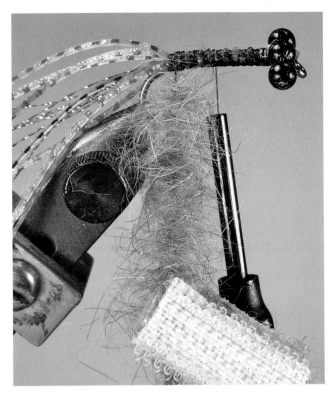

13. Close the thread loop and twist it until it forms a dense dubbing rope. Thoroughly rake out the dubbing rope so that it is as bushy as you can make it before wrapping it onto the hook shank. When raking softer or shorter-fibered dubbing, I prefer to use a homemade dubbing brush made by sticking adhesive-backed Velcro around the end of a pencil.

14. Wrap the dubbing rope forward onto the hook shank. Be sure to sweep back the longer dubbing fibers with your non-wrapping hand between each turn of the rope so as not to trap any fibers and so the body of the fly stays as bushy as possible. Wrap this dubbing rope up about one-third of the hook shank and stop at a point roughly even with the hook point. Tie the dubbing rope down at this point and trim the excess—if done right, there will not be any wasted dubbing, but it is not the end of the world if there is.

15. Create a second thread dubbing loop at the same point on the hook shank that you ended the first part of the dubbed body. This second loop should be longer than the first—roughly 4 inches (10 cm). Wax the thread loop. Bring the thread forward and park it and the bobbin immediately behind the bead chain.

16. Load the thread loop with the Crawdub. Put a bit more dubbing into the loop than you think you need, as you want the forward two-thirds of the fly to be as thick and bushy as possible.

17. Close the thread loop and twist it until it forms a dense dubbing rope.

18. Crawdub has much longer and coarser fibers, so it really binds up tight when twisted into a dubbing rope. I take extra time and use a much heavier dubbing brush for raking out this type of dubbing—and it needs to be raked out very well! Dennis Collier custom wire brushes are my favorite.

19. Once you have the dubbing rope raked out and as bushy as you can possibly make it, begin wrapping it forward onto the hook shank. Take deliberate measures to sweep back the long dubbing fibers with your non-wrapping hand with every turn. There is no point in brushing out the dubbing rope if it is just bound back into a tight clump on the fly. This also is the reason I do not utilize the rotary function on my fly-tying vise—maybe if I had that third hand I always wanted. Tie off the dubbing rope once it is wrapped up to the bead chain. On the last wrap I like to bring the dubbing rope over the top of the bead-chain tie-down area and secure it in place there—this eliminates the slight material gap between the dubbing and the bead chain.

20. Tie a whip-finish knot behind the hook eye, cut the thread close to the knot, and add a small drop of head cement or Zap-A-Gap to the finish knot. I find it much easier to tie the finish knot on this pattern if I cock the fly slightly toward me and turn the vise so the hook eye is facing me slightly—this way I can get the whip-finish tool around the length of bead chain. This is only possible if you are working with a rotary vise on a pedestal base.

21. Use a sturdy bodkin to pick out the dubbing. No matter how thoroughly you raked the dubbing loops before wrapping them onto the hook shank, there is still work to be done—this fly needs to be *bushy!* Take a good minute or two to really pick out all the bound-down dubbing fibers you can.

22. Once you have used a bodkin to pick out as much of the dubbing fibers as you can, use a coarse wire dubbing brush to rake all the fibers so they sweep back toward the rear of the fly.

23. Remove the fly from the vise and trim all the dubbing from the bottom, or "belly," of the fly. This is easily

accomplished if the fly is held firmly by the hook bend with one hand and trimmed with scissors from the rear of the fly (against the "grain," or direction the dubbing fibers are lying) with your other hand. It is important that this fly gets a tight belly trim, as this is crucial in making the fly swim hook point up the way it is supposed to. The tightly cropped belly will allow the fly to glide or dart back to the bottom of the lake or river during a fishing retrieve as well—like a spooked crayfish. The trim job also exposes the color variation of the two dubbings used, which is nice.

PATTERN VARIATION

BALL PEEN CRAW (SOFTSHELL)

Hook: #6 Tiemco 3769

Thread: Tan 140-denier UTC Ultra Thread

Tail Flash: Bonefish tan Krystal Flash

Tail Rubber: Pumpkin/black flake Sili Legs

Eyes: Gold bead chain (medium)

Adhesive: Zap-A-Gap

Wax: BT's Tacky Dubbing Wax

Body, Rear 1/3: Softshell saltwater Dave Whitlock
    SLF Dubbing

Body, Forward 2/3: Tan Crawdub

Head Cement: Zap-A-Gap

TRI-MINNOW

I met Thomas Ziegler in a fly shop in Boulder, Colorado, in the spring of 2007. I liked the guy right off—he seemed to know his way around the shop I was working at (although it was his first time in) and he actually stopped talking after asking a question. *Crazy.* It certainly helped that we shared a distinct Midwest humility and love of warm water.

The Tri-Minnow with articulation and lead eyes up front has an action that can best be described as a bucking bronco when retrieved.

Thomas Ziegler perfected his skills at the vise and on the water during his college years at the University of Missouri, where he studied fisheries and wildlife. *Ted Calcaterra* photo.

I believe one of the first questions he ever asked me was along the lines of "How is the bass fishing out here?" accompanied by a facial expression that told me he feared the answer and the answer was not going to be good—he was a new arrival in Rocky Mountain trout country, after all. However, by pure happenstance, he had just run into another serious bass angler.

Tom is an avid fly tier (I gathered that much right from the start, based on the things he came in to buy), and eventually I figured out he was a quite good fly tier. Soon, and for selfish reasons, I coerced him into hosting some of the Saturday morning fly-tying demonstrations. It was during one of these weekend demos while Tom was entertaining the troops with his vise and stories that I eavesdropped and learned more about him. Turns out he had managed a fly shop for a few years back in his home state of Missouri. *No wonder.* This made me like the guy even more—not just because we shared some basic work history, but because

it took me almost a year to learn about it. In an industry where it is not uncommon for customers to fill you in on their experience and expertise within minutes of walking into your fly shop, Tom's unpretentious style was refreshing.

Born in 1971 to an angling father, Tom grew up fishing in the Missouri Ozarks with the occasional, but highly anticipated, summer trips to the Catskills, the Adirondacks, and the wilds of Montana. He learned to tie his own trout flies while peering over his father's shoulder, and it did not take long before he was using his talents at the vise to finance his fishing. Tom Hargrove, the well-loved owner/operator of St. Louis's T. Hargrove Fly Fishing, Inc., once commissioned an order of 500 scuds from the young Ziegler boy and paid him with a brand-new 7-weight Sage.

Tom and his angling both came of age during his college years at the University of Missouri, where he studied fisheries and wildlife. This era in his life was what he describes as his "warm water, wild trout, and Pearl Jam phase." Tom

Wade fishing for smallmouth bass in moving water may be the most fun an angler can have with a fly rod. Ted Calcaterra on the Huzzah River, Missouri. *Thomas Ziegler* photo.

and his Mizzou classmates would take road trips to explore some of the state's spring-fed streams that held wild rainbows. These waters also provided Tom an introduction to smallmouth bass. As it turned out, the trout streams were an hour and a half to two hours from his college apartment, but there were a plethora of old reclaimed strip-mining pits a mere 15 miles away loaded with largemouth bass—after this discovery, it was lucky Tom ever graduated. He and his roommates acquired a 14½-foot red Old Town canoe, and they would spend their off days (and skip days) exploring the sprawling labyrinth of man-made ponds.

After college, Tom drifted a bit, as those freshly released from institution are prone to do. He spent a couple years in Yellowstone cleaning hotel rooms and fishing, but the lure of Missouri and the vibe he liked around Columbia brought him back. Tom found work as an environmental toxicologist for a while, but soon fell into the fly-fishing industry he had been tap-dancing around for years. He began managing the Clearwater Fly Shop in Columbia in 1996, the same year he married his wife, Teresa. But, as a new husband with intentions to become a family man, Tom quickly realized "shop life" was not going to cut it. He had to find more respectable work, and did, as a project manager at Boeing in St. Louis—the company that also paid for him to go back to school and earn his MBA.

On a fortuitous family vacation to Colorado in the summer of 2006, Tom and Teresa (and by then their son Bobby and daughter Katie) hatched their plan to move west. As they drove through the town of Longmont, Colorado, they looked at each other and said, "We should retire to a place like this." And then they decided, on the spot, they would live where they wanted immediately. *Why wait?* By April of 2007 Tom had landed a job with Ball Aerospace in Boulder and found a house in Broomfield for his family. All that was left was to track down a local fly shop and get acquainted.

That's when I met Tom.

The more I got to know him, the more I liked him. Tom was smart and easy to talk to, and it helped that he liked to fish for bass. He was a darn fine fly tier as well. The Tri-Minnow pattern of his caught and held my eye the longest. At first pass I was confused as to the rationale behind a fly made almost entirely of tightly packed and trimmed deer hair, but with heavy lead eyes at the front. It seemed like a hydrodynamic oxymoron . . . as well as one heck of a mouthful for the fish. Upon further scrutiny, and alone time with it on the water, I figured out why it worked and why I loved it. Sure, the hair wanted it to float and the eyes wanted it to sink, but that conflict gave the pattern somewhat of a neutral

buoyancy that kept the fly in the desired zone longer and gave it the opportunity for more erratic and unpredictable movement—all virtues in a bass fly.

The Tri-Minnow was first made for the largemouth bass in the ponds near Tom's college apartment and further tested on the stream smallmouth of Missouri. The fly gained brief notoriety in an article Tom wrote for the June/July 1998 issue of *Warmwater Fly Fishing*. In the article, a fly-tying tutorial is included, and as I sit now and look over it I realize just how far the pattern has evolved. Back then the Tri-Minnow was only tied on a single hook—the articulation didn't happen until later. The version Tom first showed me in the fly shop was very similar to the one I now fish (and which is featured in this book), but both hooks remained intact. The 1998 version utilized lead wire around the hook shank instead of lead eyes, which gave the fly a more horizontal, Slug-Go jerk bait action in the water, whereas the newer Tri-Minnow with articulation and lead eyes up front has an action that can best be described as a bucking bronco when retrieved. I recommend experimenting with all manifestations of this streamer, even unweighted topwater variations.

TRI-MINNOW (WHITE)

Hooks: Two #4 Tiemco 811S

Thread 1: White 3/0 Danville's Waxed Monocord

Tail Flash: Pearl Flashabou

Tail: White rabbit strip

Adhesive: Zap-A-Gap

Thread 2: White 200-denier UTC G.S.P.

Body: White deer belly hair

Eyes: Fluorescent chartreuse painted lead dumbbell eyes (medium)

Hook Connector: RIO Powerflex Wire Bite Tippet (.016"/20 lb.)

Gill Slit: Red deer belly hair

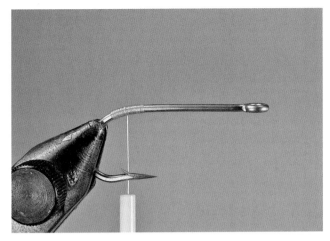

1. Mount a hook extra firmly in the jaws of the vise. Anytime I am going to be packing large amounts of spun deer hair onto a hook, I will mount the hook deep into the jaws to avoid movement or hook breakage while applying force during the act of packing hair. Begin the 3/0 waxed monocord thread between the hook point and the rear point of the barb, and wrap a solid thread base that extends back slightly onto the bend of the hook. Wrap the thread forward and let the bobbin hang so that the thread rests in the middle of the thread base.

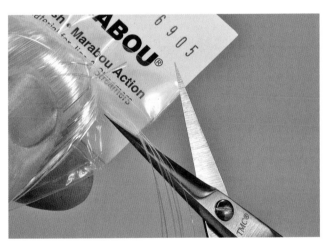

2. Select six strands of Flashabou to use as tail flash.

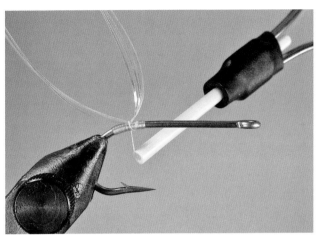

3. Tie down the six strands of Flashabou in the middle of the thread base you have built. Standard Flashabou comes in clumps of 10-inch (25 cm) strands, making the six you select plenty long enough to be tied down at their middle and folded over—giving you 12 tail strands of flash that cannot be easily pulled out. You will only need less than a 3-inch (8 cm) clump of the Flashabou, so technically you could save waste by getting three flies' worth out of each six-strand clump, but Flashabou reacts spastically to static electricity. As much as I like to conserve tying materials, in this instance it is seldom worth the hassle.

4. Trim the forward end of the rabbit hide strip into a point. The forward end is the end that was closest to the head of the rabbit. Hair "flows" to the rear. You *have* petted a cat before, right?

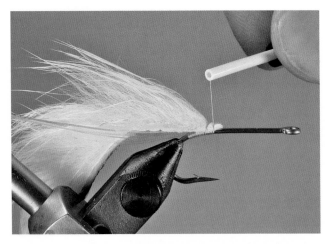

5. Tie the prepared rabbit strip down on top of the thread base. Let the trimmed tip of rabbit hide lie at a point a tad forward of the thread base and even with the tip of the hook point. Trimming the hide to a point and offsetting the tie-down location give the tail tie-in area a gradually sloping base that will be easier to pack deer hair onto later.

6. Use a half hitch or whip-finish knot to tie off the thread and then trim—you will be switching threads after this step. An extended-reach whip-finish tool is helpful when tying thread off so far back on a hook shank. Trim the rabbit strip so the hide extends behind the tie-down point 1½ inches (38 mm). Be sure to use the tips of your scissors and only sever the hide, not the actual fur—the fur should then extend farther behind the fly. Trim the 12 strands of Flashabou to the same length as the rabbit hide.

7. Trim the severed end of rabbit hide into a point. I always take the extra time to do this, as squared-off tail leather has an unnatural appearance.

8. Apply Zap-A-Gap to the entire tie-down area. Don't forget the underside.

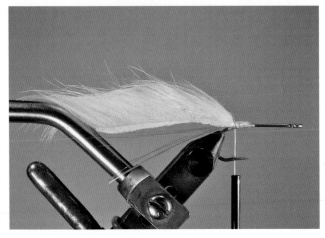

9. Quickly, before the Zap-A-Gap has a chance to dry, switch threads to the G.S.P. Begin the thread wraps just in front of the existing thread base and wrap back over the entire tie-down area. If you dally and allow the Zap-A-Gap to harden, this tie-down area will become unnecessarily bulky and the new thread will not have the durability advantage of being anchored in adhesive. The 3/0 waxed monocord is a round, abrasive thread better suited for mounting material firmly to a hook shank, whereas the 200-denier G.S.P is strong enough to allow you to crank down hard on a clump of deer hair and is slick and flat enough to make pushing (packing) the deer hair clumps back onto themselves much easier. In this tutorial I use a white ceramic bobbin for the waxed monocord and black for the G.S.P.

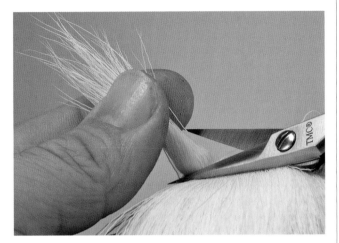

10. Cut off a fat clump of white deer belly hair.

11. Use a hair comb to help remove all the soft underfur and any broken or short hair from the base of the clump of deer hair.

12. Tie the first clump of deer hair in at the very rear of the tail tie-down area. Lay the deer hair down onto the top of the hook shank so that all the hair tips extend to the rear, out over the rabbit strip tail—this is done so, once the fly is finished (trimmed and shaved), there will be a few hairs remaining over the tail. This photo is taken after the hair has been allowed to migrate all the way around the hook shank, but before any thread tension has been applied—the hair will splay outward and stand up once this happens.

13. Cut, prep, and tie in several more clumps of deer hair. After each clump has been secured, be sure to compress the hair back onto the hook shank as much as possible. You can use just your thumb to do this if you wish, but a hair-packing tool will make this chore easier and avoid the inevitable sore thumb. Continue this process until you reach the hook eye. The more hair you can cram tightly onto the hook, the better.

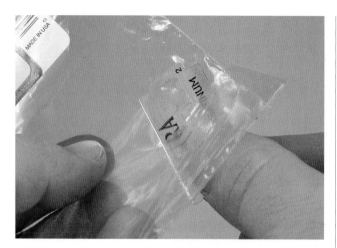

14. Once you have so much deer hair packed onto the hook that the last clump is bulging out over the hook eye, cut a short slit in a piece of plastic (the bag that the deer hair came in is perfect). You will slide this over the eye of the hook to push back the hair and allow you to more easily tie the whip-finish knot.

15. Slide the thread and hook eye through the slit in the plastic bag, pushing the deer hair back and out of the way. A couple extra thread wraps between the plastic and the hook eye will keep the plastic in place. Tie a tight and thorough whip-finish knot and trim the thread. Apply a small drop of Zap-A-Gap to the knot with the aid of a bodkin. Remove the hook from the vise and temporarily set this rear half of the fly aside.

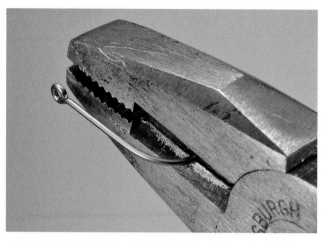

16. Take the second hook and clip it in the middle of the bend. Use heavy pliers with cutters for the job and be prepared for both pieces of the hook to fly off across the room . . . never to be seen again. Hold the shank and aim the point into a trash can.

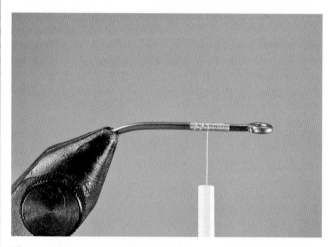

17. Insert the pointless hook into the jaws of the tying vise and clamp it as firmly as you did the first hook. There should be just enough of the hook bend remaining to allow a solid grip of the hook—this remaining bit of hook bend will also serve as a keel marker for the fly once you are done tying it and have moved on to the shaving and shaping of the finished Tri-Minnow. You could leave the point of the hook to be clipped once the fly is complete, but it will get in the way of both the hair packing and shaping. Begin thread wraps (back to the waxed monocord) one hook-eye width behind the hook eye and create a solid thread base that extends approximately two hook-eye widths down the hook shank. Bring the thread to a resting point in the middle of the thread base.

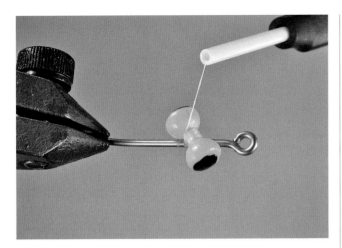

18. Rotate the hook shank and mount the lead dumbbell eyes onto the bottom of the thread base. If you are using a non-rotary vise, you will have to reposition the hook. The initial mounting thread wraps should be tight and leave the barbell eyes cocked at an angle on the hook shank. Once this is done, use a thumbnail to force the eyes straight, or perpendicular to the hook shank, and use additional tight thread wraps to secure it in place.

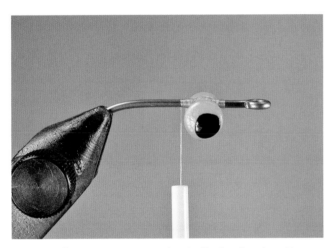

19. Once the eyes are mounted onto the hook, return the vise to the starting position and wrap the thread to the rear of the thread base and let the bobbin hang.

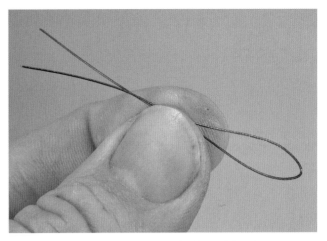

20. Cut a 4¼-inch (114 mm) length of wire bite tippet—use the same pliers used to clip the hook. Fold the wire in half.

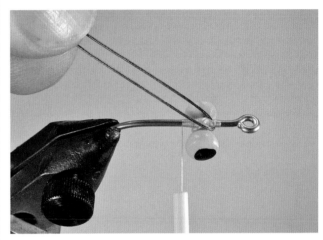

21. Take the loop of wire and "lasso" the front of the hook and pull back so the wire catches on the tied-down lead eyes.

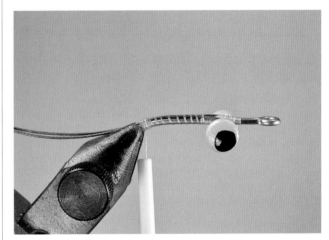

22. Tie both ends of the wire down over the top of the hook shank. Leave as much gap between each turn of thread as possible. Once you reach the end of the straight hook shank, wrap a short but solid band of thread to secure the wires in place. The wide spiral thread wraps are made to ensure the liquid adhesive you apply later will seep right down to the hook shank. Leave the bobbin hanging at the rear of the hook shank.

23. Locate the rear half of the fly that you temporarily set aside and thread the two ends of wire through the eye of the rear hook. Be sure the hook is pointed down, as the bushy deer hair will be completely hiding the hook and it is easy to make this mistake. Fold the two wire ends back over the top of the hook shank and secure them in place with thread wraps wound forward, stopping directly behind the lead eyes. There should be a small wire loop at the rear of the hook shank that is just big enough to allow free movement of the rear half of the fly, and the two ends of wire should extend out past the front of the hook eye.

24. Take each end of wire separately and wrap it over the lead eyes, under the hook shank, and then back on top of the hook shank. Use a couple tight wraps of thread to hold the wire in place. Repeat this process with the other end of wire, but in the opposite direction. The wire ends should be just long enough to extend over most of the hook shank but not interfere with the loop joint of the articulated streamer—this eliminates the need to clip off any excess wire.

25. Tie down the two ends of wire. Wrap the thread forward and tie off with a whip-finish knot. Trim the thread—you are now done with the waxed monocord.

26. Switch threads one last time to the G.S.P. and begin the thread wraps directly behind the lead eyes. Brush on a liberal amount of Zap-A-Gap. There should be ample amounts of the wire exposed, allowing sufficient gaps for the adhesive to soak all the way down to the hook shank—this ensures you have a very sturdy streamer. Before the adhesive dries, wrap the thread back to the rear of the hook shank.

27. Begin adding and packing in more clumps of deer hair from the rear of the hook shank all the way forward to the lead eyes—it will take several clumps of hair to reach this point. It will be harder to pack the hair clumps back onto themselves this time around because the hair is being tied down over the wire and thread base, but pack it in as best you can. Pause once you reach a point approximately one hook eye width behind the lead eye.

28. Cut out a clump of red deer belly hair and prepare it (brush out the underfur) the same way as all the other clumps of hair used on the body of this fly.

29. Rotate the fly so the lead eyes are on top, making it easier to tie in the clump of red deer hair—this will create the pronounced "bloody" gill slit once the fly is finished and shaved. Hold the clump of hair in place on the top side of the hook shank while tightening down with the thread in order to keep any of the hair from rotating around to the wrong side of the fly.

30. Pack at least two more clumps of white deer hair in behind the lead eyes before moving forward and tying in hair in front of the eyes. Hair should be bulging out over the eyes on both the top and bottom. It is crucial to get a large clump of white hair crammed in between the red hair and the lead eyes, as this is what will compress the red hair and push it back—this gives it a naturally arched gill-line shape once the fly is shaved.

31. Pack in as many clumps of deer hair as you can make fit on the front side of the lead eyes. The hair should now be bulging well over the hook eye. This will once again make the whip-finish knot difficult, so utilize the plastic-bag trick to wrap up the fly. Trim the thread once the knot is complete and add a small drop of Zap-A-Gap to the knot with the aid of a bodkin.

32. The tying portion of this fly is now complete—on to the shaving and shaping. Most of the finishing touches will be done after you remove the fly from the vise; however, the general Tri-Minnow shape should be made while the fly is still secure in the jaws of the vise, as this is the easiest way to know for sure the exact top and bottom of the streamer. To begin, shave the top of the fly flat.

33. Next, shave the sides at an angle, with the bottoms of both sides meeting to form a belly like a V-hulled boat of sorts. Be careful not to shave the painted pupils off the lead eyes.

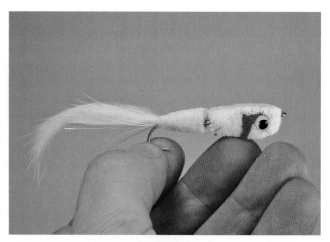

34. Once the general shape of the fly is achieved, remove the fly from the vise and finish shaving. The body of the Tri-Minnow should be triangular in shape (hence the name), viewed both broadside and head-on. It is very important that this fly be shaved down to the proper size—if it is slightly too fat or bulky, it will not sink. At no point in the head or body should the fly be wider than the lead eyes. The head should not be larger than ½ inch (13 mm) measured from the flat top to the angled bottom. The base of the deer hair body should be shaved down as slim as you can make it without severing any thread. I use cheap, double-sided razor blades to shave the fly into shape because I go through so many (one blade per fly). Use one side of the razor blade for all the rough cutting and save the other side for all the delicate work to finish up the fly.

PATTERN VARIATIONS

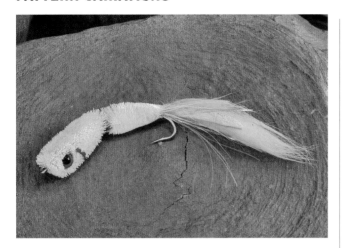

TRI-MINNOW (YELLOW)

Hooks: Two #4 Tiemco 811S

Thread 1: White 3/0 Danville's Waxed Monocord

Tail Flash: Yellow Flashabou

Tail: Fluorescent yellow chartreuse rabbit strip

Adhesive: Zap-A-Gap

Thread 2: White 200-denier UTC G.S.P.

Body: Fluorescent yellow deer belly hair

Eyes: Red painted lead dumbbell eyes (medium)

Hook Connector: RIO Powerflex Wire Bite Tippet (.016"/20 lb.)

Gill Slit: Red deer belly hair

TRI-MINNOW (TAN)

Hooks: Two #4 Tiemco 811S

Thread 1: White 3/0 Danville's Waxed Monocord

Tail Flash: Gold Holographic Flashabou

Tail: Tan rabbit strip

Adhesive: Zap-A-Gap

Thread 2: White 200-denier UTC G.S.P.

Body: Tan deer belly hair

Eyes: White painted lead dumbbell eyes (medium)

Hook Connector: RIO Powerflex Wire Bite Tippet (.016"/20 lb.)

Gill Slit: Red deer belly hair

TRI-MINNOW (OLIVE)

Hooks: Two #4 Tiemco 811S

Thread 1: White 3/0 Danville's Waxed Monocord

Tail Flash: Pearl Flashabou

Tail: Olive rabbit strip

Adhesive: Zap-A-Gap

Thread 2: White 200-denier UTC G.S.P.

Body: Olive deer belly hair

Eyes: Yellow painted lead dumbbell eyes (medium)

Hook Connector: RIO Powerflex Wire Bite Tippet (.016"/20 lb.)

Gill Slit: Red deer belly hair

TRI-MINNOW (BLACK)

Hooks: Two #4 Tiemco 811S

Thread 1: White 3/0 Danville's Waxed Monocord

Tail Flash: Black Holographic Flashabou

Tail: Black rabbit strip

Adhesive: Zap-A-Gap

Thread 2: White 200-denier UTC G.S.P.

Body: Black deer belly hair

Eyes: Gold painted lead dumbbell eyes (medium)

Hook Connector: RIO Powerflex Wire Bite Tippet (.016"/20 lb.)

Gill Slit: Red deer belly hair

TEXAS RINGWORM

I did not accidentally create the Texas Ringworm. I spent days curled into the fetal position on an old futon in a tiny, overpriced studio apartment in Boulder, Colorado, drinking cheap red wine and brainstorming. I was a single guy back then, living in that one-room rental (I stored belly boats in the bathtub) with a cat my sister left me when she fled the country.

The Texas Ringworm won the first-ever Best of Show trophy for a freshwater fly at the International Fly Tackle Dealer Show.

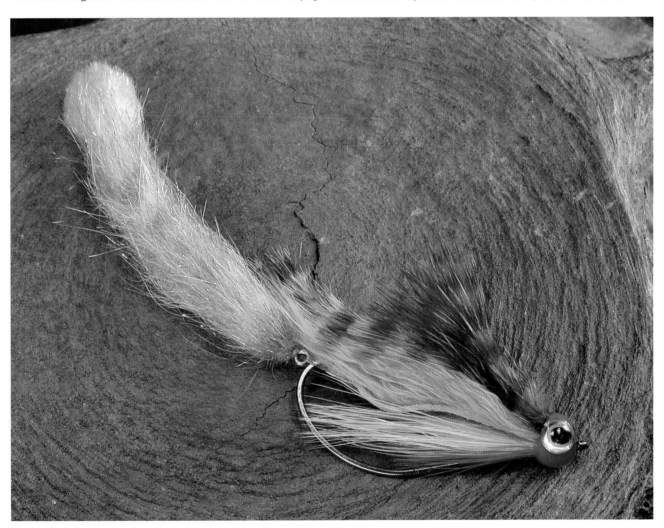

The Texas Ringworm uses a gangion to lock the hook into a weedless position like a properly rigged soft plastic and will disengage during the hook set, allowing the entire spear and bend of the hook to penetrate the mouth of the bass that eats it.

I was guiding for a local fly shop that paid just enough to keep my pickup running and me off the street. Money was scarce, so I was looking to earn a buck wherever and however I could. I was sending how-to articles to fishing magazines and giving casting and fly-tying lessons, as well as collecting meager royalties from fly patterns I had invented.

Umpqua Feather Merchants had already picked up a couple of my patterns and I had a new one, the Geezus Lizard, coming out in the wholesale catalog that year. This was a subsurface bass fly that got Umpqua's attention

because it had a unique, multicolored furled dubbing loop tail. I knew as soon as the catalog hit the steps of fly shops nationally, my new tail idea was going to be on the radar of every serious fly designer in the country. There would be knockoffs coming from smaller fly wholesalers with marginal scruples (that was a given), but what I was most worried about was someone taking my idea and making it better. It was going to happen. There are some amazing and talented fly tiers holding brooms and flipping Closed/Open signs on front doors of shops around this country, and as stimulating as being a part of this loosely assembled creative community can be, it is downright *competitive* when you are a starving trout bum (or bass bum) hoping the next royalty check will have enough left for cat food after the rent is paid.

I have a long history cluttered with different styles of angling. My grandfather taught me how to throw a seine when I was barely old enough to tie my own shoes, and I ran trot lines with my own father before I started kindergarten . . . I have bait fished, commercially fished, trolled, snagged, trespassed, and even used conventional bass gear. We all have a past and some of them are not polite table conversation, but it is what we glean from those experiences that can turn embarrassments into *know-how*.

The deadliest trick I ever learned while holding a spin rod was how to rig soft plastics. I would collect and covet these "rubber worms" that came in big, slimy, self-sealing bags (to keep the contents fresh like a pouch of Beech-Nut). To rig one, first you chose the right-size lead bullet weight to slide onto the line, then you would tie on your worm hook. You picked your favorite plastic from a bag, threaded the hook through its nose, and brought the hook point back and buried it farther down into the soft body of the lure. This is known as a Texas-rigged rubber worm—maybe the most dangerous and weedless bass rig ever pitched into lukewarm water.

As I lay there on my futon deep in trout country, I remembered those long summers in the South and bags full of artificial worms, grubs, and salamanders. I had already perfected a way for a fly tier to emulate one of these long, soft plastic lures using thread and dubbing, but now I had to invent a way to turn that Geezus Lizard tail into a Texas-rigged worm. My overly romantic imagination had me convinced I was on the hunt for the holy grail of bass flies. I had cheap wine and lots of time—all I was missing was a squire with coconuts.

The fly I came up with is the Texas Ringworm. It does all the things it needs to do. This fly fishes just like a 4½-inch soft plastic worm—it is flexible and undulates in the water, and the size 2 hook stays inverted (hook point up) with only the very tip of the spear sticking out of the body. The long furled tail makes up the rear half of the fly, while the big secret up front is the thin wire, flexible hook attached to the tail with a fluorocarbon "gangion" (a term used for a short, stout line attached to a longline, which I used when I worked as a commercial halibut fisherman). The hook uses this gangion to lock into a weedless position like a properly rigged soft plastic and will disengage during the hook set, allowing the entire spear and bend of the hook to penetrate the mouth of the bass that ate it. The Texas Ringworm is light enough to be easily cast with a stiff 5-weight fly rod and floating line when on a small farm pond, but can be equally deadly when cast with a heavier rod and a sink-tip fly line in rivers or deeper bodies of water. Many times an aggressive fish will take it and run while the fly is still sinking. This fly is every bit as effective as any soft plastic I have ever fished, with the added luxury of never having to be replaced like a chewed-up rubber worm.

The Texas Ringworm was picked up by Umpqua Feather Merchants and won them their first-ever Best of Show trophy for a fly at the International Fly Tackle Dealer Show. I now only teach classes when I want to, have three well-fed cats . . . and have long since left that little apartment in Boulder.

Even if it is for just an hour after work, any time on bass water is rewarding.

TEXAS RINGWORM (SUNFISH)

Hook 1: #4 Tiemco 105

Thread 1: White 3/0 Danville's Waxed Monocord

Wax: BT's Tacky Dubbing Wax

Tail Dubbing 1: Minnow belly Dave Whitlock SLF

Tail Tip: Yellow Senyo's Laser Dub

Tail Dubbing 2: Dragonfly nymph olive Dave Whitlock SLF

Adhesive: Zap-A-Gap

Gangion Tube: Light olive tubing (standard)

Gangion: RIO Fluoroflex tippet (.017"/25 lb.)

Main Body: Light olive Hareline Olive Barred Magnum Rabbit Strip

Hook 2: #2 Tiemco 8089

Thread 2: Olive 6/0 UNI-Thread

Throat 1: Fluorescent red marabou blood quills

Throat 2: Shell pink marabou blood quills

Top Body: Olive grizzly marabou

Head Resin 1: Yellow Loon UV Fly Paint

Eyes: Orange/black pupil Hareline Oval Pupil 3D Eyes ($\frac{3}{16}$")

Head Resin 2: Red Loon UV Fly Paint

Head Resin 3: Loon UV Knot Sense

Head Cement: Hard as Hull

1. Before mounting the first hook, prepare some of the materials for this fly. It is a time-saving practice to cut all the rubber tubing and fluorocarbon leader material for the dozen or so Ringworms you intend to tie, but it is only essential you prepare the three dubbings used for the furled tail (as you will have only one hand free once the process begins). Most important is the Laser Dub used for the tip of the tail—hand stack a clump of the material to form a clump with all the fibers straight and somewhat even. In the case of the black eel color variation, you will need to blend two dubbings to get just the right color.

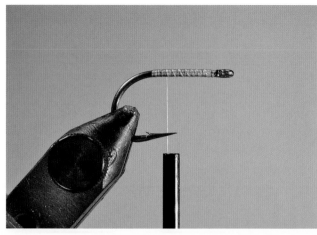

2. Once the tail dubbing is prepared and at the ready, mount the first hook (#4 Tiemco 105) firmly into the vise and create a solid thread base using thread 1 (white 3/0 Danville's Waxed Monocord). The thread base should begin immediately behind the hook eye and extend the entire length of the straight hook shank. Leave the bobbin hanging so the thread is slightly behind the tip of the hook.

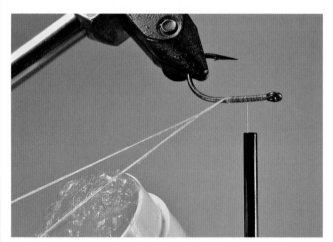

3. Rotate the vise so the hook point is up and out of the way. Pull long lengths of thread from the bobbin, one length at a time, creating a long three-strand thread loop around the index finger of your non-tying hand. Three strands of the 3/0 thread is needed to give the finished tail the proper stiffness (once furled, the tail will have 12 strands of thread running through it). Once the thread loop has been created, wrap the thread forward slightly and let the bobbin hang so the thread is in the middle of the thread base. Wax the entire thread loop in preparation for the dubbing.

4. Fill the waxed thread loop with the three separate dubbings that were prepared earlier. Begin with the lighter of the two tail dubbing colors, add the Laser Dub tail tip in the middle, and then finish with the darker of the two tail dubbings. The overall length of this dubbing loop should be 5½ inches (14 cm).

5. Twist the dubbing loop until the thread at the butt of the loop (right at the hook) begins to bunch up onto itself and is in danger of breaking. After the first two or three rotations in the twist, stop and fold both sides of the tail tip dubbing onto the same side of what is now a dubbing rope. Stop twisting occasionally throughout the process to brush out and loosen the dubbing fibers on either side of the middle tail tip that are getting bound up tight by the twisting. To avoid "cross-pollination" and to conserve dubbing material, clean out the dubbing brush and save the excess before moving down and brushing out the other side.

6. Once the dubbing rope has maximum twist, rotate the vise (so the hook point is down) and pull back on the tail tip piece (like drawing a bowstring) and let the dubbing rope furl over itself. You will feel which way the rope wants to wrap if you give the tip section a tiny bit of slack. Once you establish which way it wants to go, encourage a tighter furl by twisting the tail tip as you go. Hold the terminal end of the dubbing rope up at an angle to better control the spacing of the color segmentation as the rope furls and forms the tail.

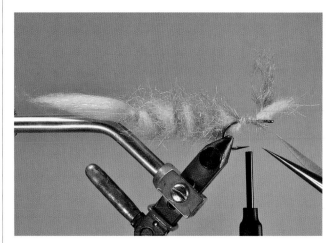

7. Do not mount the tail in place once it is finished—the butt end will be too narrow and you can never perfectly predict how long it will be before you start. Grasp the butt end between the thumb and index finger of your non-tying hand (to prevent unraveling) and trim the tail from the hook shank. Then mount the tail on top of the hook shank so it is the proper length. The end of the furled part of the tail (butt of the tail tip) should be 2 inches (5 cm) from the lead edge of the hook eye—this will make the entire tail section of the fly 2½ inches (64 mm) long once the tail tip is trimmed. Cut away the remaining two butt ends of the furled tail.

8. When tying the base of the furled tail down, the tension of the thread wraps will want to push the tail off to the side of the hook shank—let it! This hook will be clipped before the fly is finished and the tail will be mounted sideways. Having the tail tied in on the side of the hook shank will keep the fly from being minutely lopsided. Leave the thread resting at the very rear of the tie-down area and coat the entire area with Zap-A-Gap.

10. Create another waxed thread loop at the rear of the hook shank, then bring the bobbin forward and let it rest immediately behind the hook eye. This time the thread loop can be shorter and need only be one strand. Once the thread loop is properly made and waxed, insert some of both tail dubbings—a bit of the dark dubbing first, then the light, and then the dark again. The finished dubbing loop should be at least 2½ inches (64 mm) long.

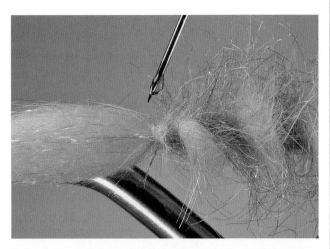

9. Apply a small drop of Zap-A-Gap at the base of the tail tip section of the tail. Brush back any of the long dubbing fibers from the furled section of the tail to avoid getting the adhesive anywhere other than the intended spot. Once the Zap-A-Gap has been applied, roll that area of the tail quickly between two fingers to immediately set the adhesive. This will prevent the Laser Dub fibers used in the tail tip from slipping out when under the duress of use.

11. Twist the dubbing loop into a tight rope and loosen up the long dubbing fibers with a wire brush before wrapping the dubbing rope forward onto the hook shank. The three-part color configuration of this dubbing rope will mimic the segmentation of the rest of the tail created by the furling process.

12. Once you wrap the dubbing rope forward and reach the hook eye, tie down the dubbing rope, trim away the excess, and secure everything with a whip-finish knot. Trim the thread and apply a small dab of Zap-A-Gap to the finish knot.

13. Cut the tail tip section of the tail to about ½ inch (13 mm) and take time to taper it to a blunt point. It is a good idea to pick out this Laser Dub material with a bodkin before trimming, just to be sure it is all straight and cooperative.

14. Remove the tail from the vise and use heavy side cutters to clip off the entire bend of the hook.

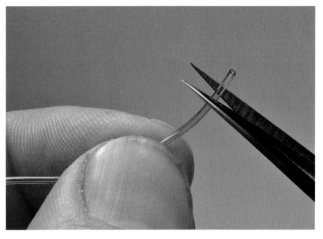

15. Cut a ¼-inch (6 mm) piece of standard rubber tubing in a color that matches the fly you are tying. If this piece of tubing is cut too long, it will be frustratingly difficult to thread the fluorocarbon through the second time, as you will need to do in step 17.

16. Cut a 6-inch (15 cm) length of Fluoroflex tippet. Thread the fluorocarbon tippet through the previously cut piece of tubing, then thread it through the hook eye of the tail section of the fly. Trim the tip of the fluorocarbon into a point—the longer the point, the easier it will thread back through the rubber tubing. Stick the trimmed tip into dubbing wax to lubricate it, making it easier to push all the way through the rubber tubing—it is a tight fit.

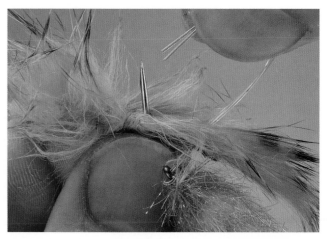

17. Bend the sharpened and waxed tip of fluorocarbon tippet over and thread it back through the short length of rubber tubing—this may take a moment of work. Pull the tippet material through until both ends are even. If the sharpened end is a bit bent and ratty, it is a good idea to trim off a tiny bit just to make threading both ends through the holes in the rabbit hide easier (that happens in the next step). Pull the piece of rubber tubing down close to the hook eye. Leave a loop of fluorocarbon between the hook eye and tubing about the size of the outside radius of the hook eye.

19. Once the two ends of tippet are through the first hole in the rabbit hide, bend them both back and thread them through the second hole, this time from the hairy side of the rabbit strip. The bodkin is still in place to make finding the hole possible. The easiest way to find the hole is to lick your fingers and then use your damp fingers to pull back all the hair around the protruding bodkin. Position the handle of the bodkin between your knees to keep it upright and slowly pull the rabbit strip up and off the bodkin while immediately following it with the two ends of tippet.

18. Cut a piece of magnum (wide) rabbit strip to 1½ inches (38 mm) long. Be careful to just cut the hide and not any of the fur. Use your bodkin to poke two holes through the rabbit hide. The first hole should be ³⁄₁₆ inch (1 cm) from the rear end of the rabbit strip; the second hole should be ⁹⁄₁₆ inch (3 cm) from the rear end of the rabbit strip. Make each hole slightly wider by forcibly wiggling the bodkin around once it has penetrated the rabbit hide. Leave the bodkin in the second hole, as you will need it to act as a guide in the next step. Thread both ends of the fluorocarbon tippet through the first hole from the bare side of the rabbit strip.

20. Pull both ends of the fluorocarbon tippet straight and position the rabbit strip back against the rubber tubing. Brush out any trapped rabbit hair from the top side. Set the tail with connected rabbit strip aside temporarily.

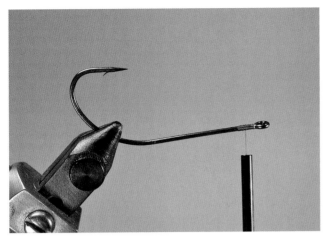

21. Mount the second hook (#2 Tiemco 8089) firmly in the vise. Mount the hook so the hook point is up and the straight hook shank is cocked upward at a slight angle. Switch bobbins to the one holding the second thread in the recipe (olive 6/0 UNI-Thread) and create a solid thread base immediately behind the hook eye. The thread base should be only a hook-eye length long. Leave the bobbin hanging so the thread is in the middle of the short thread base.

22. Select the two full marabou feathers to be used as the "throat" of the streamer. The bottom of the two feathers will always be a bright red, but the color of the second feather will change depending on what variation of Ringworm you are tying.

23. Mount the two marabou feathers one at a time on top of the short thread base. It is easiest to wet the marabou and slick it back to form a condensed, straight, and well-behaved feather before mounting. Use two tight thread wraps to mount the bottom feather so the tip is shy of the hook point by about the length from the hook point to the back of the barb. Mount the second marabou feather directly on top of the first, but have the tip go back as far as the outside arch of the hook bend. Pull both the tip ends and butt ends of the two feathers up and wrap several tight thread wraps around the base of the tie-down area, between the hook shank and the material. These last thread wraps help bunch up the feathers as well as kick them up at a greater angle off the hook shank. Leave the thread resting between the tie-down area and the hook eye. Trim the butt ends of marabou tight to the tie-down area.

24. Thread the tail and rabbit strip section of the fly onto the hook. The loop in the fluorocarbon tippet (between the rear hook eye and the band of tubing) should easily slip over the hook point. Slide the loop all the way down until it is stopped by the jaws of the vise. Take the two ends of tippet and thread them into the front hook eye from above.

25. Tie down the two ends of fluorocarbon firmly behind the front hook eye. Grasp the furled tail and force it back up and over the outermost bend of the hook (but not all the way off the hook point). This will pull the two pieces of fluorocarbon through the tight thread tie-down just far enough to allow the tail section of the fly to slide back and forth over the outside of the hook bend. The tail section should only be able to slide over the hook bend if encouraged to, but not on its own accord—you should hear a slight "click" sound when the rear hook eye passes over the outside bend of the front hook. The "up" position (shown in the photo) is how the tail section of the Ringworm should ride while being fished (keeping it weedless). The force of the hook set will push the tail section into the "down" position, allowing the entire spear and bend of the hook to penetrate and hold.

26. Once the two ends of fluorocarbon have been "calibrated" to just the right length, rotate the vise around (so the hook point is down). Bend the two strands of tippet that are threaded through the forward hook eye back onto the hook shank and tie them down firmly. This will lock the two strands of fluorocarbon tippet in place and not allow them to budge. Trim the butt ends of the fluorocarbon. It is OK to leave a bit of both sticking out, as they are clear and leaving tags will make them harder to pull out. Apply a small amount of Zap-A-Gap to the entire thread head tie-down area behind the forward hook eye.

27. While the Zap-A-Gap is still wet, tie the forward end of the rabbit strip down behind the forward hook eye.

28. Select three full-bodied olive grizzly marabou feathers.

29. Tie the grizzly marabou feathers down on top of the fly. Tie these feathers in one at a time—one off to the side, one in the middle, and one off to the other side. It is easier to manage these feathers if they are damp and slicked back to show their true length. The tips of these three feathers should be even with the tip of the longest of the two marabou feathers tied in on the bottom. Trim away the butt ends of the three feathers.

30. Build a solid thread head over the trimmed ends of the three olive grizzly marabou feathers. Tie a whip-finish knot and trim the thread. Because all the materials have been tied in on top of each other, the thread head should be much taller than it is wide—this will allow you to put dome eyes on either side of the head, and the result will be a somewhat round finished head.

31. Coat the entire thread head with a heavy layer of yellow Loon UV Fly Paint—when put over olive thread, the yellow UV resin will be more green chartreuse. It is much easier to get an even coat of resin over the head if you are using a rotary vise, as you can turn the fly while applying the resin. Before curing the UV resin (with a UV lamp), move the resin around with a bodkin tip (as you continue to turn the vise) to be sure the entire thread head is covered. The curing time will depend on the power of your UV lamp—the best ones only take a few seconds.

32. Stick the eyes on either side of the head. The eyes are sticky on the back side, so they will hold in place temporarily. Rotate the vise to expose the underside of the head and drip on a small dab or two of red Loon UV Fly Paint. Use a bodkin to encourage the wet UV resin to slide down all around the eyes. Give it a moment to allow the resin to seep down into and fill the cracks and voids, then rotate the vise back over to let the wet resin bulge out slightly. As soon as the wet resin bulges out slightly (it only takes a second), zap it with the UV lamp.

33. Use Loon UV Knot Sense (or their clear fly paint—it's the same stuff) to fill in the top of the head and add a clear coating to the entire head, to include covering the two eyes. You will need to use your bodkin to push the wet resin around to ensure complete coverage, but be careful not to get any in the hook eye. Once the head is as round as it can get, cure it with the UV lamp.

34. Often the UV resin is left a bit tacky even once cured (even the stuff claiming to be "tack free"), so brush on a light coat of Hard as Hull or other head cement and let dry.

PATTERN VARIATION

TEXAS RINGWORM (BLACK EEL)

Hook 1: #4 Tiemco 105

Thread 1: Dark brown 3/0 Danville's Waxed Monocord

Wax: BT's Tacky Dubbing Wax

Tail Dubbing 1: Peacock Poul Jorgensen SLF Salmon & Steelhead Dubbing

Tail Tip: Green chartreuse and fluorescent chartreuse Senyo's Laser Dub (blended together)

Tail Dubbing 2: Claret black Poul Jorgensen SLF Salmon & Steelhead Dubbing

Adhesive: Zap-A-Gap

Gangion Tube: Brown tubing (standard)

Gangion: RIO Fluoroflex tippet (.017"/25 lb.)

Main Body: Black rabbit strip (magnum)

Hook 2: #2 Tiemco 8089

Thread 2: Olive 6/0 UNI-Thread

Throat 1: Fluorescent red marabou blood quills

Throat 2: Golden olive marabou blood quills

Top Body: Olive grizzly marabou

Head Resin 1: Yellow Loon UV Fly Paint

Eyes: Red/black pupil Hareline Oval Pupil 3D Eyes (³⁄₁₆")

Head Resin 2: Red Loon UV Fly Paint

Head Resin 3: Loon UV Knot Sense

Head Cement: Hard as Hull

STUNTMAN EDDY

The Stuntman Eddy is a costly fly, both monetarily and in the amount of time it takes to tie, but is the most realistic in appearance and action of any baitfish streamer I have ever tied or fished. It takes over 40 minutes to tie, but may be more daunting than that . . . it is *tedious*. Half the time it takes to make is spent repeating the same four tying steps over and over again, then the other half is spent trimming what you have tied into the proper shape. But it is worth every minute you slave at the vise or over the trash bin—or dollar you spend at the fly shop. This is my all-time-favorite fly.

Once you have seen a Stuntman do its tricks, other streamer patterns will look to you like old socks being towed through the water.

The Stuntman Eddy can be tied to whatever size works best for your bass waters and will work well in most any color pattern you can dream up at the vise. *Erin Block* photo.

I tied the first prototype Stuntman sometime in 2006. I was working at a fly shop on the south side of Boulder, Colorado, and the then-owner of the shop was preparing for a family vacation to the Baja Peninsula in Mexico. He had fished there in the past and was hoping to get out on the water at least for a day or two. He was lamenting over all the flies he had yet to tie. There was an exorbitant amount of Sierra mackerel in the area he intended to fish (in addition to the targeted roosterfish), and these mackerel are notorious for destroying big rooster streamers. He claimed the teeth of just one of these fish would make any fly it touched basically worthless—this was the reason for needing to bring so many flies, even for a meager couple days of fishing.

I knew nothing of Sierra mackerel and how destructive they were, but I did know how to make sturdy flies, so I sat down that night and crafted the most bombproof baitfish pattern on stainless steel I could come up with. The result was a 5½-inch chartreuse and white fly with two joints and two hooks. It was a large and bizarre fly when seen in trout country (keep in mind, this was still a few years before the big-streamer craze struck the freshwater scene). Ten days later the fly was returned to me. It looked like a well-enjoyed puppy toy, but was still intact and still serviceable. And it had landed and handled *seven* Sierra mackerel.

For a while after the initial success of my new jointed streamer, it went by the name "Mac Proof Mullet," although the original had few similar characteristics to an actual mullet. It was a *working title*. The pattern was far from finished. Because of the fly's proven durability and the fact that it was a baitfish pattern, the idea was perfect for a northern pike fly. The next spring I began fishing a 4½-inch scaled-down version of the fly in some of the Front Range lakes that held pike. They were small pike but plentiful, and few of them could resist this new streamer—and none of the flies ever showed any wear, even after multiple days and dozens of pike attacks. It quickly became my go-to big baitfish streamer, so naturally finer tuning ensued. Soon I had a 3½-inch bass version and several species-specific color schemes. I made baby bass with dark lateral lines, creek chubs, perch, shad, and trout. The flies were time-consuming to tie but never fell apart, and because I almost always fished them with ultra-heavy leaders, I rarely lost any.

At some point a year or two after the fly's creation, I saw a slasher/thriller Quentin Tarantino film called *Death Proof.* Kurt Russell played a professional body double who rigs his car so the driver can survive a crash, but the hapless woman passenger is not so lucky. I don't remember much more of the movie, but the name sounded a bit like "Mac Proof," so

the fly was on my mind when I watched it. The fly needed a new name, too, so I was already on the prowl for inspiration. I renamed the fly Stuntman Eddy after the Kurt Russell character. It was maybe another entire year later, while sitting around talking flies and fishing with friends Clint Johnson and Greg Keenan, that I realized I had misremembered the name from the movie. Clint and Greg are both movie buffs (especially gory ones), and they gave me funny looks when I told them the origin of the fly's name. Stuntman *Mike*, they said. The guy's name was *Stuntman Mike!* But it was too late. The name had stuck.

The Stuntman streamer is tough—that was the key specification for the pattern right from the start—but years of tinkering have perfected both the look and action of the fly. The EP Fibers that make up the main body of the fly are a strong synthetic material and just stiff enough to maintain shape when trimmed appropriately short, yet soft enough to look and feel natural. The flashy dubbing cropped short along either flank give the streamer a baitfish flash without being too gaudy. The shape of the fly is its most deadly attribute—not the fly's side profile, but the front profile. The double articulation allows the swimming motion when retrieved, but the thinness of the fly allows the erratic, darting action of a wounded or scared fish. This latter attribute is what triggers the predatory nature in bass. Once you have seen a Stuntman do its tricks, other streamer patterns will look to you like old socks being towed through the water.

STUNTMAN EDDY (RAINBOW TROUT)

Hook 1: #6 Gamakatsu B10S
Thread: White 100-denier UTC G.S.P.
Tail Dubbing: Pearl Ice Dub
Tail Feather: Olive marabou blood quills
Adhesive: Zap-A-Gap
Hook 2: #1/0 Umpqua U401
Wire Connector: RIO Wire Bite Tippet (.018"/30 lb.)
Top Fiber 1: Golden olive EP 3-D Fibers
Bottom Fiber: Bucktail white EP Fibers
Lateral Dubbing 1: Orange Ice Dub
Top Fiber 2: Olive EP 3-D Fibers
Lateral Dubbing 2: UV pink Ice Dub
Hook 3: #2 Tiemco 600SP
Eye Adhesive: Bish's Original Tear Mender
Eyes: Yellow adhesive holographic eyes (5/16")

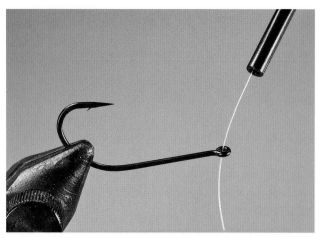

1. The Stuntman Eddy takes three separate hooks. Begin by mounting the rear hook (#6 Gamakatsu B10S) firmly into the vise "upside down," or hook point up—this is how the rear hook will ride when the fly is finished. Because all the materials on this rear hook will be mounted on a very short section of the hook shank directly behind the hook eye, they have a tendency to slip down the shank after being fished for a while. The G.S.P. thread used to make this fly as durable as possible also contributes to the potential material slippage on the tail. To prevent this you must create an "eye-locked thread base." Begin by inserting the thread into the hook eye . . .

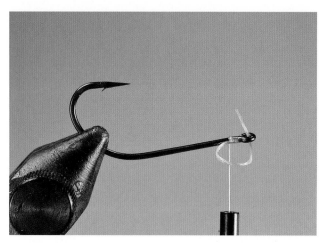

2. Once the thread has been inserted through the hook eye from above, wrap four turns of thread over itself and the hook shank. Fold the tag end of thread back over the short thread base and insert it once again through the hook eye—this time from below.

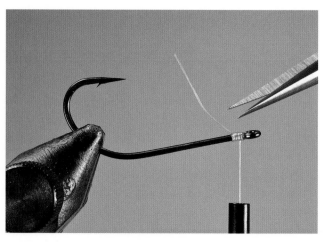

3. Pull the tag end of thread all the way through the hook eye and use a couple more thread wraps over the thread base to secure it in place. The overall thread base should be no more than the length of the hook eye. Trim the remaining tag of thread. This is the eye-locked thread base that will not slip or be pulled down the hook shank.

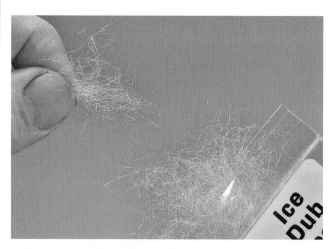

4. Pull out a healthy tuft of Ice Dub and hand stack it so that most of the long flashy fibers are extended to the point that if you grasped the now-elongated tuft firmly at its center, it would be difficult to pluck loose fibers from either end—this allows it to be tied down at its center without shedding fibers of dubbing.

5. Fold the tuft of Ice Dub over the exposed thread between the tip of the bobbin and the hook shank, and use the thread to draw the material down into place on the hook shank directly behind the hook eye. Use two thread wraps to secure the Ice Dub in place, then fold the forward end of the dubbing tuft back to make one clump of dubbing extending back and away from the hook eye. Make one more tight thread wrap between this and the hook eye.

6. Select one large marabou blood quill (one with long, fine fibers as opposed to one with bushy, short fibers). Break the feather into two pieces—save both.

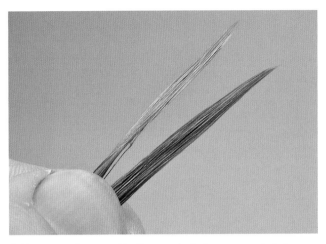

7. For ease of use and better control, dampen and slick down both pieces of marabou. Keep the larger of the two (usually the rear section) in hand and set the smaller section aside for later.

8. Tie the larger of the two marabou pieces down onto the top of the Ice Dub tuft. Before doing this, lick your fingers and slick back the tuft of Ice Dub so you can be sure you are laying the marabou down with all the material tips somewhat even. Use two tight thread wraps over the top of the marabou to secure it in place, then pull both the rearward clump of Ice Dub and marabou as well as the forward butt end of marabou up together. Use two or three additional wraps of thread around the outside of the base of all this material—this will cock the materials up off and away from the hook shank. Tie the thread off with a whip-finish knot and trim.

9. Trim away the forward butt end of the marabou feather. Leave a small stump of marabou directly behind the hook eye, as this makes it less able to come out from its fairly small thread tie-down. Apply Zap-A-Gap adhesive to the underside of the thread base and the marabou stump on the top. This will increase the durability of this rear tail section of the fly and keep the materials cocked permanently upright on the hook shank. Remove the hook from the vise and set it aside for later.

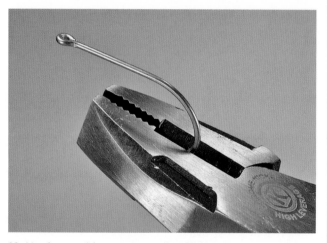

10. Use heavy side cutters to clip off the entire spear of the second hook (#1/0 Umpqua U401). Be sure to leave plenty of the hook bend, as you will need this to properly mount the hook into the vise. Only the hook eye and straight shank are needed for the finished fly, but the bend is needed temporarily as a purchase point in the vise. Tying is made easier and safer with the spear of the hook removed. The rest of the bend will be removed later.

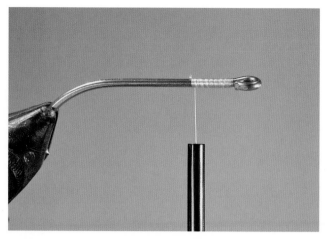

11. Mount the clipped hook in the vise, then begin a solid thread base directly behind the hook eye and extend it back on the hook shank at least two hook-eye lengths. Let the bobbin hang at the rear of the thread base.

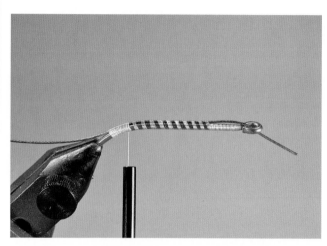

12. Use side cutters to snip off a 3½-inch (9 cm) length of RIO Wire Bite Tippet. Thread one end of this length of wire through the hook eye (from above) so that about ½ inch (13 mm) of the wire protrudes out past the forward end of the thread base. Use wide spiral wraps of thread down the hook shank to secure the wire in place. Once the thread tie-down wraps have reached the rear end of the straight hook shank, build a solid thread base from there, extending slightly down onto the bend of the hook. Return the thread to the forward end of this short rear thread base.

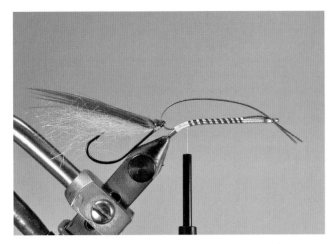

13. Thread the tail hook onto the wire that is extending off the rear of the hook shank—be sure the rear hook is oriented hook point up. Once the tail is attached, thread the end of the wire into the front hook eye alongside the other end of the wire.

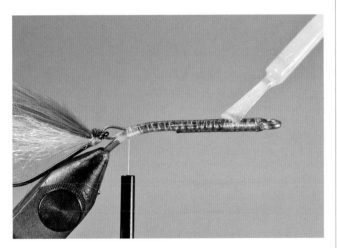

14. Tie the wire down onto the hook shank, then fold the two wire ends back onto the underside of the hook shank and tie them down as well. The rear loop of wire you have created off the back end of the hook shank should be slightly larger than the front hook eye and rest ever so slightly back onto the bend of the front hook—this ensures the tail will remain in line with the lateral line of the finished fly. Once all the wire has been tied down, apply Zap-A-Gap over the entire thread base and wire tie-down. The reason the main stretch of the wire tie-down was done with well-spaced spiral thread wraps was to allow the adhesive to quickly soak through down to the bare hook shank.

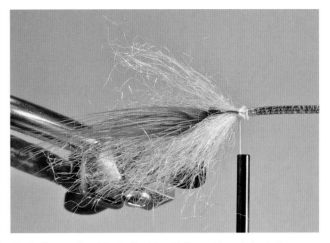

15. Pull out a healthy tuft of Ice Dub and hand stack it so that most of the long flashy fibers are extended to the point that if you grasped the now-elongated tuft firmly at its center, it would be difficult to pluck loose fibers from either end—this allows it to be tied down at its center without shedding dubbing fibers. (This is exactly how the Ice Dub was prepared before mounting it onto the tail hook.) Fold the tuft of dubbing over the exposed thread between the fly and tip of the bobbin and use the thread to draw the material down onto the side of the hook shank directly forward of the wire loop joint. After one securing wrap of thread, brush the forward end of the secured dubbing tuft back to join the rear half and make a couple additional thread wraps over the fold in the dubbing to lock it in place. Repeat this entire process on the other side of the fly. Now the entire joint of the articulated tail should be concealed, but not inhibited, by the Ice Dub.

16. Retrieve the tip section of marabou that was removed and set aside when making the tail and tie it down at the top/rear of the hook shank. The tip of this marabou should be even with the tip of the original. Trim the excess butt end of the marabou feather.

17. Begin building the EP Fiber body of the fly. Start with a section of what is listed as Top Fiber 1 in the fly recipe—in this case, it is the golden olive EP Fibers. The sections of EP Fiber used for the entirety of this fly should be no larger around than a no. 2 pencil—maybe slightly skinnier. EP Fiber comes in bundles of 10-inch (25 cm) fibers, and you can pull out between 20 and 24 appropriate-size sections. Mount each section of EP Fibers to the fly in a similar fashion as you mounted the Ice Dub tufts, by folding them around the exposed thread and then using the thread to pull the material down onto the hook shank in the proper place. Each section of EP Fiber will be long enough for several applications, so do your best to conserve the material. Mount the first section on the top of the hook shank directly on top of the thread tie-down for the two side dubbing clumps and marabou. Use one wrap of thread to draw the material down onto the fly, then a second wrap to better secure the EP Fiber section in place. Trim the long end and set it aside to use later.

18. Mount a similar section of the bottom EP Fiber (in this case, the bucktail white) to the bottom of the hook shank directly opposite where you mounted the top section. Use the initial wrap of thread to draw the material onto the hook shank, then use two more tight thread wraps to better secure it in place. When making the initial wrap, follow the same thread path used for the two wraps that are holding the top section of EP Fibers in place. On the successive two wraps, do not go over the top fibers, but just in front

of them. Then pull all the EP Fibers from both the top and bottom sections to the rear and make four more thread wraps as tight as possible directly in front of them. This ends up being nine thread wraps in all, with three of the wraps securing each of the two sections of EP Fiber (one of the wraps is shared by the top and bottom) and four locking wraps placed right at the forward edge. Trim the long end of this section of EP Fibers and set it aside for the next go-round. This step is made easier if you are using a rotary vise and can turn the fly over.

19. Cock the fly onto its side and apply a small dab of Zap-A-Gap to the thread tie-down for the two sections of EP Fibers. This is an important step to not forget after every series of EP Fibers mounting, as this adhesive is what makes this fly indestructible and will make the lateral dubbing (which is about to be tied in) stick flat to the sides of the fly. Be sure some of the Zap-A-Gap bleeds into the upright EP Fibers—just not too much. This is the opportune time to make any slight adjustments to the positioning of the EP Fibers.

20. Tie in a tuft of the Lateral Dubbing 1 (in this case, orange Ice Dub) on either side of the hook shank. Prepare and mount these dubbing tufts the same way all the past dubbing tufts have been mounted—by hand stacking them, folding them onto the thread, drawing them into place onto the flank of the fly, and then brushing back the forward end. During the thread wrap that is securing the dubbing tuft in place, pull the thread forward slightly (thus pulling the dubbing forward slightly)—this will place the actual tie-down location of the dubbing tuft slightly forward of where it needs to be, allowing you to back wrap a couple turns of thread over the folded dubbing to better secure it.

21. Repeat the last four steps until you reach the hook eye. In this trout variation of the Stuntman Eddy streamer, the bottom EP Fiber remains constant, but the top EP Fiber and the lateral dubbing will alternate between two different colors. It should take 10 to 12 full rounds to reach the hook eye. Once finished, the EP Fibers on the top and bottom should be packed in densely and be leaning out over the hook eye—this ensures the forward joint of this articulated fly will not have a visible gap. Tie a whip-finish knot behind the hook eye, trim the thread, and apply a dab of Zap-A-Gap to the finish knot. Remove the partial fly from the vise.

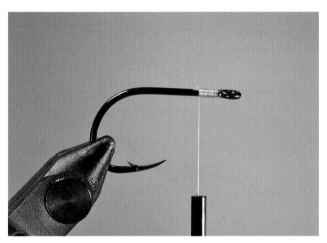

22. Clamp the third and final hook (#2 Tiemco 600SP) firmly into the vise. Build a solid thread base from directly behind the hook eye to about a hook-eye length back on the hook shank. Leave the bobbin hanging so that the thread rests at the rear of the short thread base.

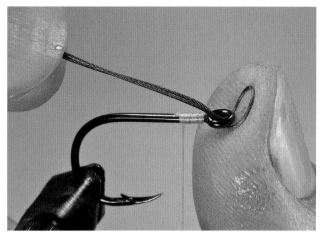

23. Use side cutters to snip off a 5-inch (13 cm) length of RIO Wire Bite Tippet. Fold this piece of wire perfectly in half and thread both ends into the hook eye (from below). Draw the doubled-over wire through the hook eye, and when the loop at the end is nearing the hook eye, use your thumb to push the loop up over the hook eye. Draw the wire tight, cinching the loop tight behind the hook eye.

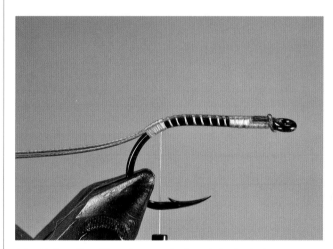

24. While still pulling the set of wires tight, lock them in place by wrapping a tight base of thread (about another hook-eye length long) over the wire. Once the wire is secure and won't budge, continue wrapping the thread to the rear. Use wide-spaced spiral wraps until you reach the rear of the straight hook shank, then begin building another solid thread base over the wire down onto the hook bend. This rear solid thread base should also be a hook-eye length long. Bring the thread forward and let the bobbin hang so the thread rests at the forward end of the rear thread base.

25. Attach the rear portion of the streamer by threading the two ends of wire up through the rear hook eye and then folding them back over the front hook shank and tying them down. The rear hook eye should be snug up against the front hook, but still have room to move freely. Two strands of wire are used for this joint not for additional strength, but to prevent twisting or listing of the rear end of this articulated streamer. When tying the two ends of wire down, encourage them to rest one on either side of the existing set of wire tied down onto the top of the hook shank—this will spread the two loops of wire at the joint, further preventing any twisting or listing. Spiral wrap the thread tie-down forward until you force the two ends of wire up against the back side of the wire loop created two steps ago. Build a solid band of thread at this spot.

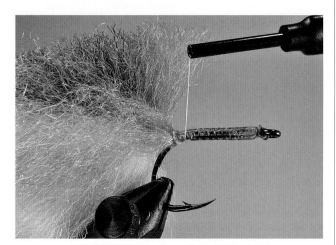

26. Fold the two ends of wire down onto the bottom of the hook shank and tie them down. Coat the entire wire tie-down with Zap-A-Gap. Bring the thread back to the rear of the hook shank, where you will then tie in two more lateral tufts of Ice Dub just forward of the wire joint. If the Stuntman variation you are tying calls for two colors of lateral dubbing (as this one does), the color of these tufts will be determined by—and be opposite of—whatever color you left off on at the forward end of the last hook. Use extra-large tufts of dubbing for these two tufts, as they are needed to conceal the joint and fill in any excessive gap between the two hooks.

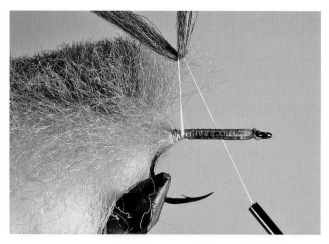

27. Continue building the body of the fly by repeating the four-step process (top EP Fibers, bottom EP Fibers, Zap-A-Gap, and lateral dubbing tufts).

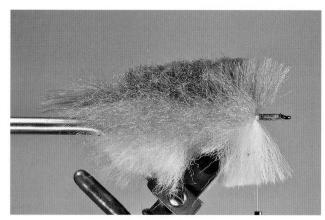

28. Once you have built the fly body up the final hook shank to a point about even with the front hook point, make a slight adjustment to the color combination of the top EP Fibers—leave out the lighter of the two colors and continue on with just the darker color (in this case, the olive EP Fibers). This makes the top of the head of the streamer slightly darker than the rest of the body.

29. When you reach the hook eye, tie off with a whip-finish knot, trim the thread, and apply a dab of Zap-A-Gap to the knot.

30. Now that the tying phase of creating a Stuntman is complete, remove the fly from the vise and trim it into a small fish. It would be easy to quickly cut this ball of EP Fibers down into a manageable fish shape if it were not for the heavy 600SP hook hidden deep in the belly of this fibrous mess. The best way to proceed is to locate this hook and carve a gap in the belly fibers to expose it, thus establishing a belly line for the fly and preventing you from ruining your scissors.

31. Continue trimming the belly EP Fibers, which will eventually expose the partially clipped bend of the second hook. Use heavy side cutters to clip the remainder of this hook bend down close to the rear joint in the fly. Be careful not to accidentally cut the wire loop of the joint.

32. Trim the top fibers down to a desired fishlike shape. Periodically hold the streamer nose up to get a good visual of how each of the three sections of this fly will line up while moving through the water.

33. Once the bottom and the top fibers are trimmed down to create the desired broadside silhouette, take extra time and care in trimming the lateral dubbing sides down to make the fly as narrow as possible. The proper head dimensions of a Stuntman Eddy should be no more than ¾ inch (19 mm) tall and ⁵⁄₁₆ inch (8 mm) wide. The overall length of the fly should be 3¾ inches (95 mm).

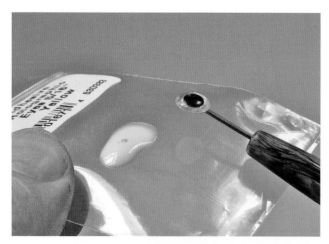

34. Select two adhesive holographic eyes to finish off the fly. Stick an eye onto the end of a bodkin (the adhesive back will help) and dip it into a small puddle of Tear Mender to coat the entire back side of the eye. Pour the puddle of Tear Mender onto the small plastic bag the eyes came in, as it is handy and this particular adhesive will easily peel off plastic once dry.

35. Place each of the eyes and squeeze them together to achieve as narrow a head profile as possible. Allow the Tear Mender at least a full day to dry before fishing.

PATTERN VARIATIONS

STUNTMAN EDDY (THREADFIN SHAD)

Hook 1: #6 Gamakatsu B10S

Thread: White 100-denier UTC G.S.P.

Tail Dubbing: Pearl Ice Dub

Tail Feather: Fluorescent white marabou

Adhesive: Zap-A-Gap

Hook 2: #1/0 Umpqua U401

Wire Connector: RIO Wire Bite Tippet (.018"/30 lb.)

Top Fiber 1: Bucktail white EP 3-D Fibers

Bottom Fiber: Bucktail white EP Fibers

Lateral Dubbing: Pearl Ice Dub

Top Fiber 2: Sage EP Fibers

Hook 3: #2 Tiemco 600SP

Eye Adhesive: Bish's Original Tear Mender

Eyes: Super pearl adhesive holographic eyes (⁵⁄₁₆")

STUNTMAN EDDY (YELLOW PERCH)

Hook 1: #6 Gamakatsu B10S

Thread: White 100-denier UTC G.S.P.

Tail Dubbing: Fluorescent yellow Ice Dub

Tail Feather: Cream marabou

Adhesive: Zap-A-Gap

Hook 2: #1/0 Umpqua U401

Wire Connector: RIO Wire Bite Tippet (.018"/30 lb.)

Top Fiber 1: Baitfish Bally EP Fibers

Bottom Fiber: Baitfish Bally EP Fibers

Lateral Dubbing 1: Fluorescent yellow SLF Prism Dub

Top Fiber 2: Golden olive EP 3-D Fibers

Top Fiber 3: Black EP Fibers

Lateral Dubbing 2: UV hot orange Ice Dub

Hook 3: #2 Tiemco 600SP

Eye Adhesive: Bish's Original Tear Mender

Eyes: Gold adhesive holographic eyes (⁵⁄₁₆")

STUNTMAN EDDY (CREEK CHUB)

Hook 1: #6 Gamakatsu B10S

Thread: White 100-denier UTC G.S.P.

Tail Dubbing: Copper Ice Dub

Tail Feather: Olive brown marabou

Adhesive: Zap-A-Gap

Hook 2: #1/0 Umpqua U401

Wire Connector: RIO Wire Bite Tippet (.018"/30 lb.)

Top Fiber 1: Tan EP Fibers

Bottom Fiber: Baitfish Bally EP Fibers

Lateral Dubbing: Golden brown Ice Dub

Top Fiber 2: Golden olive EP 3-D Fibers

Hook 3: #2 Tiemco 600SP

Eye Adhesive: Bish's Original Tear Mender

Eyes: Gold adhesive holographic eyes (⁵⁄₁₆")

BELLYACHE MINNOW

Rob Kolanda from Longmont, Colorado, tied the first Bellyache Minnow sometime in 2008. Right around that time, Rob also caught the plague while walleye fishing. He was out most of the night in a float tube on Boulder Reservoir casting streamers on a heavy sink-tip fly line and the next day did not feel well. His wife nagged him for a day or so and eventually made him get looked at and sure enough . . . *black death*. I kid you not. I and all the other guys who worked with him at the fly shop went to see him in the hospital. It was serious. He looked bad. We all joked about him coming down with whirling disease. Rob did not die of the plague and I was glad. I liked working and fishing with him.

The Bellyache Minnow is perfect to use at the edge of a steep drop-off where you need the fly to sink fast.

Erin Block releases a bass at the edge of a lake. It is always best to keep a fish at least partially in the water while you remove the fly.

I watched this baitfish streamer be invented. I saw almost every stage in its early development as it rose from the primordial fly tier's detritus and turned into a viable fly. Softex and other random fly-tying goops, hooks, and materials were piled on our shop tying bench like toys and comic books on a messy child's bedroom floor. Rob would come into work early back then because he had a toddler at home and preferred to tie away from curious little fingers that were apt to become wacky rigged to a 1/0 hook. I would sometimes come in after Rob and see him in the back, intently focused on his latest creation. A new "midden" layer of tying materials would have usually formed over the already cluttered bench like refuse under an ancient rock shelter. Rob would finish the fly with me peering over his shoulder, and we would then analyze the design and material choice. Sometimes we would go so far as to fill a container with water from the back sink and test how it swam. At some point I would show him whatever flies I had been working on at home the night before, we would further compare ideas and get new ideas, and the creative circle would continue throughout the workday.

The Bellyache Minnow is a simple streamer and a lot like a Zonker at first glance, but has internal intricacies that make it a greatly improved version of that now almost 40-year-old streamer pattern. The rabbit strip over the top of the fly may be the most visually distinctive trait, and it is this that begs a comparison to the Zonker. The belly of the Bellyache is tied with a very healthy amount of long-fibered Ice Dub that gives the streamer a fluid and lifelike look. Rob would create a simple dubbing rope by waxing the thread and rolling on the Ice Dub for his original Bellyaches. This made a slimmer, more compact fly that appeared more leechlike than fishlike in the water, and over time it would get worn thin by contact with rocks and gravel and a bald spot would begin to appear at the bottom. I like to put the dubbing on with a well-groomed (brushed out) dubbing loop, as this makes the belly more durable and adds girth to the fly. The hazards of adding more substance to what you want to be the bottom of a fly you are trying to make swim hook point up is obvious once it hits the water—drag force often makes the fly swim sideways or even upside down when retrieved. It is worth tying this fly with a more pronounced belly, for both appearances and durability, but you must be careful and considerate about the amount of weight you have tied in at the start of the tying process.

The ribbed tungsten scud/shrimp body in the guts of the Bellyache were originally made (as their name suggests) to add weight to small crustacean patterns, but the Bellyache was the first streamer to use this style of weight to sink a baitfish pattern. The tungsten bodies I have been stocking in fly shops for well over a decade have changed slightly over the years, as well as been occasionally mislabeled, so be cognizant of this when you sit down to tie a batch of Bellyaches. The tungsten bodies in size large used to be (circa at least 2008) between .99 and 1.05 grams, but now they are between .82 and .90 gram—this is not really a problem, as the new, lighter-weight "larges" are the perfect weight for this fly. The serious problem comes when the medium bodies (.55 to .58 gram) are accidentally packaged in the bags labeled large. If this streamer is tied the way I like to tie it, with the body dubbing as bushy and lively as possible, and the counterweight is too light (significantly less than .80 gram), the fly will swim sideways. The safest thing to do is weigh all your bodies beforehand and create separate little bags for each varying weight.

If done right, the Bellyache Minnow will sink fast, and then swim very realistically. Between just Rob and me, we have landed almost every freshwater fish species in the country using this fly, from carp, walleye, wiper, brown trout, rainbows, brookies, and cutts to northern pike, largemouth and smallmouth bass, and every panfish and crappie we have come across. I will always have a few variations of the Bellyache Minnow on me when I am bass fishing, and when one day they find me dead of the plague along a riverbank or reservoir, there will likely be one tied to the end of my line.

BELLYACHE MINNOW (OLIVE)

Hook: #1/0 Gamakatsu SC15

Thread: Red 140-denier UTC Ultra Thread

Weight: Ribbed tungsten body (large)

Adhesive 1: Zap-A-Gap

Wax: BT's Tacky Dubbing Wax

Body Dub 1: Pearl Ice Dub

Body Dub 2: Pearl Ice Dub

Body Dub 3: Olive brown Ice Dub

Throat Dub: Minnow gills Dave Whitlock SLF

Back 1: Olive variant Black Barred Rabbit Strips

Adhesive 2: Tear Mender

Back 2: Black rabbit strip (magnum)

Head Top Color: Black Sharpie marker

Eyes: Yellow holographic eyes (5/32")

Head: Epoxy or UV-curing resin

Head Cement: Hard as Hull

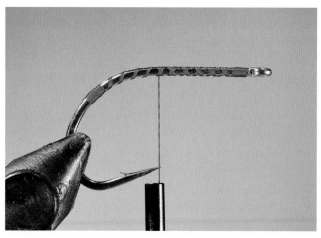

2. Once you have created a short, solid band of thread at the rear of what I will call the "usable hook shank," spiral wrap the thread forward to the hook eye and create another short, solid band of thread, then spiral wrap the thread back to the rear. Stop the rearward thread wraps just past the middle of the hook shank and let the bobbin hang so that the thread is perfectly even with the very tip of the hook point. Trim the tag end of thread at the rear of the thread base. The two solid bands of thread are to secure the starting wraps (rear band) and ensure the spiraled thread wraps will not slide back on the hook shank (forward band). The thread and bobbin have been stopped at this exact spot in preparation for mounting the ribbed tungsten body in the exact place every time.

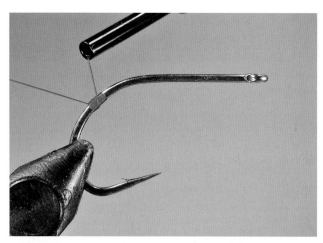

1. Clamp the hook securely in the vise with the hook shank horizontal. Begin the thread wraps well back onto the bend of the hook. It is important that the thread be started at this spot because this will mark the point where the rear of the "minnow's" belly will be tied, and it has to be this far back on the hook in order to swim correctly when finished.

3. Mount the ribbed tungsten body onto the top of the hook shank so that the middle of the grooves lines up with where the thread and bobbin have been left. Make two tight wraps of thread in this center groove of the tungsten body to hold it in place.

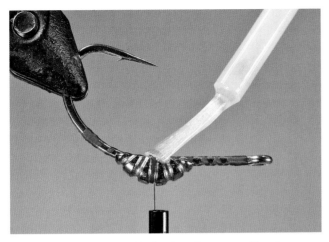

4. Rotate the hook into the hook-point-up position (remove the hook and reposition if you are using a non-rotary vise). Apply a liberal amount of Zap-A-Gap to the underside of the ribbed tungsten body—this ensures the weight stays centered, even after days of being bounced off logs and rocks. Be sure to get a little of the adhesive on the thread base to the rear of the body weight—this will help lock in the first big tuft of body dubbing.

6. Rotate the hook back to the hook-down starting position and wrap the thread back to the rear edge of the ribbed tungsten body weight—be sure to get at least a couple wraps of thread through the second groove from center, but do not worry too much if the thread will not catch in the very last groove. Tie the clump of dubbing in right at the rear of the body weight. One wrap of thread over the middle of the dubbing clump will suffice.

5. Pull out a healthy tuft of the first body dubbing—in this case, it is the pearl Ice Dub. I like using the longer-fibered Ice Dub for the rear of this fly because I can hand sort/stack the dubbing into one long clump that can be tied in at the middle and will not "shed" and lose too many fibers.

7. Fold the forward end of the dubbing clump back over itself, forming one larger Ice Dub "tail" off the back of the hook shank. Wrap the thread back to the rear end of the original thread base.

8. Rotate the hook once again to the hook-point-up position. Create an 8- to 9-inch (20 to 23 cm) thread loop extending from the rear of the thread base. Wrap the thread forward and leave the bobbin hanging so that the thread is about a hook-eye length behind the hook eye. Wax the thread loop in preparation for dubbing.

9. Fill the waxed thread loop with dubbing. The first 5 inches (13 cm) should be the second body dubbing in the recipe—in this case, the pearl Ice Dub. The second 2 inches

(5 cm) should be the third body dubbing in the recipe—in this case, the olive brown Ice Dub. A high school wrestling coach once told me about a desperation move he called the "five on two" . . . I use that old advice as a way to remember the proper amounts of each dubbing to put in the loop.

10. Twist the dubbing loop by hand or with a dubbing twirl tool until it forms a solid dubbing rope. The more evenly you stack the dubbing into the thread loop, the more consistent the finished rope will be. Pull the rope tight and use a coarse wire dubbing brush to rake out and "fluff up" as much of the trapped dubbing fibers as you can.

11. Wrap the dubbing rope forward, covering the thread base and the ribbed body weight. The color shift in the dubbing rope should happen just before the ribbed tungsten body is completely covered. Make the first wrap snug up to the dubbing tail created in step 7, so all the like dubbing blends. Make each wrap as tight as possible and be sure to sweep back the raked-out dubbing fibers with each wrap so as not to trap them under the wrap—you want the body of this fly as bushy as possible. Sometimes I will brush a small amount of Zap-A-Gap over the top of the ribbed tungsten body before I begin these wraps of dubbing rope to ensure they don't slip slightly and expose some of the "guts" of the fly later when the fly is being fished. This will not alter the effectiveness of the fly, but will affect my confidence in its ability to work, which is almost worse.

12. Wrap the dubbing rope to a hook-eye length behind the hook eye and tie it down. Trim the excess.

13. Pull a small clump of the throat dubbing (minnow gills Dave Whitlock SLF dubbing) from its bag and hand sort/stack it so that all the fibers are generally aligned—this will allow you to tie the clump down by the middle and not have much of it shed or fall out.

14. Rotate the fly to the hook-point-down position and tie the clump of prepared dubbing in by its middle right behind the hook eye. One or two thread wraps is all you need.

15. Fold the forward end of the dubbing tuft back over itself so that it joins the rest of the red dubbing at what will be the front bottom of the minnow fly. Secure it in place with multiple tight thread wraps. In theory, this color replicates flared or even bleeding gills of a young baitfish, but in reality, it has more to do with "bin appeal." Tie a half hitch or quick whip-finish knot with the thread before moving on, as you will soon be temporarily removing the fly from the vise and the knot will keep the thread from accidentally unraveling.

16. Rotate the fly into the hook-point-up position and thoroughly rake out the dubbing body with a coarse wire dubbing brush. By the end of this step, you want all the long dubbing fibers to be swept back away from the hook point—there should actually be a slight "part" down the hook shaft, as there is an even amount of swept-back dubbing on either side.

17. Select a strip of barred rabbit. I look for the lengths within a particular rabbit strip that have the most pronounced barring.

18. Grasp the unfinished fly by the raked-back dubbing belly and remove it from the vise. Stab the hook point through the underside of the rabbit strip. Be sure to poke the hook through at least 1 inch (25 mm) back onto the rabbit hide, to have enough to tie down over the top of the fly.

19. Secure the hook back into the jaws of the vise. Squeeze a small amount of Tear Mender onto the underneath side of the rabbit strip (the part that will be making contact with the top of the dubbed belly of the fly). *Do not* apply the Tear Mender directly to the dubbing body—it is very easy to squeeze out too much, and it will quickly soak into the entire mass of dubbing and ruin the fly.

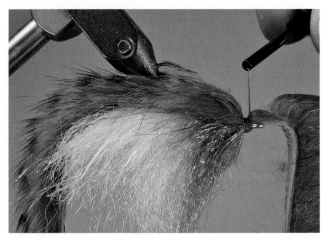

20. Rotate the fly to the hook-point-up position and lay the prepared rabbit strip down over the top of the fly. Tie the rabbit strip down behind the hook eye. The Tear Mender will lock the rabbit hide down onto the fly permanently.

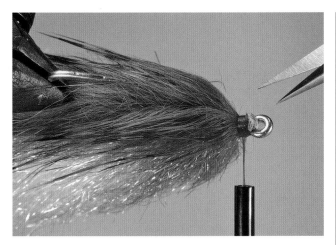

21. Trim the excess rabbit strip from the front of the fly. Be sure to leave the hook eye clear of material and thread.

22. Trim the rabbit strip at the rear end of the fly. Be sure to cut only the leather of the rabbit strip, not the hair. I also take the time to make the end pointed, not squared off, because it looks more natural. The overall fly should be 3 inches (76 mm) long if it is being tied on a Gamakatsu SC15 size 1/0 hook.

23. Trim a tuft of hair from the dyed black rabbit strip. I try to trim off as much as I can hold between my thumb and forefinger. I prefer to use a magnum rabbit strip because

they are cut wider and this allows me to grasp more hair in one pinch.

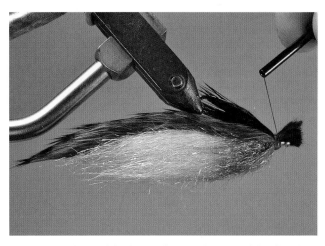

24. Tie the black rabbit hair tuft onto the top of the fly. The tips of the rabbit hair should extend back to just past the outside bend of the hook. Make a couple tight turns of thread over the black rabbit hair, then trim the excess off the front before continuing the tie-down—this ensures you do not "crowd the head" and obscure the hook eye. I like to dab a small drop of Zap-A-Gap onto the trimmed ends of rabbit hair before wrapping thread over them to allow the adhesive to soak back into the hair, permanently securing it into place.

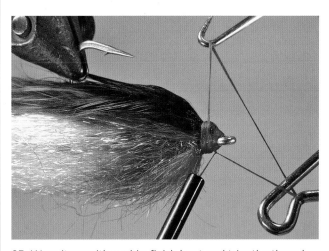

25. Wrap it up with a whip-finish knot and trim the thread.

26. Use a black Sharpie permanent marker to darken the top of the thread head. This will make the top of the head match the black rabbit on the top of the fly and the remaining red thread match the "throat" dubbing on the bottom side of the fly. This is the sole reason I tie this fly with red thread.

28. Use epoxy or the UV-curing resin of your choice to create a clear and durable head on the minnow. Cover both eyes entirely to be sure they never come off. If the UV resin cures with a slight tackiness, brush on a light coat of head cement.

27. Put the eyes in place. The eyes are sticky on the back, so will hold in place nicely.

29. Once the Bellyache Minnow is finished, I will grasp the hook with pliers or forceps and hold the fly nose first under a stream of scalding hot water for one full minute. This slightly straightens out each synthetic dubbing fiber, which compacts the body and ensures it swims true. This also puts a permanent kink in the tie-down spot where each dubbing fiber is trapped, making the body less likely to fall apart after extended use.

PATTERN VARIATIONS

BELLYACHE MINNOW (BROWN/TAN)

Hook: #1/0 Gamakatsu SC15

Thread: Red 140-denier UTC Ultra Thread

Weight: Ribbed tungsten body (large)

Adhesive 1: Zap-A-Gap

Wax: BT's Tacky Dubbing Wax

Body Dub 1: Tan UV Ice Dub

Body Dub 2: Tan UV Ice Dub

Body Dub 3: Rusty brown Ice Dub

Throat Dub: Minnow gills Dave Whitlock SLF

Back 1: Light brown Hareline Black Barred Rabbit Strips

Adhesive 2: Tear Mender

Back 2: Black rabbit strip (magnum)

Eyes: Gold holographic eyes (⁵⁄₃₂")

Head Top Color: Black Sharpie marker

Head: Epoxy or UV-curing resin

Head Cement: Hard as Hull

BELLYACHE MINNOW (WHITE)

Hook: # 1/0 Gamakatsu SC15

Thread: Red 140-denier UTC Ultra Thread

Weight: Ribbed tungsten body (large)

Adhesive 1: Zap-A-Gap

Wax: BT's Tacky Dubbing Wax

Body Dub 1: Minnow belly Ice Dub

Body Dub 2: Minnow belly Ice Dub

Body Dub 3: Hot yellow Ice Dub

Throat Dub: Minnow gills Dave Whitlock SLF

Back 1: White Hareline Black Barred Rabbit Strips

Adhesive 2: Tear Mender

Back 2: Black rabbit strip (magnum)

Eyes: Red holographic eyes (⁵⁄₃₂")

Head Top Color: Black Sharpie marker

Head: Epoxy or UV-curing resin

Head Cement: Hard as Hull

BELLYACHE MINNOW (FIRE TIGER)

Hook: #1/0 Gamakatsu SC15

Thread: Red 140-denier UTC Ultra Thread

Weight: Ribbed tungsten body (large)

Adhesive 1: Zap-A-Gap

Wax: BT's Tacky Dubbing Wax

Body Dub 1: Hot yellow Ice Dub

Body Dub 2: Hot yellow Ice Dub

Body Dub 3: Orange Ice Dub

Throat Dub: Minnow gills Dave Whitlock SLF

Back 1: Black/orange over yellow Hareline Tiger Barred Rabbit Strips

Adhesive 2: Tear Mender

Back 2: Black rabbit strip (magnum)

Eyes: Gold holographic eyes (⁵⁄₃₂")

Head Top Color: Black Sharpie marker

Head: Epoxy or UV-curing resin

Head Cement: Hard as Hull

SNAPBACK

There is no conversation I enjoy more than one with a fellow fly tier who completely nerds out about flies—not necessarily about new hooks, materials, or how the flies look, but how they act. I like someone who asks questions of metal, fur, and feather and uses the vise to figure them out . . . then uses water and fish to keep figuring it out. I know rather quickly when I meet someone who obsesses about fly tying as much as I do. I know by the way they inspect a fly pulled from a stranger's box, or the way they use their hands to describe what one of their own flies does in the water. You can't fake geek. And I can peg my own from across a room.

The Snapback is a big fly but lightweight enough not to break your back casting it all day long.

Or from the other side of a boat.

I knew David Goodrich was of my tribe long before that evening Erin Block and I stood on either end of his boat heaving giant musky flies into a New Mexico reservoir. Erin and I had known David for years before that evening, fished with him in the Colorado high country, and spent late nights tying carp flies together at our kitchen table. I always looked forward to our conversations, be they over the Internet or a table covered in bucktail and tools. However, having one of our fly-tying conversations as we stood together on the boat was like playing catch with a MLB pitcher while he described (no, *showed*) the break his slider could get.

Erin and I had come to David's home water unprepared. We had enough rods, reels, and rain jackets to fill the Bargain Cave of a big-box, but lacked any real musky flies. I had rounded up all of my largest pike flies a few hours before starting out on the nine-hour drive from our home in Colorado that morning, but they all proved to be embarrassingly

inadequate. They were too small and moved wrong. David found one of his own flies entwined with outboard motor parts and empty cans of energy drink. It was a large brown and green streamer that had served a tour or two, seen some action. I could tell because it was ratty and had long ago lost both its eyes. David had not planned to fish himself that evening, content to play host since he had us shacked up at his fly shop for another three days—there would be plenty of time. But we had to see what was wrong with our pitch. And we saw. And it stung a bit when it hit the mitt. Standing together on the carpeted deck, we looked down into the murky reservoir and talked about how a large streamer should move. Glide. Pause. It had been a decade since I had learned so much in one day.

Luckily Erin and I had packed fly-tying equipment. That evening we fished until dark then crashed hard, all three of us crammed into a small room at the back of David's fly shop. He was living at his shop at the time. There was just enough

Tiger musky and large northern pike gave David Goodrich confidence in using big flies for bass. Large fish eat other fish—it's a hard-knock life.

room for our sleeping bags between a mini-refrigerator that did not work and a half-table/half-fly-tying-bench with a giant jar of pickles placed like a centerpiece. We grilled some meat in the gravel parking area out front and ate while tying two flies each to use the next day. David provided 5/0 hooks and schlappen of a proper length (SPL), and we added deer hair, High Life, and Flashabou until we had a pitch so wicked that even the Willie Mays of musky was going to get caught reaching. We brought 58 tiger musky to the boat before going home to Colorado.

David Goodrich was born in Illinois but came to Grants, New Mexico, with his family when he was 10 years old. He and his older brother, Nate, would take tubs of chicken livers to a local reservoir to catch catfish. One day they caught a trout, and neither knew what it was. David learned what it was by searching through microfiche at a public library. He also noted that every old article about trout contained a mention of fly fishing. He deduced that to better catch this new fish, he must use a fly. So he became a fly fisherman—or a fly fisherboy—with a $20 W.W. Grigg fly rig from Wal-Mart and his mother as a valet. He would try convincing her to drive him up to Bluewater Creek, that inlet into the reservoir, every day after school, even during the cold months. Young David would break the ice in the creek and come back a little later to cast his size 14 Blue Dun dry fly into the current. There were genuine rainbow trout in that little creek, sometimes as long as 6 inches.

Years later, life would take the Goodrich brothers away from the pleasant waters of their childhood. Nate would do time in the desert with the Big Red One (1st Infantry Division), and David would gig around the state in a heavy metal band with some high school buddies. He played guitar. Later his brother, fresh back from the war, would join the band. Nate was on bass. They played bars and the occasional festival and eventually—emotionally burnt out, divorced, and living in an apartment in Albuquerque—David was left with nothing but family and fish. His brother and father dragged him back to the reservoir where he had learned how to live. One of them hooked a giant channel catfish that day, but lost it right at shore. David jumped in fully clothed and came back with the fish and, in a sense, re-baptized as a hard-core angler. He bummed around New Mexico and Colorado for a while (this is when Erin and I met him) but would eventually open a shop in Prewitt, New Mexico, with Nate . . . right next to the Bluewater Reservoir that both raised him and saved him.

When David and Nate opened Tumbleweed Fly & Tackle, the nearby reservoir had recently undergone a serious identity

The most fun time to tie flies is just before a much-anticipated fishing trip. However, the *best* time to tie is during or immediately after the trip. It is then that you know *exactly* what's needed!

overhaul. The catfish and trout had been overrun by orange goldfish (introduced by shore anglers with live bags of bait), and the state fish and game department countered with mass stocking of tiger musky (a sterile cross between northern pike and muskellunge). The result was predictable—a mass of well-fed fish-eaters and two suddenly serious musky fishermen who were brothers. Nate remained a focused gear angler, while David stuck to his fly rod. This time the dry-fly hooks and size 14 hackle were put away, replaced with halibut-size hooks and bales of bucktail.

By the time I got around to making the trip down to check out the shop and fish with David, he had completely dialed in the now several-year-old musky fishery. He seemed to be able to see below the brown water and know where the larger fish were waiting, and knew exactly what would entice them to attack. Erin and I took full advantage of our friend's knowledge during the course of that long weekend. What has stayed with me almost more vividly than the memory of that fishing trip was the fly-tying theory I had learned by witnessing firsthand. Of course, I went home to Colorado and tied a lifetime's supply of musky streamers, all with just the next trip in mind. The musky pattern of David's I tied was his X-Tail, a 12- to 14-inch streamer on a 5/0 Gamakatsu heavy-cover worm hook with a 40 mm Blane Chocklett's Big Game Shank at the front (David does a fly-tying video series called *Fly Hacks*, and this fly is featured in episode 5). But once the surge of post-trip adrenaline wore off, I began tying flies of a more practical size for my own everyday bass and pike purposes.

David's Snapback is a 6-inch (15 cm) scaled-down variation of his larger X-Tail musky fly. The Snapback derives its name from its ability to "snap back" into a straight position every time it bends at the articulation point (where the rear hook is connected to the forward shank), whereas most large jointed streamers tend to jackknife radically—which can give them an erratic, wounded baitfish action in the water, but drastically hinder the forward momentum of the moving fly. The larger the streamer, the more this subtle trait becomes important. When the angler jerks the line during the retrieve, it pulls the fly forward and the front half of the fly slows down, but the heavier rear end doesn't slow down as quickly. The rear end pushes the front, forcing a bend at the hitching point (think of the aerial news footage of a train derailment). The tubing material that is pulled over the joint in the fly is the secret step. David has since incorporated this "Snapback style" into some of his older musky patterns such as the X-Tail and other Bohen- and Popovics-esque patterns. Because this concept in fly design began on a streamer made for large, toothy critters, the tubing material David has used to restrict the movement of the fly's joint has always been some form of heavy-duty clear vinyl tubing purchased at a hardware store—this is true even on the 6-inch bass Snapbacks he ties. I usually use the E-Z Body material from Hareline Dubbin because it can be found in a fly shop and compresses on the Blane Chocklett's Big Game Shank, making it easier to tie and lighter weight.

The Snapback in various color combinations has become my go-to pike fly, and when big, aggressive bass are in the area, this fly will draw out the biggest and meanest. It is always a wise idea to have at least one large bass streamer in your possession when near bass water—the Snapback is the big one in my box.

SNAPBACK (BLACK & WHITE)

Hook: #2/0 Gamakatsu B10S
Thread: White 200-denier UTC G.S.P.
Adhesive: Zap-A-Gap
Inside Tail Feather: Shad gray schlappen
Outside Tail Feather: White schlappen
Rear Hair: White bucktail
Flash: Silver Holographic Flashabou
Shank: Blane Chocklett's Articulated Big Game Shank (40 mm)
Tubing: Pearl E-Z Body (medium)
Center Feather: White schlappen (afterfeather)
Flank Feather: Natural grizzly schlappen-esque hackle feather
Front Hair: Black bucktail
Topping: Strung peacock herl
Marker: Black Sharpie
Eyes: ½ Tempt Clear Cure Adhesive Eyes (12.7 mm)
Head Resin: Loon UV Knot Sense

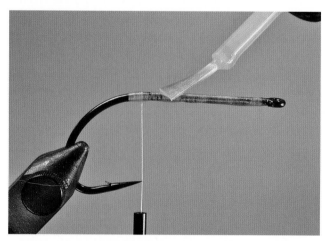

1. Clamp the hook securely in the jaws of the vise. Start a thin but solid thread base immediately behind the hook eye and extend it all the way back to the rear of the straight hook shank. Wrap the thread forward slightly onto the thread base and let the bobbin hang free so the thread is even with the hook point—from this point back to the rear of the thread base will be the tie-down spot for the tail feathers. Brush a light coat of Zap-A-Gap adhesive onto the entire thread base—this provides a solid base for the rear of the fly and creates a slick surface to more easily slide the deer hair into place around the hook shank.

2. Select four schlappen feathers: two white and two gray. I look for solid, wide feathers that taper to a quick point at the tip. The tips of schlappen feathers can vary, however, and you will tie with most of them, so the main criteria in choosing the four feathers for the rear of this streamer are that the outside feathers (white) are wider than the inside feathers (gray) and that both feathers in each color pair are roughly the same size and shape. Choose one of the white feathers that is extra long and has plenty of fluffy, marabou-like afterfeather on the base half of the quill and trim off this feather base to use later.

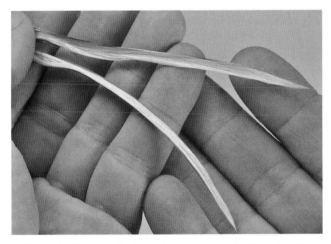

3. Separate the four feathers into two gray/white sets. Wet each feather and then lay both gray feathers down beside each other on your tying bench concave side down. Next, lay the white feathers on top of their gray mate—also concave side down. Be sure the feather tips are even.

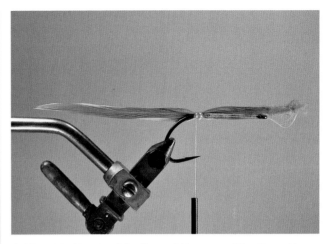

4. Mount both sets of feathers at the rear of the thread base so they extend out behind the fly two hook-shank lengths. Pictured here is just the first set, mounted on the far side. The feather quills should be on the side of the hook shank, not the top. Mount each set of feathers so the natural curve arcs inward. Once both sets are tied in, they will curve into each other, both gray feathers on the inside.

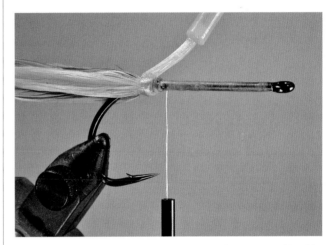

5. Trim away the butt ends of all four tail feathers and build a small bump of thread over the tie-down area. Leave the bobbin hanging so the thread is just at the forward side of the thread bump. Coat the entire thread bump with Zap-A-Gap. Brush some of the adhesive onto the base of the tail feathers—this will stiffen the four tail feathers, reducing the likelihood they will foul in the hook gap when wet and the fly is being vigorously cast.

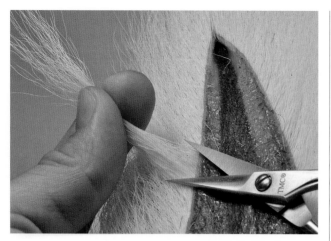

6. Select and cut a clump of white bucktail.

7. Mount the clump of bucktail to the top of the hook shank using three wraps of thread (the wraps should not be too tight). The tips of deer hair will not all be even (as they are not "stacked") but should be roughly two-thirds the length of the tail feathers. Three wraps of thread are just enough to hold the hair in place, yet loose enough to allow the hair to be pushed with a thumbnail down onto both sides of the hook shank. Be sure to leave the bottom of the hook shank bare of deer hair—this keeps hair from fouling the hook and negatively altering the way the finished fly will swim.

8. Select a bundle of six full-length strands of Flashabou. This flash material is notoriously difficult to manage once out of the plastic sleeve it comes in, so cut a small slit at the top (just below where it is stapled to the paper hang card) and use the hook at the end of your whip-finish tool to pull out just what you need. Once a bundle of six strands is selected and pulled free, run them all through your mouth to temporarily stick them together. While you are at it, pull out and prepare six bundles total (six strands each); wet them and lay them aside.

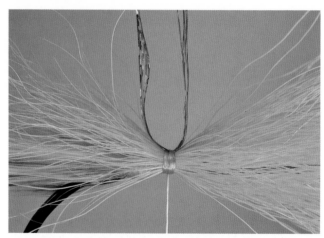

9. Tie the first of the six Flashabou bundles down on top of the first bucktail tie-down area. Once the Flashabou is in place, fold back the forward-facing side and tie it back with a couple more wraps of thread. Trim all 12 ends of Flashabou even with the tips of tail feathers.

10. Once the Flashabou is in place and trimmed to the proper length, build up a narrow bump of thread right at the tie-down spot—this bump of thread will prevent the next clump of deer hair from ever lying down flat to the hook shank. Lift the butt ends of deer hair up off the hook shank and cut them off—be sure to make the cut at an angle to make the thread transition off the hair as smooth as possible. The clumps of hair used on the back hook of this fly will be smaller than the ones that will be used on the front shank and only cover three sides of the hook shank (the bottom is left bare), so one cut of the butt sections should suffice. Two cuts will be necessary to trim the butt ends of deer hair on the forward shank. Before wrapping the thread forward over the angled butt ends of hair and into position to mount the next clump of hair, apply a small dab of Zap-A-Gap to the bump of thread and the trimmed ends of hair. Use only three or four wraps of thread to tie down the butt ends, and leave the thread resting about a hook-eye length forward of the first thread bump.

12. The underside of the rear hook should have parts of the original thread base and all the thread bumps exposed. This goes against most aesthetically driven fly-tying instincts, but it is necessary to keep the fly swimming and performing correctly. Remove the hook from the vise and set it aside.

13. Select a 40 mm Big Game Shank and take a close look at it. One loop end is larger than the other—this is the loop that will be attached to the hook eye. The small loop end will become the "hook eye" of the finished fly. Also take note of how both loop ends are positioned in relation to each other. Because the hook eye is straight (thus horizontal), the rear loop of the Big Game Shank will be vertical once threaded onto the hook eye—this means the front loop of the shank needs to be oriented opposite if it is to act as the hook eye of the fly once finished. If the streamer is going to swim properly, this opposite orientation must be perfect . . . and it rarely is right out of the bag. Usually they are off by about 30 degrees. Sight down the shank and use two pliers to get it right.

11. Repeat the process of preparing a clump of bucktail, mounting and positioning it, tying in a clump of Flashabou (although only add the flash every *other* time), building a small thread bump, trimming away the excess hair, adding adhesive, and advancing the thread a total of five times. This should exhaust half of the six prepared bundles of Flashabou (each bundle should be trimmed slightly shorter than the previous one) and fill out the entire length of hook shank. Build a large round thread head behind the hook eye and apply Zap-A-Gap to all sides of the head.

14. Hook the large shank loop through the hook eye, then clamp the large loop firmly into the jaws of the vise. There will be just enough room on the rear shank loop to get a solid purchase with the vise and keep the hook eye in the loop, although the rear part of the fly will be kicked up at an angle. Use a rubber band looped around the hook bend and some rear part of the vise to hold the hook in line, yet out of the way.

15. Melt the end of a roll of Hareline Dubbin E-Z Body material. Melting the end will ensure the woven tubular material will not come unwoven while in use, but will also slightly shrink the outer circumference, which will allow the tubing to lock onto the rear part of the fly once the melted end pops over the round thread head created behind the hook eye.

16. Cut an exactly 1-inch (25.4 mm) length of E-Z Body material and thread it (melted end first) onto the Big Game Shank. Be sure to always melt the end of tubing before measuring and cutting, as the melting process will shrink the material.

17. Restart the thread behind the forward loop of the Big Game Shank and build a solid thread base back until it reaches the forward end of the E-Z Body tubing. Push the tubing back on the shank until the forward end of the tubing is even with front end of shank metal that has been bent back to form the forward loop in the shank—this will jam the melted end of the tubing up against the jaws of the vise and the tubing will not be able to extend fully over the fly joint until the fly is finished and removed from the vise. Tie the tubing down in place with thread wraps that extend all the way back to the point where the rear loop of the shank begins. Leave the bobbin hanging with the thread resting at the very rear of this new thread base.

18. Select and trim a portion of the white schlappen tail feather set aside in the early stages of this fly and tie it in by the fat end of quill. Advance the thread up the shank one hook-eye length (the hook eye of the actual rear hook).

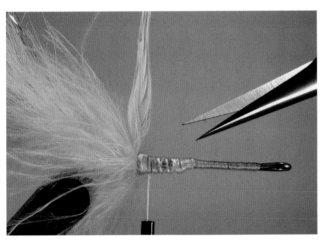

19. Make at least two complete turns of the feather around the hook shank and tie it down—this will create a marabou-like "skirt" just forward of the joint in this articulated streamer that will blend in with the white bucktail body of the fly, yet subtly mask the joint and add a slight bit of movement and undulation mid-body. Trim away the excess feather. Build a slight thread bump at the forward edge of the wound feather and let the bobbin hang with the thread right at the forward edge of the thread bump—this is the position the thread needs to be in to continue placing clumps of deer hair.

20. Continue the process of preparing a clump of bucktail, mounting and positioning it, tying in a clump of Flashabou (although only add the flash *every other time*), building a small thread bump, trimming away the excess hair, adding adhesive, and advancing the thread a total of five more times. The clumps of hair you cut and prepare for this forward half of the streamer should be twice as large as the ones used at the rear, as you will need enough hair to push all the way around the shank—the bottom should not be left bare as it was before. This should exhaust the rest of the prepared bundles of Flashabou (each bundle should be trimmed slightly shorter than the previous one) and fill out most of the Big Game Shank. There should be just enough space behind the forward shank "eye" for one more clump of bucktail.

21. Select two long grizzly hackle feathers to be used as flank feathers on the top/sides of the streamer. David Goodrich originally used nothing but the longest schlappen feathers because they were the only feathers long enough for the 12- to 18-inch musky flies he was tying. With these smaller bass versions of the fly, I have found several types of feather that will suffice—shorter schlappen, extra-long Whiting Bugger Hackle, and my favorite, the wide-based long-tipped oddity feathers on the back side of most Hebert Miner rooster saddles. There are only a handfull of these perfect feathers on each saddle. I will often pluck them as soon as I acquire a new saddle and pair them up for future use. The natural black and white grizzly feather is the easiest to find, but dyed feathers that fit the bill for this pattern are often more difficult to track down. If you are planning a large batch of one particulare color, it may be worth making a dye batch, but do not be above taking a permanent marker to a couple naturals to get the color you want.

24. Use three wraps of thread to loosely mount the black deer hair to the front of the fly. Push the hair evenly all the way around the head.

22. Mount the two flank feathers. They need to be on either side of the fly, but as high up as they can be without being on the top of the fly. Be sure to mount each feather so the inside, or cupped side, of the feather is hugging the body of the fly. The tips of these feathers should extend back past the tips of the tail feathers. Because each pair of these schlappen-esque flank feathers is so unique, you will need to be the judge of how far they should extend behind the fly. As a general rule I try to keep this streamer about 6 inches (15 cm) long.

25. Once the black deer hair is spread evenly around the head of the fly, make several more thread wraps (much tighter this time) to lock the hair in place and flare it slightly. Trim away all the butt ends of hair, brush a small amount of Zap-A-Gap onto the trimmed butts, then tie them all down tight—this will create a slight thread "head" at the front of the fly.

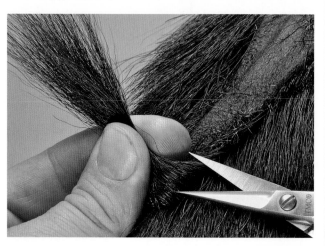

23. Select, cut, and prepare a fat clump of black bucktail for the head of the fly.

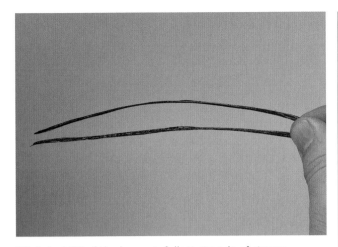

26. Select 20 of the longest, fullest strands of strung peacock herl. Separate the herl into two clumps with all their tips lined up evenly. Wet both clumps of herl (I run them through my mouth) so all the strands stay together neatly and you can see which way each clump wants to arch.

27. Mount both clumps of peacock herl on top of the fly, between the two flank feathers. Two clumps of herl mounted beside each other creates a flatter, wider top to the streamer than if they were all mounted together in one 20-strand clump. If the strands of peacock are all long enough, tie them in so the tips are even with the two tips of the flank feathers. If they are not long enough to do that, make the tips of peacock even with the tips of the four tail fathers. Trim away the butt ends of the peacock herl.

28. Apply a dab of Zap-A-Gap to the trimmed butt ends of peacock herl, then build an evenly tapered thread head over the tie-down area. Tie a whip-finish knot and cut the thread. Pat down the head to be sure the adhesive is fully dry, then use a black Sharpie marker to color the entire head.

29. Position two Clear Cure Adhesive Eyes onto the side of the thread head. The sticky backs of the eyes will hold them in place temporarily, but try to get some UV-cured resin dripped in between the eyes and cured as quickly as possible to secure them in place more permanently. Squeeze the two eyes tight to the head just before using the UV curing light for the first time, as this will ensure the head stays as narrow as possible and thus will be able to cut through the water better.

30. On the heads of large streamers such as these, I will often use at least three separate applications of UV resin before the desired shape is achieved. If you try to get all the resin on and cured in one go, it will more than likely end in disaster—or at least an oddly and ugly shaped head. The final coat of resin should completely cover the head of the fly, to include the facing sides of the eyes—this ensures the eyes will never pop off. Be sure the head is sturdy, but do your best to keep the resin as minimal as possible. A head that is too bulky will be heavy and can negatively affect the way the fly swims.

31. If the UV resin used on the head of the fly is still a tad tacky once cured with a UV lamp, brush on a light coat of head cement and let it dry. Be sure to properly position the E-Z Body tubing at the fly's joint once the fly has been removed from the jaws of the vise—the hook at the end of your whip-finish tool is perfect for coaxing the tubing out over the thread head behind the rear hook eye. When the tubing is pulled out straight, it will prevent the fly from bending too much, which will allow it to "glide" for greater distances when being retrieved.

PATTERN VARIATION

SNAPBACK (CHARTREUSE & WHITE)

Hook: #2/0 Gamakatsu B10S

Thread: White 200-denier UTC G.S.P.

Adhesive: Zap-A-Gap

Inside Tail Feather: Chartreuse schlappen

Outside Tail Feather: White schlappen

Rear Hair: White bucktail

Flash: Chartreuse Dyed Pearl Flashabou

Shank: Articulated Big Game Shank (40 mm)

Tubing: Pearl E-Z Body (medium)

Center Feather: White schlappen (afterfeather)

Flank Feather: Chartreuse grizzly schlappen-esque hackle feather

Front Hair: Light olive bucktail

Topping: Strung peacock herl

Marker: Black Sharpie

Eyes: ½ Raptor Clear Cure Real Eyes (12.7 mm)

Head Resin: Loon UV Knot Sense

INDEX

ABOUT THE AUTHOR

Jay Zimmerman has been tying flies and chasing bass since he was a child. He has worked in the fly-fishing industry for many years as a guide, casting and fly-tying instructor, fly-shop manager, and commercial fly designer for Umpqua Feather Merchants. This is his fourth book; his previous book, *The Best Carp Flies* (2015), was the first comprehensive book on tying the best flies for carp and helped push a once-disrespected gamefish into the mainstream.